Mrs. Lemons,

I thank God for the opportunity to meet you. Be encouraged! Tell your story as the Lord would have you to tell it! Do not be afraid! Your story will help to save *many*!

God Bless You!

[signature]

i

Diary of a BROKEN Praise Dancer

Aries Winans

Destiny House Publishing, LLC
Detroit, MI

Diary of a Broken Praise Dancer

Published by Destiny House Publishing, LLC

Copyright © June 2011 Aries Winans
International Standard Book Number:

Unless otherwise stated, all scripture quotations are from the Holy Bible, New King James Version. Scripture references that do not have the Bible version noted are the author's paraphrase.

Original printing 2011

Cover design: RLSmith Designs

Photography: Elle McGraw's Creative Couch

Editing and Publication Layout:
Destiny House Publishing, LLC

For information:
Destiny House Publishing
www.destinyhousepublishing.com
P.O. Box 19774 Detroit, MI 48219
888.890.4555

DEDICATIONS

To my cousin, Deyja Fitzgerald, I love you. Keep moving forward!

To every minister of the arts (song, dance, mime, pageantry, theater, etc), from the minister to the member

To all those that may be bound by the spirit of rejection, lust, fornication, homosexuality, perversion and/ or mind-control

This book is for you

THANK YOUS & ACKNOWLEDGEMENTS

If it had not been for the Lord, who was on my side, I don't know where I'd be! To my Lord, my God, My Redeemer, The Lifter of my head, My Healer and My Savior- Jesus, I love you, more than life itself! You hold my world in Your hands. I will bless You forever.

To my amazing husband, Tony Winans: I bless God for the day you were created. I love you with everything in me. Thank you for always covering me in prayer and for demonstrating the love of God to me daily. You are mine and I am yours. Marriage for a lifetime!

To our son, Anthony Winans - I love you and I am so proud of the young man you are becoming. Continue to take a stand for the Lord.

To all of my wonderful parents- Sheila Urum-Eke, Joseph Urum-Eke, Joceline Bronson, Prentice Bronson, Joyce Underwood, Charles Underwood, and my god-mothers, Julia Thomas and Carolyn Collins. I love you all so much. I couldn't have asked for better parents. I am so blessed to have all of you as my parents. Your love for me is unconditional. I want you to know that I am so grateful for your never-ending support, prayers and hugs!

To all of my siblings: Shelita, Vernan, Emory, Tamika, Emmanuel, Taneshia, Ike, Grace, Westley, Mary, Will and Bianca. I love you all dearly!

To my pastors, Apostle Oscar & Prophetess Crystal Jones- Words cannot express how truly grateful I am to have you as my pastors. I thank you for every prayer, every word of wisdom, every rebuke, every hug, every kiss, every word of encouragement, for always being honest with me no matter how bad it hurt. Thank you for all of the time sacrificed for me. I am grateful for it all! You two are just amazing people in general! I love you with all my heart.

Janice Perez-Rivera- Mi favorite amiga! You are the BESTEST friend anyone could ever ask for. I thank God for connecting us. I asked Him for life-long friends that have a heart for God and here you come! You are my BBSFAC for life! I love you. I thank you and I appreciate you!

Dana Snell & Amanda Van-Meter Burch: Thank you for being great friends and for always making me laugh. You two rock! Continue to take the dance community by storm- in Jesus name!

Judith Casmier, Olivia Ojo & Danielle Lathrup: Thank you for always making me feel welcome and for taking care of me when I couldn't take care of myself. I appreciate you and love you.

Rochelle Smith: Thank you for being a true friend. I love you so much. You have no idea how much of a blessing you are to me.

LaToya Dawn, Isadora Harris, Lorna Marshall, Dashawna Sheridan, Tiana Horton, Jasmine Robinson, Tiffany Wellons- You ladies are irreplaceable. I thank God for our life-long friendship. Thank you for always being supportive of me and loving me. I love you all!!!

Special Thanks to:
Moma (Sheila Urum-Eke) - I love you. Thank you, thank you, and thank you for always being there for me. No matter what the situation was, if at all possible, you were there. I thank you for being the one to comfort me and encourage me when I felt like I couldn't go on. Thank you for your unfailing love, prayers, support and for being in my corner. When it comes to verbally expressing just how grateful I am for you, I get speechless because simply saying "Thank You" just won't do. I thank God for you and the relationship that we have. I'll always be your baby girl.

Ma (Joceline Bronson) - In order for me to properly thank you for all you've done and just for who you are to me, I'd have to write another book just for you! I thank God for you. Thank you for being my ma. I don't consider you a step-mother because there's no step or distance between us. We have a bond that is uncommon between step-mother and step-daughter. I intend to keep it that way for the rest of our lives. You are a priceless gem in my life that can never be replaced. You are and have always been my prayer partner, my shoulder to cry on, the person I can call on for anything, my support system, my encourager, my closest friend and more. I thank you for always covering me in prayer, for being patient with me and for loving me through everything. I love you with all my heart.

Prophetess Crystal Jones - I love you…I love you…I love you… Thank you – for everything! It's too much to name. You are an amazing woman to me and I count it an honor to have you as my pastor. Thank you for always caring for my soul, covering me in prayer, thank you for the countless conversations, wisdom given, the time you gave me, for demonstrating God's love toward me and for never giving up on me. You are irreplaceable.

Dr. Mayra Leon, Elect Lady Rufus, Lady Suzi Brooks, Mrs. Nicole Leonard and Minister Rekesha Pittman - You ladies have been such a tremendous blessing to my life. I THANK YOU so much for covering me in prayer, counseling me, checking up on me, taking time to listen to me and give me Godly advice. I appreciate you so much more than you know. I thank God for you!

CONTENTS

My Journey

Thank you for choosing to read my testimony. I know the title of this book is about a "broken" praise dancer, which indeed, I was! Please allow me to help you understand how being broken by the enemy was turned around for my good and how I am now broken for the Master's use.

Rejection, lust, mind control, rebellion, fornication, disobedience, homosexuality and hatred – in a nutshell, SIN, is what caused me to get to the point of brokenness. I wanted to give up on the call God placed on my life. If I could, I would have given back all the gifts He's placed in me. I felt hopeless and helpless. But thanks be to God! He delivered me out of it all! By the end of this book, you will see that I went from being broken due to my own sin, to being broken for the Lord. This broken is what the Bible speaks of in Psalm 51:17 -
"The sacrifices of God are a broken spirit; A broken and a contrite heart, O God, Thou wilt not despise."

God desires a broken and contrite heart which is the true sacrifice of one who determines to turn from sin, to forsake sin, and to abandon it. Where I was once full of myself, I am now empty, and available for the Lord to fill me with more of Him. I realize I am nothing apart from the Lord. So I offer Him my nothingness.
Before diving into the story, I need to shed some light on my past so that you will understand the spirit of rejection, lust and homosexuality did not just "appear" in my life. It had a beginning.

Starting with a generational curse; both of my parents were molested when they were teenagers by relatives. My older sister and brother were also molested as children. I was raised in a single parent home – with my mother playing the role of mother and father for 3 children, me being the youngest. I was only 10 days old when my father was taken away to prison. I did not see him again that I recall until I was 10 years old. This is how the spirit of rejection was able to enter into my life.

As a child, I learned about sex before I even fully understood where babies came from. I was introduced to pornography at a very young age. Often, I'd hear my relatives having intercourse while I tried to sleep. Although I did not know what it was at the time, I quickly put the pieces together on my own. This is one of the ways lust was able to take root in my life. By the age of 11, I was already watching pornography with my older brother and my mother's boyfriends' children, and I had already begun engaging in homosexual acts.

At the age of 12, lust was fully present in my life and had showed up in many ways, even though I was still playing with Barbie dolls and I thought boys were the most disgusting things on earth. I remember crying many nights for my father as a teenager. I just wanted to know him and know that he loved me as his own child. Over the years, he made many attempts to come see me. Some were successful, but most were unfulfilled promises which took a bigger blow at my already rejected heart. At the age of 14, I began to have dreams of a tall, dark figure having intercourse with me. I remember it felt like fire in real life. I didn't know what it meant at that time. But not too long after the dreams started, I lost my virginity. I remember when I was 15 years old; my big sister told me she had a girlfriend. I was utterly grossed out and I vowed to never be a homosexual. I was too good for that. Without fail, I fell. This is why the Bible warns us not to think more highly of ourselves than we ought. The very thing I said I would never do was the very same thing I made haste to do as often as I could.

I believe I began to have an interest in girls at the age of 17. I was turned out by a woman I had just met through a girl I went to school with but barely knew; however, everyone knew she was openly gay. From there, I became bisexual. I had a boyfriend who did not care if I slept with women. My mind soon turned - - - I felt like I was on a mission to turn out the world. There were no limits! Whoever I set my eyes on, that's who I was going after. I felt like I had to introduce women everywhere to this lifestyle. So, I slept with females I met online, through friends from school, through hear-say, and even from my boyfriend. One of the women was married and the other was my closest friend. Since I did not understand my worth, I allowed both men and women to handle me in ways that were never intended. Lust was no struggle for me during my teenage years because I was completely given over to it.

After I graduated from high school, I planned to visit my family in Michigan before I went off to college in Colorado. God had other plans for me. When I got to Michigan, my intent was never to stay, only to visit. I went out a few times with a woman I met online earlier in the year. She took me to her job a few times (a strip club) and invited me to go hang out with her and her friends. She seemed pretty cool. I was only 18 at the time. My parents did not know all of this was going on. I lied and said I knew her from my hometown and she moved to Michigan a few years ago. One day, she picked me up to go to a party with her and her friends. For some reason, we ended up not going, but went to her friend's house instead. Long story short, while I sat there in a room, watching, something came over me and I immediately got disgusted and wanted to leave. She tried to have sex with me, but I refused.

September 11, 2001, as I watched the Twin Towers falling on the news, I thought to myself, I know if I die right now, I'm going to hell. Mind you, I wasn't saved, nor was I thinking about living saved. I was having the time of my life. I had not a care in the world. But this day changed my life. After weeks of my parents asking me to go to church with them (and me declining), I finally said YES! That night, I gave my life to the Lord and I joined my parents church the following Sunday (I love my church family!!!!!!).

The journey for me to lay down the lifestyle of homosexuality began. That was

SOOOO HARD! It seems like, in an instant, I had to change my entire life: my wardrobe, my hairstyles, phone number, email address, close down my Black Planet page and let go of my friends. Not only this, but God changed my heart and I wanted to move to Michigan. I am so grateful He changed my plans because had I stayed where I was, I'm not sure how long I would have lived.

I knew that I needed to be delivered from homosexuality because I knew it was something God hated. I knew it was wrong. And I wanted it out of me. Every single time I went up for prayer, I would ask God to please reveal that spirit and let someone call it out of me and pray for me in that area. To my dismay, it didn't happen. I believe the spirit of lust was called out instead. At that time, I didn't understand how the two were connected. So I felt like that wasn't good enough. I began praise dancing in 2002 per my pastor's request. I had never danced in church before and had no desire to either. I didn't know anything about dance ministry, dance garments, I had no prior training, wasn't sure how I should dance in church, or even how to select a song. Needless to say, I had a LOT to learn! I remember being so nervous the first time I danced solo. It was for our 1st service at our new church location. I wore a white leotard, white sports bra, white skirt and white tights. Yes, I was super holy. Lol. After service was over, my mom had to sit me down and explain to me about modesty in dance ministry. I thought I was modest. My leotard came up to my neck, my arms and legs were completely covered. But some of the men made comments that they had to leave the service while I danced to avoid looking at me lustfully. After I finished crying, stopped blaming myself, and listened to my mom, I was able to understand and realized the importance of layering my chest and even wear a wrap if necessary so that no one is distracted by my body while ministering in dance.

The next time I ministered a solo piece, I was careful to implement everything my mom told me, down to the letter. I even bought a pink sweater wrap to make sure I was modest. The last thing I wanted was for someone to lust after me while watching me minister in dance. At that point, it's not ministry, but a distraction. My mom prayed with me before I went out to minister and the Lord took over from there. That day, I realized how dance ministry is really another form of ministry. People's lives were changed…and the Lord used dance to portray His message. From that point, I sought to learn more about dance ministry. Keep in mind that I still hadn't been delivered from the spirit of homosexuality, lust, fornication or rejection.

In 2003, I went to Perfecting Church's annual Holy Convocation. Pastor Donnie McClurkin was preaching this night. God changed his message, seemingly right in the middle of his sermon. He ended up ministering on homosexuality. At that time, I thought I was fine because I wasn't doing anything homosexual and I wasn't having sex either. But when he finished speaking and made that alter call, a war began to rage in my body. The person sitting next to me (a friend I made a few days prior) got up and went down to the alter. I started screaming within myself, "No wait! Wait for me!" My mom was sitting a few rows away from me. I caught a glimpse of her rocking back and forth, praying….for me.

I finally got up and made my way down the steps. When I finally reached the main floor, all these thoughts started flooding my mind, saying, "Don't go down there! You can still go back to your seat! What if someone from your church sees you? What will they think? Turn around stupid!" But I kept going. Felt like I was taking baby steps. My body was trembling so much that I stumbled over my own feet. After what seemed like 20 minutes of fighting just to get to the already crowded alter, I finally made it! There were men and women down there of all ages! I had never seen anything like that before. I just lifted my hands and began to cry out to the Lord to save me, cleanse me and heal me. Within minutes, I heard screams from people being prayed for and the pastors (Pastor Marvin Winans and Pastor Donnie McClurkin), along with the ministers were praying and laying hands on the people. Before I knew it, one of them put their hand on my head and said something along the lines of, "Freedom in the name of Jesus!" and kept moving. My body just dropped. I started crying and screaming and praying…. There was so much going on. Some of the ministers helped me up and somebody prayed for me. That part is a blur. But all I remember was before it was all over, I was jumping and screaming to the top of my lungs as if I had lost my mind. Just like that, the Lord freed me.

Even after the service and the entire drive home, I could not stop crying because I had never felt the Love of God for me, so heavy and so real before. He loved me enough to deliver me! Since deliverance is a process, I had to continue to walk circumspect, daily.

As I continued to walk through my deliverance, I noticed how God shifted my dance. He anointed it and even used me to dance prophetically (before I even knew what prophetic dance was). The Lord blew my mind! I had no idea how powerful dance could be! The only dance I was familiar with was secular dancing. Lord literally taught me everything I knew. Wait, let me back up. My pastor and mom taught me about dance and ministering, which was greatly needed and extremely helpful! The Lord gave me choreography, ideas for garments, and He even graced me to be able to pick up a streamer for the 1st time and use it as if I had been ministering with it for years.

Over the next few years, I found myself constantly battling with my pastor because as she was mentoring me, she tried over and over again to get me to see areas of pride and idolatry in my life. They mostly showed up within the dance ministry, but ultimately affected every area of my life. I denied it every single time. In addition to the pride, I also became very rebellious. An example of this rebellion regarding dance ministry would be on several different occasions, I would be invited to go and minister in dance at another church. When I asked my pastors if our dance ministry could go, their response was, "no." Well, I took that as them saying the dance team couldn't go, but that didn't mean I couldn't go. So I went without my pastor's covering. I soon stopped asking if I could go places to dance, and I just went. Needless to say, I was sat down many times for this. And I deserved to be! I had a desire to be seen. I was operating in false humility (by saying, "I don't want to be seen. I just love dancing for the Lord!"), pride, rebellion and witchcraft (*Rebellion is as the sin of witchcraft* 1 Samuel 15:23) while dancing at these other churches. This was a very dangerous place to be.

Earlier, I mentioned that my pastor attempted to get me to see how I was "star crazy", which was idolatry. It just sounded terribly harsh, so I put it out of my mind. I totally disregarded her counsel in that area. But once again, I was wrong. I WAS star crazy. Even my mom told me the same thing about me being crazy about celebrities. Being around celebrities was exciting to me! No matter who it came from, I'd always blow it off and sum it up as the person telling me was jealous because I had favor. For example: I was able to get me and my friend backstage to meet Donnie McClurkin and Yolanda Adams after their concert - without backstage passes. I met Joanne Rosario, talked with her, took pictures with her and once, she rode on the same plane as me and gave me an autographed book of prayers that her father wrote. Another instance was when I was able to get backstage and meet Fred Hammond after a concert. I was the "hype girl" for a new Christian radio host in Detroit. I was crazy about Dorinda Clark-Cole and her ministry.

In 2006, my mom kept telling me that there is residue of lust in me and I need to get rid of it. At times, I denied it and pretended as if she was wrong. Reason being, I wasn't doing anything lustful. I did not have a boyfriend. I was not sexually active. As a matter of fact, I had just celebrated my 4th year of celibacy! I knew I couldn't be dealing with lust. But once again, I was wrong. I should have listened to the warning because I knew she was right. I found myself allowing my eyes to look at soft pornographic TV commercials just a few moments more. I took "second looks" when I knew I should have walked the other way. I entertained lustful thoughts. I did pray. Don't get me wrong. However, I did not guard my spirit like I know I should have.

I'd say things like, "Lord, take these thoughts away from me" and "Oh God! I shouldn't be looking at that. I'm not gay. I'm not dealing with stuff like that. I'm saved. Devil leave me alone!" Ok, realistically, I could understand if the enemy laughed at me. Where was the Word? Where was the authority? Why didn't I plead the Blood of Jesus over my thoughts and take control over them? Speak the word over them? It's because I got comfortable with my walk. I disobeyed wise counsel. I ignored it. I put confidence in my own flesh. Little by little. I forgot about the dreams, the warnings, the prophecies the Lord gave me over the last few years. They were written in my journal, neatly tucked away on a shelf.

I thoroughly enjoyed dancing for the Lord. However, the combination of the arts and lust became another world for me. Over time, I had gotten to the point where I loved dance so much, it became an idol for me. I was so focused on "dancing" that I lost sight of the whole purpose of dancing, which was supposed to be for the Lord. I became a prideful, glory stealer. I denied it every time it was brought to my attention. I became greatly discouraged to the point where I was ready to give up on dance completely.

Here begins my story…Diary of a Broken Praise Dancer.

As you continue to read my story, I pray that you are able to follow along. "Diary Of A Broken Praise Dancer" is comprised of emails and journal entries. I have combined these two in order to tell the story and for the reader to be able to see how I fell off. You will find at the end of some entries, there is a special section titled, "Looking Back." This is where I wanted to bring light to these specific situations, speak on God's grace, expose the enemy, and to show you – the reader, through the Word of God, how my actions were wrong. For every sin that plagued my soul, there is a remedy in the Word of God.

I pray that each reader is able to find something in my story to identify with, see the need for repentance, healing and deliverance, and understand the importance of forgiveness. I pray that you will realize the need to tell your secret, repent, give your life whole heartedly to the Lord and ask God to deliver you from whatever it is that may have you bound. Even if there's just residue, deal with it! I pray that you will not allow the enemy room in your life. Please, do not put any confidence in your flesh. Pride is real and it will kill you if you don't submit your gifts, your ministries, your talents and your life to the Lord. After all, He gave it to you. So why not trust Him with it? Why not submit it to Him? He wants it all.

I have learned so much while writing this book. I see how God literally saved my life in so many ways. I can see how His grace and mercy kept me. I am so grateful that He loves me STILL! Even now, as I write this, I am still walking out my deliverance. I repeat: deliverance is a process. I did not go to the altar, receive Christ as my Lord and Savior, get prayer for lust and homosexuality, and then get delivered on the spot. No. I did receive salvation and my leaders agreed with me in prayer for my deliverance, but it's up to me to walk it out.

I pray that each person sees the difference in salvation and deliverance. You can be saved but not delivered. I accepted Christ as my personal Lord and Savior, but there were still many things that I had not been delivered of yet. As long as I live, I will always be striving to be more like Christ. Thus, I will forever be walking out my deliverance. By this, I mean that I don't want to get comfortable to the point where I feel like I'm now fully delivered and I don't have to fight anymore. The day I decide to let down my guard, guess who's going to be right there waiting for me? Yep! All those spirits that I was delivered from want to come back. Not so! I will continue to fight the good fight of faith all the days of my life and in the name of Jesus, I will snatch my brothers and sisters out of the fire as I'm walking this thing out!

I thank God for His forgiveness, redemption, grace and mercy. It is only by the grace of God that I am able to share this story in hopes that it will bless you, encourage you, and remind you that God CAN and He is MORE than able to deliver you out of any situation. No matter how big, deep, uncontrollable or hopeless it may seem for you. There is nothing too hard for God. What is impossible with man is possible with God. He is limitless. He is all powerful. He can heal your broken heart. He alone has the power to deliver your soul. He is the hope of Glory. He can redeem the time for you! He has power over the enemy and He can give you the strength to fight back! I can say it with boldness because He did it for me! Since God is no respecter of persons, I know He will do it for you!

This book is not about exposure of a person or persons, but exposure of the enemy. There are many stories like this all over the world. Light must be shed on them so that all parties involved can be free in the name of Jesus! There are a LOT of things like this that go on behind closed doors in the Christian Arts Community. Sadly, a lot of it goes unspoken. People learn to suffer in silence because often times it's your word over theirs. But that is another lie from the pit of hell. If you pray and ask the Lord to be with you every step of the way, open your mouth, speak the truth- only, the Lord will vindicate you. The Bible says that if we acknowledge Him in ALL of our ways, then He will direct our path. That "ALL" is all-inclusive. So even in situations where you have to expose yourself for the sake of being free from the snares of the enemy, acknowledge Him first! Take it to the Lord. I wouldn't advise taking it into your own hands. Seek wise counsel and take heed! In the multitude of counsel, there IS safety.

Above all, I pray that this book will help someone. I pray this isn't just another book that will collect dust on a shelf. I encourage you to pass it along to someone else that needs it once you are done. The enemy must be exposed. I give God praise in advance for your complete healing and deliverance. Amen.

This book is based on a true story. All names and locations have been changed to protect the innocent and the not-so innocent.

A dream
July 26, 2005

I remember this dream, so clearly. *I was inside a building that didn't look familiar to me. I stood at the end of a long hallway that had beautifully designed carpet, cathedral ceiling, and ivory, sky-blue and silver on the walls. All of a sudden, this angelic-like being, wearing an all white flowing garment, starts running in front of me. So I began to run after this angel. It seemed like the hallway had no ending. But as I ran, I couldn't help but notice the huge writing on the wall. It read in impeccable silver cursive writing, "An angel of light." As I kept running, the words continued, "An angel of light, An angel of light." I kept running. The words dropped off. "An angel of..." Then when I saw, "An angel...??????????" That made my heart drop and I stopped running and stood there facing the writing, just staring.*

In an instant, the entire scene changed and this "angel" and I were in a restaurant. I remember it was an old burger joint set up with black & white checker floors. We were sitting at a white table with benches on both sides. The "angel" sat on one side and I sat on the other. The angel was holding my hand, gently stroking it with its thumb. Then within seconds, this angel's head began to shake, turning into something distorted. Every 3 seconds its head shook and became more demonic and with each transformation, its grip tightened on my hand. Then I woke up.

*I asked my ma what this meant and she interpreted it for me. The dream meant that I would allow someone to get so close to me that I would trust them with my intimate, personal business. This person would soon turn on me. So that put me on guard for a long time! Later on, while searching the scriptures, I stumbled upon the scripture in **2 Corinthians 11:14 which says** "And no wonder, for Satan himself masquerades as an angel of light." (NIV)*

LOOKING BACK
The Lord forewarned me about a toxic relationship that was to come, back in 2005. This was exactly one year before I met Rollanda. The dream came to pass in my life just as clear as it played out in my dream. Everything in the beginning seemed to be so perfect. It seemed to be from God. So much so, that this person took on an angelic appearance in my eyes (2 Corinthians

11:14) *And no wonder. For Satan himself masquerades as an angel of light. NIV).*
But just as quickly as I let my guard down, this person surely turned on me
and began to show their true colors.

Although I never forgot this dream, I surely ignored it. I did not apply it to the
relationship between Rollanda and I because **I wanted** it to be right. I wanted
that relationship to be one that was lifelong. But after I fell in sin with her, I
totally put the dream out of my mind because of my own desires. I ignored the
warning of God. Please take heed to your dreams. Especially if you know God
speaks to you through dreams. I encourage you to write your dreams down in a
journal, and date them. If you are unsure about what your dreams mean, pray
and ask the Lord to give you understanding. Or like in my case, you could ask
someone that has the gift of interpretation.

November 16, 2007
Dear Diary,

*When I woke up the next morning, it was another beautiful day in sunny
Florida. Only this day was different. Around this time yesterday, I was so
happy to be here in Florida. I would go outside every morning and sit on the
side walk and enjoy the warm sun on my skin and breathe the fresh air, just
thanking God for the beauty of the new day. But this morning, I was afraid to
even open my eyes for fear of what I might see. As I laid there in the bed,
eyes closed but fully awake, I thought to myself "I'm going to hell." That's
the only thing that came to mind at that moment. I raised my hand in front of
my face and opened one eye, I'm still alive! I wiggled my fingers and opened
my other eye. Thank you Jesus for not taking me in my sleep! Five minutes
passed...I'm still laying very still in the same bed sin and extreme shame took
place in just a few hours ago. This is what came to me as I lay in the bed.
"RUN...RUN! Get up, grab your things, get in the car and drive away until
you run out of gas and don't look back. Call someone to come get you. Just
GO!" Sounded like a great idea! I didn't want to see anyone in the house. I
didn't want to pet the dog. Didn't want to take another shower first or eat
any breakfast. Just RUN.*

*Instead of running, I just laid there and the deterioration of my mind, passion
and drive to dance, to live solely for Christ, to trust leadership, or even look
at myself as anything worth loving- began. For the rest of the day, images of
the night before danced in my head. I replayed every moment over and over
again, trying to figure out where did I go wrong? Was my innocence simply
me being naïve and oblivious to what was really going on? Did I just walk*

into the biggest web of my life? From the moment she came into the room, I sensed no danger. Was I desensitized to it? Why was I blinded to the obvious? She got into bed with me, just to chill with me for a little bit. I was already half asleep. She said to me "I'm so glad that you're here." I said me too. I think she asked me for a hug. I gave her one of my famous bear hugs (but the half sleep version). She moaned a little and asked me for another. So I gave her another hug, not even paying attention to nor was I aware of what was to come next. My mind wasn't prepared for it. In an instant, she had climbed on top of me and started grinding on me, whispering things in my ear. I just laid there, kinda whimpering with my hands up near my shoulders, in total shock. Within 2 minutes she was done. She sat on the side of the bed and said "Sorry mama" and walked out the room.

Chapter 1
Preparation

Dear Diary,
October 19, 2006

I can't believe it! Oh my goodness! Whew....I gotta calm down. Ok, (inhale...exhale) so yesterday, my friend sends me an email about this dance conference coming to town in just a few days, right. I looked at the flyer and instantly got super excited! So much so, that I printed the flyer and ran out of the office to go call the number for more information. I'm going to fast forward to today. How about, I'm still really excited?!?! My friend deserves a huge hug for this. She knows how close I am to giving up on dance all together. Man, this is so right on time. When I got to work today, I had an email from the conference host waiting for me. This is what the email said:

Sierra, thank you for contacting us at The Dance Challenger. I look forward to personally meeting you. G-d has spoken a word to me that a spirit of healing and deliverance will sweep the city like a Tsunami...Get ready for the Tsunami, Sierra!!!! Please tell as many people as you can about this conference. I'll send you a flyer in the next e-mail. Please come and introduce yourself to me. Ok. I'd like to meet you. Be blessed.

Living w/ purpose. Walking in Destiny
Rollanda Robertson-Anchorage ~ Author, Speaker, Success Coach
www.TheDanceChallenger.org
Live well, Love more & Dance more...you'll live longer (:-

Dear Diary,
October 20, 2006

My goodness this lady is fast! Lol. Talk about prompt responses :0) I responded to Rollanda's initial email, then she responded right back! To illuminate confusion, my response to her email makes up the majority of this entry. Her response to me is in bold. She put her response in the body of my email. Never had that happen before. Lol. So, here's the email convo:

Hello Rollanda!

What an honor! Thank you for responding to my e-mail. I must admit my pleasure! I am SOOOO excited about this conference that I could barely write the information down because I couldn't stop jumping up and down!

However, I am a little discouraged because I have to work during most of the conference. I would be able to attend Thursday evening, Friday about 4pm, and Saturday after 11am. *orrrrr too bad Sierra. You'll miss all of Friday's workshops. We have some awesome workshops during the daytime. Can you ask for 1/2 day off or something? Hey ask G-d to favor w/ the time off w/ pay. Helloooooooo! He is a BIG G-d.* I want to be at every single thing that goes on at this conference because I so desire to learn about the Lord of the dance! My spirit yearns to dance for Him. But there's so much that I do not know and I've been searching for a conference like this for well over a year now. Although I might not be able to attend every workshop, I am going to do my best to get there and I can't wait to meet you. Your ministry is such an encouragement to me already! *That's encouraging to hear. I am happy to know that you are blessed by what G-d has called us to do. I'm just walking in destiny...when we are in the right vein of life G-d moves and he uses us in ways, we could not imagine or ways that's not normal even to our personality. He only is G-d. Amen!*

PS: Can you recommend a church with a great praise group in the area? Since you are in the gospel capital of the world... I know Detroit has the badness groups on earth. Let me know. I need a praise team. There's been a cancellation.

Have a blessed day!!!
Sierra

October 31, 2006
Dear Diary,

I am just so ecstatic today! Every single day since the dance conference, I've been dancing before the Lord everywhere that I go! I'm so glad I pressed to go! Before the conference, I remember telling my friends how I was considering not dancing anymore. Reason being, it's like, I just can't seem to anything right! Eh, that's another story for another day. But YESTERDAY, I decided to post my experience while at the dance conference on the DC website. It was just THAT GOOD! This is what I sent to Rollanda:

Good morning Ms. Rollanda!

I'm not sure how to post a testimony for the conference I just attended in Southfield, MI, so I'm taking a chance by sending it through this e-mail. Below is my testimony:

I would like to first thank Rollanda and the DC staff for all of their hard work. Thank you all for allowing God to use you to pour into the lives of other dancers that has a passion and a desire to dance for the Lord- around the metro Detroit area. This conference has really been life changing for me and has stirred up the hunger for God even more so than before. I went there for the word- and I got that. I've known that there's more to dancing for God than simply moving around gracefully. I wanted meat, and I was not disappointed! Each class I attended, I received a wealth of knowledge. I could sit at the feet of these teachers for hours and just soak in it. God is just so awesome! I learned so much!

WOW! WOW! WOW! God is AWESOME! The power of God was so strong in that place! I thank God for each person I met there! Each of the ministries represented there! My God! You could see the heart of God through the ministry of dance! It was amazing! I could go on and on but I don't want to write a novel on the DC website! Oh and I had so much fun modeling your garments! Thank you for the opportunity! As you can see, it was hard for me to part ways with them! I am looking forward to the conference in Canada and the next one that comes to Michigan!!! Bless God!!! Oh, Ms. Ah'shely, your class is still with me today. I enjoyed it so much! I felt the presence of God as we ministered that song in the class. Sunday when I went to church, I was able to worship using sign language. It was beautiful!!! Not in the sight of others, but the language of sign is beautiful especially when used to worship God- which I had never done before. I plan to teach the children at my church the song you taught us. I'm so excited about it! Thank you sooooo much!!!

Sierra- Detroit, MI

I was so shocked that she responded as quickly as she did! Later the same day, she sent me this email response:

Sierra, thank you for your kind words. I soooooo enjoyed meeting you Ms. Fashion Model (: We appreciate you taking time to let us know that you were blessed by our conf. thank you also for the nice card. You are so gracious w/ your words. May you be blessed in return for blessing us this weekend. We'll post your testimony on the site in a day or so. I'll past this on to Ah'shely as well. It was really cool getting to know you a bit. Please, please keep in touch.

Thanks a million for your effort in assisting w/ finding a praise and worship leader. Your help did not go unnoticed. Be blessed. Rollanda

November 4, 2006
Dear Diary,

I know I'm grown but, I wish I could run away from home. I'm always frustrated while I'm here. I feel bad for my step mom because she's always stressed out. But because of everything we went through at my last two apartments, um, our relationship hasn't been the same since. I wish I could take my little sister away from all this drama and help her to have peace of mind. Well, both of us have peace of mind! My job has been my safe haven. I love going to work, everyday and talking to my co-workers, taking pictures, meeting new people, just being there in general. I'm glad I'm in dance school, too. So now, I have another excuse to stay away from home longer. I feel bad, kinda sorta but not really, for staying away until like 9:30pm then coming home and preparing for the next day. I love my family but…I guess it's more so my daddy that makes everyone want to run away…including me. It's a long story. But since I feel like I can't trust my pastor to discuss it with her, I don't have a best friend to confide in, I…I guess I'll just keep it to myself until God teaches me how to deal with it without losing my mind.

From: Sierra
To: Rollanda
Sent: November 8, 2006
Subject: Hello Rollanda!
(Rollanda's response to Sierra in bold/italic font)

Hey Rollanda!
I'm just sending you a short e-mail to say hello. I'm sure you're extremely busy so I won't keep you. I'm still looking forward to the conference in Canada since it's somewhat close to me. I know the conference in Tampa is going to be a great success! DC consists of a group of awesome people. I so enjoyed you all! ***Thanks Sierra***

Quick question… are the pictures that were taken at the conference in Detroit going to be put online as well? Just wondering. :0) ***yes. It will be posted in about one week.*** Hope to hear from you soon…(Oh… and your book is THA

4

BOMB! I'm not done yet. ***Thanks lady. I appreciate the compliment.*** But it's hard to go from day to day. I want to read it all at once*!) **Don't cheat.***

Read one day at a time

Have an awesome day-
Sierra

From: Sierra
To: Rollanda
Sent: November 15, 2006
Subject: Good afternoon!

Good afternoon mighty woman of God,

Wow... I'm still reading the book and I'm learning so much! I have got to recommend this book to be read by every dancer I know. Even as I read, the Lord began to give me little things to do for what He has given me to do. But it's kinda scary beginning. He has told me to begin teaching dance class. He gave me the name of the class/studio, and now I'm working on a format. He sends confirmation after confirmation about having a studio. My issue is I feel like I don't know enough. But when I told the Lord that, I got a sharp reply "You know Me." When you have time, could you give me some pointers and/ or even briefly tell me how you got started with your ministry? I am presently in dance school and I'm loving it. (My very first performance is coming up in a few short weeks.) Oh, and I contacted Joannie Dougehousen yesterday in regards to joining her dance classes- mainly because it is Christian based and I need the meat, not only technique. I believe once I do what He said, the little dancers are going to come from all over the city. People have been asking me for a few years where I teach dance at. That was before I began teaching anyone- even at church. I know its God and it's not about me in no shape, form, or fashion. I have put it off for quite some time for fear of stepping out on what He told me to do. But I have recently picked it up again and began to pray on clear direction on what He wants me to do, how to carry it out, where to have it, what format does He want me to have, things like that.

Your book reminded me that it's not about me. Yes, the gift is in my hands, but I'm not in control of the gift, the gift-giver is in control. These are His ideas, not mine. So I must consult Him. Whenever you have time... :0)

I was also wondering, how was the conference in Tampa? I think I told Mrs. Ah'shely that if I could, I would go to every city with you all so that I can learn, learn, and learn some more!

Have an awesome day!!!!
Sierra

From: Rollanda
To: Sierra
Sent: November 16, 2006
Subject: Re: Hello Rollanda!

Sierra, WOW!!! I'm so happy to hear that you are enjoying my work. To g-d be the glory. Thanks for sharing your thoughts and vision w/ me. YOU CAN DO IT! If G-d speaks a thing it SHALL COME TO PASS!!! Please call me on Saturday between 1pm - 2pm. Thanks, Rollanda

November 29, 2006
Dear Diary,

I feel so honored! I'm also a little thrown off at the same time. Rollanda has been calling me out the clear just to chat. I mostly keep silent when we're on the phone together, just listening to her talk. Since I've been in armorbearer training, my take on leaders (especially leaders that are as busy and well-known as her) is that they are always super busy. So if they give me a moment of their time, I'm not to take it for granted, but rather glean from them. Be present, but not a chatter box. Anyways, yeah, like one day I texted her and asked if she could talk because I needed some advice. More so like I needed to vent. She called me a little while later and we talked for at least a good hour or so. The conversation was detailed, on my part. I was mad about things going on at church and dealing with the ladies I danced with (as usual) and stuff that's happening at home (as usual) . She listened and gave me some pretty good advice. I wish I could remember the whole conversation. Since the conference here in Detroit, we've been staying in contact quite a bit. She's been texting me at 2 and 3 in the morning...just to see if I'm up. Sometimes I'd lie and say yes I'm awake. Normally I'm not awake at 2 or 3 am. I'm trying to get my last few hours of sleep in before the next busy day...But there were a few occasions where I may have been half sleep or something and decided to respond to her text. One day, she called me while she was shopping for pillows at Wal-Mart. She didn't want anything at all but just to chat. I didn't know what to think of it! Lol. Another day, she kept

6

texting me until I woke up because she said she needed someone to talk to while she drove home from a dance conference. It was about 2 hours away from where she lived. I was wondering why she called me of all people; why not talk to her husband... But before I could ask, she said that her husband refused to stay on the phone with her and her best friend is asleep. I sat up in bed and listened to her talk about the conference until she got home because she said she was sleepy. It's all good though. That's fine with me. I'm glad we connected! I thank God for it all :0)

November 30, 2006
Dear Diary,

I know it's been almost a week since the conference, but I'm still thinking about everything I learned there. I've never in my life been to a conference like that. I mean, that was my first dance conference ever anyway, but it blew my mind out the water! And I gained a friend! Porsha! She lives in a city 2 hours away. And she's a travel agent. Let's see, I love to travel, she's a travel agent, both of us love to dance...I think this was another God connection! Amen! Thank you, Lord for friends. She's so nice. I'd rather think about this conference then think about the other things happening around me. Over the last 3 months alone, my apartment caught on fire, my favorite cousin was murdered, and now I'm living back at my parent's house. So, dancing and meditating on the Word are keeping me sane, right now. Gotta find something to smile about somehow!

December 2, 2006
Dear Diary,

This has been a very trying year for me. I wish my apartment didn't catch on fire. I'd still have my own space. I mean, I'm grateful to be able to come back to my parents' house and stay here til I get back on my feet but its sooooo stressful here! I need my own space and privacy, so does my little sister. I want to be able to hide away from the world whenever I need to. But I can't while I'm here. It seems like I'm tired every single day of the week. From waking up at 5 in the morning, taking my sister to school 30 minutes from home, dropping my mom off at work about an hour from home, then going to work for 8 hours, having to go pick everyone back up, take them home, then go to dance class, or church, or school or do something else that the family needs done...I'm just tired of all of this. I feel like I'm being selfish, but then again, I'm just burnt out.

December 13, 2006
Dear Diary,

Had to jot this word down! Minister Iyani kinda shocked me with this one. Oh boy, here we go!

"During this season of your life, be very careful. Do not allow the devil to trick you in any area of your life. The Bible said that God will not have us ignorant of satan's devices. So be watchful as well as pray. Don't take down your guard. Stand on the word. Increase your reading and studying and prayer. The call that is on your life, take it more serious. Only you know what all that entails. You know the prophecies that have been spoken. You know what you are called to do. Begin to line up with His word. Beware of people in sheep's clothing. Do not desire a husband. God will send yours in due time."

LOOKING BACK

This was a word given to me in December 2006. By this time, I was already in the process of developing a relationship with Rollanda, fast. Again, this was a warning to me from the Lord. He told me to be careful and not to allow the devil to trick me in ANY area of my life. This was yet another warning I did not heed. I simply wrote it in my journal and tucked it away. Right after this word was given, I was invited to Rollanda's house. During this same time, I had been told that there was residue of lust in my spirit. I ignored it. This was clearly a trick of the enemy for me. I continued my day-to-day life as though I was still delivered because I had not *acted* on anything. Granted, each time I saw a woman I felt was attractive, I gave myself a few more seconds to look before praying. Instead of turning my head when a lusty sex scene came on in a movie, I looked and entertained it for a few seconds more. I took double looks. I entertained thoughts. Little by little, I allowed it room back into my life without even realizing it.

Why? Because I let my guard down. I didn't increase my studying of the word and my prayer life began to become monotonous. Had I been in my word and had that vital lifeline of prayer with the Lord, this story may not have happened. Or, had I been obedient to His word, I would have been able to discern that this person was a wolf in sheep's clothing. I would have been able to test the spirit by the Spirit, as the word tells us to do in 1 John 4:1 *"Beloved, do not believe every spirit, but test the spirits, whether they are of God; because many false prophets have gone out into the world."*

Furthermore, I didn't heed the word from the prophet. The Bible tells us in 2 Chronicles 20:20 *"....Believe in the LORD your God, and you shall be established; believe His prophets, and you shall prosper."*

December 14, 2006
Dear Diary,

Jesus, submission hurts! Having to submit to people you hardly believe like you is hard. But just like You said…love your enemies. For if you only love those that love you, where is your reward? Even people that don't have a relationship with You do that. Lord…how is it that I can get a word of encouragement from someone saying, don't let people walk all over you and treat you any kind of way. Then another pastor says, why not? Why not be a doormat so others can get to Jesus? Who says you don't have to be? I understand both. So Lord, what do You say? Yeah, I want to obey even though it hurts. A lot of times I do and say things because I'm hurt. I'm still hurt because my flesh is being crushed but my spirit is receiving understanding.

January 19, 2007 (at home)
Dear Diary,

Ok. My brain hurts. I want so badly to move. I am sick of being the one that has to catch it every time my parents argue. It's like- my mom is being used by the devil to attack me. I could wake up, get ready for work, get in the car and I hear "You are so disrespectful…in general!" I'm like, "I didn't do anything to you. All I did was wake up!"

Why do I have to go through this? She constantly disrespects me and expects me not to say nothing. If I do or if I disagree, I'm disrespectful. Am I not 23? Okay, it's so far beyond time for me to go. But I'm stuck 'cause I'm not too sure if it would be wise for me to move. I don't want to be out of the will of God. But this is driving me NUTS! I wish I had a friend I could go stay with. If you sow disrespect you're gonna reap disrespect. She's not sowing love, that's for sure (Not right now!).

March 10, 2007
Dear Diary,

Rejection. I hate it. I really do. I am beginning to see why I do, act and say some of the things I do, act and say. It's out of rejection. I cannot give love, if I feel rejected. I cannot receive love if I feel rejected. This demon causes

9

me to feel rejected by everyone, even those that do love me and deeply care for me. Any wrong I do, I reject myself. Now – I realize why I can't even see the love of God operating in my life.

Remember that it is God who saved your life when you tried to attempt suicide at 14 years old. He said "Don't do it, I love you. Don't do it. I love you!" I feel as though today, rejection has consumed me.

March 16, 2007
Dear Diary,

Lord, I don't understand. Why am I feeling like this? I know Your favor is upon me and I am called to dance…but the connections You are placing together in my life with people of greatness, I don't understand. Also, I brought my cousin here to be blessed- to receive from You and…I know I can't see a difference in her but then again, I don't see her heart. Anyway- why am I always being put in the front? I'm trying to hide behind others but I realize that I cannot hide.

Note To Self: Rollanda said in the Prophecy in Dance class "The anointing comes in the power of my dance." Oh, and during our prophetic dance class, my partner said the Lord spoke this to her about me "He's drawing poison out of you….something that was already there."

**Talk to Rollanda about what happened when He told her to dance before Him and she knelt down instead. I'm interested to know. The Lord has instructed me to dance before Him every service. I don't have to be called to dance in order to dance for Him. But I was too afraid to do it…more afraid not to do it, so I did do it, a little bit. But not what He said to do… then the next service, I did nothing at all.

March 18, 2007
Dear Diary,

(After The Dance Challenger Conference in Ontario, Canada (March 15-17)) This conference was incredible! WOW! Okay, I got quite a bit from this conference. Wow. Well, I had a chance to talk to Rollanda about a few things and what she said brought clarity to what I believe the Lord is doing. I'm always being pushed to the front. The entire conference too! Trish had me lead the class in stretching for her while she went to get something. Rollanda had me go first on everything or lead or put me in the front row. In each workshop, the other participants pushed me to the front (while we were in groups). In dance class – same thing. Rollanda said, "Ask yourself this. Do you want to be seen? Or why do you want to be in the front? If you find you have an issue there, then you need to examine that. But maybe the Lord (paraphrasing) is saying that He has forgiven you of the prideful stuff and He's calling you to the front."

I know why. Cause I'm a leader! Lol. This- He's showing me, it's something I cannot run from. She even mentioned something about those people that see something in you and are trying to pull (or bring) that out of you. Then the next day, she put me first again (Ahhhhhh!!!! The insanity!!!) God is so good! Whatever you want Lord. It's in Your hands. Oh- and one of the instructors (the one from England) asked me if I was teaching one of the classes (at the conference). I said no. She said "You will soon!"

From: Rollanda
To: Sierra
Sent: March 26, 2007
Subject: need help w/ hotel info for MI please

Sierra, how are you lady? Would you please help me? Would you please research hotels in Detroit that might appreciate our conference this year. I need to book MI asap. Go and look at them for me. I'm looking for the level of hotel like in Toronto. Once you shoot me the names, my travel and booking cord can get on it asap. I'm excited about seeing you and the team again. Also, are you praying about armorbearing me on trips. Please let me know if G-d speaks. Thanks. Lol. Rollanda

From: Sierra
To: Rollanda
Sent: March 29, 2007
Subject: Re: need help w/ hotel info for MI please
(Rollanda's response in bold)
Rollanda-
I have prayed about armorbearing you on trips and have spoken to my pastor about it as well. And although I would love to armorbear you, I do not have peace about it at this time. I know within myself that I am not in a place to serve anyone to that capacity right now. I know you said not now, but in time. But, I just don't have peace about that at this time.

There are some spiritual issues that the Lord is dealing with me on and I must focus on that.... for my deliverance. That's about all I have for now.... I have

11

a question though. When you prayed about this, did the Lord reveal anything to you about me?

He did. However, it's not the time to share. In time we'll talk about it. Not that important for you to know right now. What is important is that you deal w/ your issues. Let Daddy deal w/ you. Get the victory and move forward in victory. Amen!? We'll talk in time if he wants us to.
Sierra

April 22, 2007
Journal entry and Word from Pastor Odetta
Dear Diary,

As of April 17, 2007, I am no longer a member of V.O.P and PO is not my mentor anymore. The first 5 days I was straight. Today, I'm okay, just thinking a lot. Pastor Odetta gave me a word from the Lord today. The word was: The enemy is coming after my mind. And after that, he's coming to take my life. Then she told me to go after God with all I've got.
That is a scary word…In addition to that, yesterday while talking to my friend via text, a scripture dropped in my spirit. Jeremiah 17:5. I knew the word, just not sure where it was. I gave it to her, not as being from God, but suggested she read it. I then felt like the Lord was saying that word was for me. Then at church today, Deacon C went straight to that same scripture for offering. Coincidence? I think not. Before that, like on Thursday or Friday, the word for the day on Bible.com was found in Hosea 10:12, "Sow for yourselves righteousness; Reap in mercy; Break up your fallow ground, For it is time to seek the Lord, Till He comes and rains righteousness on you." So I continued to read in Hosea. The analysis of the book is about God's unconditional love. *If that ain't God!!!!* Then the other words He spoke to me last summer, Laodicea and lethargic, came back to my remembrance. It's time for me to get serious about the Lord. No half-heartedness. Be real.

April 24, 2007
Dear Diary,

One of these days, I will be secure in who I am in Christ. I will be able to stand strong, make decisions the right way, consult the Lord first and WAIT for Him to answer. Don't make anything HAPPEN (on my own strength or "wisdom"). Just let God be God. Stop seeking people for what thus says the Lord. Develop a stronger prayer life of my own. Tear down the walls of rejection, anger, bitterness, hurt, disappointments and replace it with the fruit of the Spirit.

12

April 30, 2007
Dear Diary,

Ohhhh I CAN'T WAIT!!! ONLY 4 MORE DAYS!!!! I littered my calendar at home with red marks counting down each day til I go to Florida! I'm soooo freaking excited! Oh my goodness! I've never been to Florida before. I've never been to a beach nor seen the ocean before. So Rollanda and Trish are planning to take me to the beach and some other things they named. Oh gosh, I can hardly stand it! I've been packed for a week already…just waiting for the day to come. I just bought a new swimsuit, packed all the flip flops I can find, and plenty of lotion. I'm sooo ready for this. God knows I need a break from Michigan and everything in it! My job included! Geesh! Since I got this "promotion" to Executive Administrative Assistant, I have been in serious need of a vacation. This dude is difficult to work for. I'm so glad he's in Germany right now. And I'll be outta here too…in exactly F-O-U-R M-O-R-E D-A-Y-S!!!! AHHHHHH!!!!!!

May 7, 2007
Dear Diary,

I'm actually sitting on top of a building at the Indianapolis Airport writing this. Just enjoying the sunshine and preparing myself to go back home to stress and whatever I have to deal with at church. I have about 45 minutes left until my plane leaves for Detroit, so I'ma write about my time in Tampa with (smiles) Rollanda and Trish! Awww man, I had so much fun. When I arrived at the airport that night, Rollanda and Trish came to pick me up. Both greeted me with hugs (which was a surprise to me cause the first time I met Trish face to face at the conference in Canada, she shook my hand. Ha!) They put my bag in the back of the jeep and we all proceeded to get in the car. I was gonna get in the back but Trish insisted that I sit in the front. Rollanda looked at Trish crazy and said "Why'd you get in the back, love?" Trish motioned that it was ok. Soooo anyway, Rollanda said she'll take me on the scenic route to her house. We rode down one street that seemed to never end all the way from the airport to her house. We passed the football stadium, a really beautiful mall with palm trees and huge fountains in front of it and she also pointed out where her church home was. I was trying to hide my super big grin 'cause I was extra happy to be there and I was just taking t all in.

Once we arrived at their home, I was surprised. I thought she lived in a mansion. But hey, I have yet to learn about the housing market in that area. Anyway, she showed me the room where I'd be sleeping during my stay, which was the prayer room. Rollanda mentioned to me that whenever guest pastors or ministers come in from out of town, she and her husband may offer to let them stay at her house and serve them. I felt so honored to sleep in there. It was an all white room with antique things in it: an antique phone, antique bed and 2 side tables. The room was decorated with a white sheer cloth draped on the wall with a red rose in the middle. There were plenty of Christian books for me to read on the side table if I wanted. Rollanda gave me a tour of downstairs. She showed me the guest bathroom and the laundry room if I needed to wash my clothes. Showed me their office and told me to help myself to breakfast in the morning.

Every day they took me to a different beach. It was GLORIOUS!!! Oh my goodness! We went to Starbucks…my favorite hideaway spot! Man, they took me to like 3 or 4 different beaches or piers. They took me to see this pink palace that Rollanda said she got married in. We drove over this loooooooong bridge over the ocean. I was kinda scared, but I played it cool. I really freaked out when I felt the bridge start swaying. They laughed at me for being scared. So! Lol. They explained to me the history behind that bridge and why it was built to sway like that. Didn't make me any less scared but it was a nice lil' history lesson. Lol.

 While we were on our way back to the city from the Pier, Rollanda asked me a question about something…what the heck did she say??? Anyway, I have a scriptural answer (which is expected of me, right?) and she said, "Oh girl, you're too religious for me. We're free down here." Hmmm…free. Free meaning….what? Well, I did notice quite a few odd things that I guess aren't worth mentioning because I don't know them that well to speak on `em. Could be character flaws. They compromise quite a bit. Little things that I wouldn't do. But that's them. They are *different* here. I guess.
 But anyway, um, on the day I was supposed to leave, I called my moma and begged her to pay the fee so I can change my flight and stay another day. I was soooo excited when she said YES! Yay me!!! So I stayed an extra day and relaxed in the Florida sun with these fun people. They even had a tea party just because I was there visiting! Awww! Mr. Chad gave me one of the pictures he sells of his photography. It was of a sail boat in the ocean in the Bahamas. Omg! The water was so beautiful! I have a gang of sea shells to take home I got while walking along the shore with Rollanda, a nice shirt that Rollanda gave me and a few other things, plus a gang of pictures for memories' sake.

I cried this morning before I left. I gotta admit, I'm embarrassed about it now. But I was giving Rollanda a hug goodbye before her husband took me to the airport this morning, and I just started crying. I said "I don't wanna go back there! I wanna stay here in Florida!" Before I realized what I was saying, it was too late. Face on the floor. Ooops, just embarrassed myself. Oh well. What's done is done. I mean, what I expressed was how my heartfelt. I don't want to go back to Michigan. But…I gotta go back today! Lol. It was fun while it lasted. Next trip on the agenda, LAS VEGAS for the DDD Dance Conference!!!! Me and Jas are too excited. About to head to my terminal… Chow!

May 9, 2007
Dear Diary,

I just finished filling out all this paperwork and answering all these questions as part of Rollanda's mentoring program. I've never done anything like this before. Everything is so, thorough and organized. The questions had my mind going for a minute. I have to admit, I did get frustrated when she kept telling me to do it over. I had to answer the questions over because I guess she felt I wasn't being honest. But I was! Although I answered them quick, everything was truthful…to my knowledge. Lol.

She stated that before we entered into this mentor/mentee relationship I had to be able to understand and explain my definition of a mentor/coach. I was to determine the season of this relationship – which I didn't really understand what she was asking, so I didn't answer it. Lol. She asked me questions like what do I want out of ministry? What do I want out of life? What are my top 5 areas of challenge? What excites me the most and what frightens me the most. I was asked to describe myself and also describe what my paradise would be like. Name a time of my life where I felt like I was on top of the world, and a time when I felt really low. Oh, last but not least, she requested that I be open and honest with her about my spiritual walk and keep her private life, private. I mean, there were tons more questions, but those, amongst a few others really stuck out to me.

Overall, I believe I can handle this. I'm so excited! I'm gonna have a mentor!

From: Rollanda
To: Sierra
Sent: May 10, 2007
Subject: Mentor Info

I had a chance to go over your answers again thoroughly. OK. I'm ready to begin. Step one. Call me for covenant prayer and assignment one. OH BOY... Are you ready for a whirlwind year? Remember this day! Always remember this day for this is the day we covenant to be partners for our growth and for the kingdom sake. May Christ alone lead us.

Living w/ purpose. Walking in Destiny ~ Rollanda Robertson-Anchorage

May 14, 2007
Dear Diary,

Jesus...thank you for loving me despite my daily jack-ups. Your mercy truly endures forever. Each day you give me something to smile about. Because You are You, I can smile and be happy. Thank you, Lord for gradually revealing my heart to me. The reason(s) why it's so difficult for me to open up my heart to anyone. I have been wounded in pastime by those I loved, those that said they loved me and cared for me – in church and before Christ. Betrayed by family, my best friend, wounded by my parents and pastors (crushed is more like it), and rejected in one way or another by my peers. This has been throughout my life. So I unknowingly speak evasively to even those that I try to express my true feelings. By shielding my deepest secrets, I am protecting myself from being hurt like that again. By opening myself, I'm allowing myself to become vulnerable. I just don't want to feel that type of pain again. Although I know the solution isn't to not let anyone in – it's just difficult. To expose my own fears, insecurities, doubts, and weaknesses to someone is like letting them see me naked. Can they handle it and still love me? Can I handle it and still love them? Will I still love myself??

June 6, 2007
Dear Diary,

Trish just called me to chat. I thought that was very nice of her. I was quite surprised to hear from her. She told me that Rollanda really likes me...so, she guesses that makes me "aight". Our conversation was really short, but one thing Trish did tell me that kinda stuck with me was that Rollanda told her that me and Trish could never be friends unless neither one of us were a part of The Dance Challenger. I was like "why would she say that?" Neither one of us could answer that question nor do I know what she meant by that. But whatever! Lol.

July 22, 2007
My word from the Lord during Sunday service

16

I chose you from the beginning. I chose you, when you didn't even know Me. I chose you when you were in the womb of your mother. I chose you when your mother didn't even know Me. It's more than a dance. It's more than a dance. It's more than a dance. There's so much more I've put in you. There's so much more. (Bind the spirit of disappointment. I bind the spirit of discouragement. I bind the spirit of rejection!) So much disappointment. So much rejection. So much so that you reject yourself. I have not rejected you says the Lord! I love you. Feed my lambs! Feed my sheep! Feed my sheep! The dance is just a drop in the bucket. There's so much more!

August 21, 2007
Dear Diary,

I had two dreams this morning. One was about Nikki. She told someone that she wanted to fight me. There was no explanation for this. She just wanted to fight me.

Next dream: I saw a news report. The news caster said something about a traffic accident.
"Pat- Worship Expressions Your-way volunteer and someone else died in a car accident. Please send your emails of condolences to….? (Whoever her contact person was)". I saw weyregistration email address.

September 11, 2007
My word during prayer
"Run, run, run woman of God. Run after Me with all you've got. The enemy is after you. There's like a bag. A big duffle bag you're carrying and there's a trail of all of your stuff falling out. There are gifts…even gifts you had on you. You only see what's in front of you. But there's more. There is more in you. There are many gifts in you. Where much is given, much is required. I have called you as an intercessor. I called you out. There's been much imparted in you. I hear you saying "But I thought I was giving you all I've got." But there's more in you.

The enemy wants to rob/steal the anointing that is on you. Run after Me. Run, run, run after Him with all you've got. I hear you say "I am running after Him." But God said MORE! That's not all you've got. The Lord whispers to you. He whispers to you in a small voice. He speaks to you. He's gonna make this plain to you. Quiet your spirit where it's not so much in your ear. He's gonna speak to you. He knows your heart's desire. But before it can be your desire, it has to be His desire. You've asked Him for a whole lot. You've got a list of things. A long list like a Santa Claus list. The Lord

17

has revealed some things to me (Pastor Odetta) but I will only serve as confirmation. You gotta get it from God. She thinks it's a bad thing, but it's a good thing. Watch what the Lord does in her life! She doesn't realize she's being set up! The Lord is setting her up! Just tell Him yes. It's really not that big a deal. Just tell Him yes Lord. Whatever it is, YES!"

LOOKING BACK

This is yet another word I received from a prophet before I moved to Florida. Clearly, I did not take heed to this warning either. I did just the opposite! I did NOT run after God. I followed where my flesh led me - which was right out of the will of God. Instead of running after Christ with all I had, I digressed. I chose MY words over the word from the prophet. One reason was because I had not dealt with the spirit of rejection that was ruling my life. Secondly, I was offended by the one giving it to me. So again, I wrote this word down and totally disregarded it. Huge mistake. I casually dismissed the part where the Lord warned me that the enemy is after me and he's coming to rob/steal the anointing that is on me. The word "rob" is defined as "to take something from (someone) illegally, as by force or threat of violence". The word "steal" is defined as "to take (the property of another or others) without permission or right, especially secretly or by force." Apparently, the Lord was trying to warn me and get me to understand what the enemy intended to do involved great harm and pain to me, and my life. The Lord allowed this word to be given to me because He cares about my soul and He truly loves me! But - I chose not to take heed to this warning and decided to follow my own lusts and desires instead. At no point can I ever say that I was tempted or tested by God in this. It clearly was not in His will for me to turn away from Him.

James 1:13-15 *Let no one say when he is tempted, "I am tempted by God"; for God cannot be tempted by evil, nor does He Himself tempt anyone. But each one is tempted when he is drawn away by his own desires and enticed. Then, when desire has conceived, it gives birth to sin; and sin, when it is full-grown, brings forth death.*
I deemed this to be a word that was not from God (at the time), but something that was said publicly to embarrass me by the one delivering it because this person did not agree with me leaving. How wrong was I?!?!? VERY! My arrogance and pride led me to treat this word as garbage. But had I taken heed to this word, my relationship with Christ wouldn't have been lost.
Looking back, this word was so on point and it DID come to pass. This is how I see it: In the process of me carrying this duffle bag (which represents travel), not only did ALL of my things fall out (my relationship with Christ, anointing on my life, my desire to live saved, etc); I nearly lost my life as well.

Email conversation between Pastor Odetta and
Sent: October 1, 2007
Subject: Good morning

Pastor Odetta: Good Morning Beautiful Sierra,
How are you? I pray that all is well. I am looking forward to our dinner. You pick the place. I want to talk to you about some things we never got around to discussing. This move came so fast. My husband told me that you were going on with your move. I am sorry to hear that. Nevertheless, know that I love and adore you. You, my dear, will always hold a special place in my heart. I will miss you.

God does have a plan for your life and right now you are at a crossroads. And there is a serious battle going on in the spirit for your soul. I am praying for you.
Love & Prayers .... Pastor O

Sierra: Thanks Pastor Odetta. I'm sorry I forgot to put the thank you cards in the bag for you. I have them with me and will bring them to you tomorrow.

Love you too!

Pastor Odetta: Hey Sweetie, Is that all u have to say? You forgot my cards? Wow!

Sierra: LOL! I'm sorry. I don't know what else to say. Seriously. Regarding the battle for my soul: I don't know what to say because every time I turn around there's a battle for my soul. It's always been since I gave my life to the Lord. So, I mean, that's not surprising. Not to say it's cool or nothing. But I'm aware that there's a battle.

I will miss you too.
I'm sorry... I just don't know what to say from here...
Oh, about your cards. Yeah, that was on my mind yesterday....

Pastor Odetta: I thought I said intense battle. You sound like you are getting smart. But let me say this. Don't get all sour because I don't agree with your move. If you believe you are following God then why can't we discuss it like mature adults. What I was saying is that the fire is turned up.

LOOKING BACK
Indeed! I was being VERY smart and disrespectful. I was wrong on all points

19

in this conversation. 1. I laughed off the fact that I was being WARNED about there being a battle for my soul. Since when did a battle for your soul become a laughing matter? It's not. As a believer, this should have alarmed me. But because I was in a bad place, I wasn't able to receive it as such. 2. The Bible says in
1 Peter 5:8 *"Be sober, be vigilant; because your adversary the devil walks about like a roaring lion, seeking whom he may devour."*

I was in denial of the fact that the enemy was after me, that there was a battle for my soul, or even that the fire had been turned up BECAUSE I was convinced that I was right in my decision to leave my church, my job, my family (and more), and move to Florida. I did not want to even look at that as possibly being close to right. I was content with believing Pastor Odetta wanted to see me fall on my face. This too was a lie from the enemy. Pastor Odetta told me what the Lord instructed her to tell me. It was up to me to take heed or not. I chose not to. She was never against me. That was only rejection feeding me poison. I know that she loves me with the love of Christ and she cares for my soul.

Sierra: Noooo. I am soooo sorry Pastor Odetta. I wasn't trying to get smart at all. I promise I wasn't. I wasn't trying to be sarcastic either. I'm sorry. I mean you no disrespect in any way. I'm sorry. We can discuss it.

Pastor Odetta: On the contrary, Miss Sierra, you were getting smart. Telling me you already know that there is a battle for your soul. And there has been one since you got saved.

Sierra Rae Rae Brown, I have been nothing but loving and kind to you. I expect nothing less from you in return. You are **NEVER** to disrespect or dishonor me. I don't care how grown you get or how gone you get. You are still connected to me. I am your pastor/prophetess. I pray for you night and day. I cry for you and hurt for you.

You could've said, can you explain what you mean? But I feel your spirit. You must think I am going to try to talk you out of leaving. But don't worry. I gave you a word from the Lord and I am leaving it right there. This move has become a golden calf for you. I thought our relationship had grown past this.

Sierra: That's not what I meant... I apologize.

Pastor Odetta: What did you mean?

Sierra: I was trying to say, but not in a smart way- that I see there's a battle for my soul. I was agreeing with what you were saying. But it's like, whenever I'm about to do something, no matter what it is, it's the same thing. The enemy is after me. He's always after me. I wasn't trying to get smart with you in any way.

Pastor Odetta: Do you understand why?

Sierra: Sorta kinda. Not fully. Could you please explain?

Pastor Odetta: What part do you understand?

Sierra: One reason is because he's after the anointing on my life. Secondly, whenever anyone does anything for God or is even in preparation to do something for him, the enemy is always going to be after them to try and stop them any way that he can.

Pastor Odetta: Sierra, you underestimate the call on your life.

Sierra: I don't understand.

Pastor Odetta: You, Sierra Brown, are God's beautiful daughter. You have been chosen out of Tulsa, out of the midst of your sinful family to be a righteous and holy seed. God wants you to be a light to your family and to bring them to Him. God sent you here and I guess you have to determine if your purpose is completed. There is so much.

Pastor Odetta: I love you 100% for you. So does God.

Sierra: Could you break that down for me? I underestimate the call on my life. Pastor, I'm hurt. I truly, truly wish that I had your support on a lot of things I do...but I don't. I don't mean if I decide to rob a bank, I want your support... :0) But in general. And that honestly hurts.

Pastor Odetta: Sierra, I don't want you to be hurt. You are taking this the wrong way. I only told you what God told me to tell you. Before I got a word on this, I was supportive, I thought.

Sierra: Pastor Odetta, I'm having a hard time here expressing the way I feel concerning you on this matter. I don't want to say anything disrespectful to you. Not to say that I had planned on it... wait. ok, to me, when we are addressing certain things, I think it's better for me to say it vs. emailing it because I don't want it to be taken as disrespect. Nor do I want to be disrespectful in my tone.
You were supportive... in the beginning.
I....

Pastor Odetta: Call me.
Email conversation between Pastor Odetta and I
Sent: October 5, 2007
Subject: Hey

Pastor Odetta: Hi Sierra,I am sure that one day I will get to meet Miss Rollanda. But it will all be God's timing. You often pick dates that don't work for me. Our calendar is usually booked 1 year or more away. It used to be 5 years out. We had to change it because other pastors could not keep up with us. Currently our calendar is booked through Jan 2009. And we are constantly extending it. Sometimes we are able to add and take away. But we leave that to God's leading.

So it is with your party. Apostle Lydia is scheduled to come in and spend some time with me that very same weekend. We already had this planned. She will also attend church with us on that Sunday. So know that I wish you well. Mostly that you would serve God with all your heart, mind, and soul. It is my prayer that you would become a lover of the truth. No matter how painful or uncomfortable.
~ Pastor Odetta

Sierra: Ok. I understand. Thanks. Never mind the other email regarding my question.

Pastor Odetta: How do you feel? You sound a little down.

Sierra: I am. I guess there are certain things I should not push. Just let it happen in God's timing. I know that when it comes to you I tend to take things the wrong way. I believe that I do love the truth.... But I will leave that alone. I'll be fine.

Pastor Odetta: I do apologize that I have offended you. Please forgive me.

October 9, 2007
<u>Notes from Tuesday School</u>
Prophesy Seminar

Vocabulary words-
Corporate word- Words for an individual church or the church at large (the body)
Logos word- The Bible. The written word.
Rhema word- A word that is spoken from the logos. Spoken or written.
Personal prophecy- A personal word for you.
Prophet- Defender of truth. Mouthpiece, spokesperson, messenger of the Lord.

It is dangerous when you are the relative to a prophet. When you dismiss a prophet, you dismiss God. It's a blessing to have the prophet in your house. Do not become too familiar to the prophet. Your relationship to them doesn't matter you better remember who they are to the Lord.

How to handle prophecy- What to do with prophecy?
God is raising up true prophets. But you'll always have charlatans (not true prophets), immature prophets (not fully understanding), and ones that are just ignorant.

Prophets are special people to God. One of the most difficult callings to have. The prophet is not better than the rest of the 5 fold. If you fail to recognize the authority of a prophet, you refuse to hear from God.

1. When you receive a prophecy; record it, pray on it and meditate on it. You should have a book to write your prophecies in. 1 Timothy 4:14-15

2. The spoken/rhema word must line up with the logos. Read the story of King Ahab and Jehosephat. Confirmation only? No. That would mean that God can't tell you anything you don't already know.

3. Does it agree with the logos? 1 Thess. 5:20. Despise not prophesying. Test all things. Hold fast to what is good.

4. Pray. Receive the word as a possible word from God yet spoken by fallible man.

5. Seek interpretation.

23

Personal prophecy- you should always take it to the pastors. It should agree with the person that is watching over your soul. You don't act quickly on the word you receive. There is a place of waiting. (The pastors watch of your soul and protect you)

*Books to get: Prophecy and Personal Prophecy by Bill Hamon
Before you are ordained you must be tested. Proven. If you can't submit (to your leadership) then you can't lead. If you give them a hard time then it won't go well for you. Hebrews 13:17. Obey those who rule over you.

Prophecy is given to exhort, encourage and comfort.
Authority- one way we prove the word. Take it to your leaders. In the multitude of counselors there is safety. If you aren't sure about a word, put it on a shelf for a while. Go back to tending the sheep.

Prophets can pick up on people's spirit and prophecy that back to you. That what was on your heart. That's not necessarily from God. They need to learn how to skip over what they pick up and what's on their heart and speak what God is saying.
When you are clear on the interpretation of your word (and you've gotten an ok from your pastors), act in faith.

When God speaks a word- you let it happen. Don't make it happen. Personal prophecy is conditional. You can actually lose your prophecy. We shouldn't want the gift more than the Giver. Proverbs 1:20
3 Characteristics of personal prophecy-
1-Personal Prophecy is conditional. It fails because of disobedience. 1 Sam. 9:15. It can be delayed and taken away. God doesn't want your sacrifice at the expense of your obedience.
2-Unfolds over time. It is progressive. You must get the details of the prophecy.
3- I missed it...   :0(

October 17, 2007
Dear Diary,

Being a part of the Dance Challenger Team has been great! I can't wait to see the team again for the Detroit conference. Just a few more days! Then after that, off to Tampa for the next one! November 6-8! Whoooo hooooo!!! I am sooo excited! And I just can't hide it! We've all worked so hard to organize everything and have been praying diligently for the conferences (5am prayer, it's a killer! Lol). I pray a lot of dancers come from around the Metro area.

24

Lord knows we need some teaching like this in our city.

October 25, 2007
Dream

*I was at church, WGT. Rollanda came to visit. It was so weird!
I can't recall if WGT spoke to her or not. But service was over. Music was
going. People were dancing. Rollanda sat and observed. I interacted with my
church family. All of us were acting silly. Then I remembered Pastor Odetta
walking towards us. I got up and gave her a huge hug. After that, she came
and spoke to Rollanda. Once they were done greeting each other and Pastor
Odetta left the scene, Rollanda said to me "If I had (spiritual) parents that I
was wild about, I would have introduced them a long time ago. Now they
might not consider allowing me or inviting me to come back here to minister,
tomorrow." I said huh?!? "But I tried to get you two to meet. I've been
trying for the longest." (I felt bad because I never did explain what went on
between me and Pastor Odetta concerning Rollanda. I didn't know what to
do or say.)*

October 30, 2007
Dear Diary,

Well, the Detroit conference is over. Whew. Man, I can't say I'm not happy
about that! Lol. It was just a lot of work, that's all. And I enjoyed every
moment of it. But now…it's down to the wire. Time for me to pack up the
rest of my things because come next week, I'll be moving to Tampa, FL!
Yesssss!!! I can't WAIT to leave!

So anyway, the conference here this year wasn't as good as it was last year. It
was a good turn out as far as the people coming out. I think it was due to the
fact that we had to move the conference to another location at the last minute
and then Rollanda ended up having to have it in two locations, call her
website guy and have him post the info on the website about the two
locations… oh my goodness, it was quite frustrating. I'm sure a lot of people
decided not to come because of the first location. I don't blame them. I
wasn't scared tho. Shoot, I don't live too far from there. The whole crew
(minus 1 or 2 people) was here with Rollanda! It was so good to see them
again, even though I'll see them again next week. Oh, and Jas came to help
out too. She was only able to stay for one day, so she came early Saturday (at
the second location) and stayed for the leadership luncheon.

That was really nice and informative too. (I was already familiar with some of the material taught because Rollanda taught me some of the leadership stuff in the mentoring program. Needless to say, I wasn't able to fully focus on the teaching anyway because Jas and I were passing notes during the session.(Lol!) The second location was at a well known church in Detroit. What sucked to me was that I was so busy helping everyone else, serving, running from class to class making sure all the teachers were on point with their time and more, I never had a moment to enjoy the conference myself. I enjoyed helping and all, but I would have loved to participate in the conference more than I did. It's all good tho. The speaker for the evening, I won't even get on that. Yeah, I won't touch that. Anywho, I gotta wrap this up so I can finish packing. Florida, here I come!

November 5, 2007
Dear Diary,

My mom and I finally made it to Tampa! Thank God! We had to make a pit stop in Atlanta because my mother was tired and needed to take a nap. I was determined to get to Tampa and I begged for us to keep driving. Much to my dismay, we had to stop. I texted Rollanda just to let her know our progress and how excited we were to come down. Then Rollanda let me know she was in Atlanta and asked us to please stop by and see her. She was in town ministering in dance during a creative arts conference at a local church. I told her my mom was tired so I didn't think that was possible. Rollanda graciously offered her lavish hotel room to us. She said when we stop by the church, she'll give us her room key and everything. Of course, that got me super excited! I told my mom what she said, and then we made our detour to Atlanta! I was sooooo excited when I got there. I jumped out the car, ran in the church and asked some of the conference leaders if they knew where Rollanda was. They took me to her dance class, which was just ending.

We greeted each other with hugs and huge smiles. Even though we had just seen each other the week prior, you would have thought we hadn't seen each other in over a year! Ha ha ha! After giving me her hotel room key, she invited me to stay and have lunch with herself, the conference host, leaders, guest speakers and pastors. I declined. But she insisted. So I said ok. All was well with my moma. As long as she got the sleep she needed, everything was cool.

Me and my mom went on to the hotel. She took a nice little nap. I paraded around the hotel, smiling at everybody for no apparent reason. It actually made me laugh at myself. I went back to the church for lunch with Rollanda and all the leaders. I sheepishly went in and sat down. Some of the ladies from the church served all that were seated. They had a veeeery nice spread of fruits, food, breads, cheeses, and drinks. Needless to say, it was an honor to be present. Just because I know Rollanda, I get special treatment? Lol. This is lovely.

After about 2 hours, me and my mom said our goodbyes to Rollanda, then hit the road again. About 5 hours later, we made it to Tampa and checked in the hotel. I was in a rush to get my car unloaded so I called Ms. Tonya and asked if I could come over and unload my car at her house (where I was to stay for the next few months). She said it was no problem. With that, I left my moma and went on to the house to unpack my car, then went back to the hotel with my moma. I was just too excited to rest. But now that we're here, I can go ahead and chill for a minute. I have to prepare for this conference!

November 11, 2007
Dear Diary,

My thoughts while sitting on the beach (Clearwater) You, Jesus, loved me enough to die and set me free. Pieces of what Apostle Red said to me on November 9th are this (from what I remember)::: God wants to seal up those holes in me so that His love will stay in me. It's like He sends His love, I feel it but it goes through me. And I want it to remain. Rejection and my past and things present have caused the holes to form. There's like a band around me that gets tighter and tighter every time rejection or offense comes…and I've been looking for the buckle – a way to get the band off. The Lord is freeing me of this…
On another note: I am really a for real resident of Tampa, Florida. Wow. God is good! Thank you Lord for your traveling mercies. Not for me only, but all of us, moma, papa, Tammy, Rollanda and everyone else that traveled. Thank you. Now please, help me to fully understand my purpose here. I believe it's more than serving Rollanda. I need more of You, Lord. I'm starting over. Order my steps. Increase your love in me.

November 12, 2007
Dear Diary,

My moma and papa went back home today. Man, I'm gonna miss them. I'm so glad they were able to come here with me and even come to the conference and meet Rollanda. That was nice. I wanna note tho, even though I enjoyed myself helping in the conference and meeting all those people, assisting all the leaders, um one thing stood out to me that was negative. I've never heard a minister use profanity during prayer. I can't believe she said that. Rollanda called all of the staff and volunteers to stop what we were doing and come to the backroom so she can talk to us. She was so mad because of how things were going. People kept complaining, time was running short, people weren't in place, etc, etc. She said she was trying to stay calm or something but anyway, that was fine and understandable. But while she was praying, she asked God to help her not be a *****. That alarmed me. I was shocked. Like, dude, you can't talk to God like that. And you're a Christian...like, we're not supposed to use profanity. Why was that necessary? But I noticed, no one challenged it or mentioned it. Not even me.

November 13, 2007
Dear Diary,

I'm sitting on the sidewalk in front of Rollanda's house, enjoying the super awesome Florida sun on my skin and the weather down here is PERFECT today. I just got off the phone with RC. She's so crazy. She's been calling me faithfully every morning to sing crazy songs to me on her way to work. I love her. She knows how to keep me laughing. Yesterday, while I was listening to her sing, Rollanda saw me cracking up and asked what I was laughing at. So I put RC on speaker for a second so Rollanda and Trish could see why I was laughing so hard. After we got off the phone, I told them that she does this daily just to make me smile. (I love my friends!) Oddly, she gave Trish an intimate hug and asked her if she would sing to her. Weird huh?

From: Sierra
To: Pastor Odetta
Sent: November 15, 2007
Subject: Is it too late to clarify this???

LOL I'm sorry. Ok, this email is in regards to my comment, earlier; that when I got here to Tampa. I really didn't wanna call anyone because I wanted a break from Detroit and everyone in it. That's how I honestly felt. I do know that I am loved by many, many wonderful people there...like you. But there were still times that I felt like I needed a break. That's where my ME day came into play. I would take that day off for myself. I needed that peace. But in this case, that is how I felt. I had to move like 7 times within 2 weeks before I left Detroit. That's a lot to deal with, on top of losing my job and a few other things that happened with the last 2 weeks of me being there. I made it through sane...thank you Jesus. I didn't mean to sound as if I hate the people in Detroit and I was glad to get away from them. No. That's not what I meant. I just felt like I was able to breathe again. Yeah. Although I felt like I didn't wanna make any calls, I did. I called people, emailed people, and they did the same. Many of my friends, former teachers, co-workers, people from WGT and of course my family called, texted and emailed me. I have been in contact. I'm talkin to my mom, now. I knew she knew something was wrong with me. She just told me. Ok. Gotta go for now. Love you much! Sierra

Chapter 2
Chains

November 16, 2007
Dear Diary,

Man, I don't know what to say. I'm shaking as I write this. I'm still shaking and scared to death. I thank God, I didn't die in my sleep. Ok, this happened 2 days ago. I ended up spending the night over Rollanda's, because it got late and I didn't want to disturb or disrespect Ms. Tonya by coming to her house, late; so I called her to let her know I'll be staying over Rollanda's. After everyone got sleepy enough to retire to their room for the night, I went in the guest bedroom where I'd be sleeping for the night. I remember, I went to sleep grateful to be in Florida. I was halfway sleep and I remember hearing a faint tap at the door. Then it opened. It was Rollanda. She just came on in and hopped under the cover with me. I didn't mind. I was half sleep and thought nothing of it. She said "I'm so glad you're here." I said "me too. I'm happy to be here...and thanks for having me."

 She asked me for a hug, so I gave her a half sleep hug. My eyes were still closed the whole time because duh, I was on my way to sleep. I recall a faint noise coming from her when I hugged her. After I hugged her, I just laid there, eyes still closed, bout to go to sleep. She asked for another hug, so I gave her another hug and in an instant, she got between my legs and started grinding on me. Now, my eyes were wide open. I lay there, frozen. Stiff. Only noise that came from me was whimpering because I was shocked and didn't know what to think, do, say, how to feel, nothing. Within like 2 minutes, she stopped grinding on me and sat on the edge of the bed. All she said to me was "Sorry mama" and walked out the room. I never said a word. I was still flat on the bed, with my hands up by my ears, frozen. I cried myself to sleep that night.

When I woke up the next morning, it was another beautiful day in sunny Florida. Only this day was different. Around this time yesterday, I was so happy to be here in Florida. I would go outside every morning and sit on the sidewalk and enjoy the warm sun on my skin and breathe in the fresh air, just thanking God for the beauty of the new day. But this morning, I was afraid to even open my eyes for fear of what I might see. As I laid there in the bed, eyes closed but fully awake, I thought to myself "I'm going to hell." That's the only thing that came to mind at that moment. I raised my hand in front of my face and opened one eye, I'm still alive! I wiggled my fingers and opened my other eye. Thank you Jesus for not taking me in my sleep! Five minutes passed…I'm still lying very still in the same bed sin took place in just a few hours ago. "Run…run! Get up, grab your things, get in the car and drive away until you run out of gas and don't look back. Call someone to come get you. Just GO!" This is what came to me as I laid in the bed. Sounded like a great idea! I didn't want to see anyone in the house. Didn't wanna pet the dog. Didn't want to take another shower first or eat any breakfast. Just RUN. Instead of running, I just laid there.

I should have ran. But now I'm here. Still thinking about it. Instead of praying against it, I'm fighting entertaining homosexual thoughts all over again! What have I done?!!? Oh, how can I forget!?! About 2 days ago, I know it was after she came on to me so yeah, 2 days ago, while I was laying in the bed (at night), I saw a tall, dark spirit in the guest bedroom…just standing by the door. I prayed until it went away. The next day I told Rollanda there's a spirit in her house. She said "There ain't no spirits in this house. This is a Christian house." Or something like that. But I know what I saw. I know a spirit when I see one. When I got back over to Ms. Tonya's house, I sat in my car…mind blank as ever. Then I hurried and called Lenard and Pastor Odetta and told them what happened.

Of course, Lenard was trying to get me to leave Florida that same day, but I couldn't. He begged me to leave. He even offered to come get me. Plus, I don't want to go back to Michigan. I feel really horrible because I just know this is going to be really bad. Pastor Odetta told me she knew it. I guess she felt something was wrong in the spirit. I don't know. But she told me some other things that I don't recall at the moment but the one thing she did say that stood out to me was that it will happen again. Honestly, in the secret recesses of my mind, I was hoping it would. Then I was wishing she wouldn't have said anything like that and maybe I wouldn't be thinking this way. I've been fighting those thoughts ever since. I'm not blaming her. This is just a huge mess and my feet are like cement. I'm stuck.

32

November 19, 2007
Dear Diary,

Today, the loneliness of being here in Florida without my family really started to set in. Earlier this evening, I was in the guest bedroom crying to myself because my heart hurt for my family. For someone familiar. For someone that I knew. For my friends. I just needed a hug, but didn't feel like I could get one. I still feel alone. Rollanda tried to help, but I still feel alone. She texted me while I was in here to ask me what was I doing. I gave a pat answer just for the sake of responding and said I'm just laying down. I didn't tell her I was crying, but I did tell her I needed a hug and I guess I'm just missing my family, that's all. She told me to come out there with her and Trish and we can all cuddle together. So, I drug my feet and went on in the living room with her and Trish. I sat on the couch one seat cushion away from them. They were already cuddled up. Rollanda did invite me over. We all hugged each other. It was nice. They made me feel loved. After a while, we were all laughing and Rollanda was like, go get your camera! I went to the room, grabbed my camera, and we just started taking pictures. All of us, cuddled up. Faces only. Silly ones, kissy ones and a few where we pretended like we were sleep.

Then Mr. Chad came home. He grabbed his camera and started taking shots of us too. Then the dog, oh goodness, their jealous little cute dog started looking at us with those lonely puppy dog eyes because he wanted to jump on the couch with us and get some lovin' too. Rollanda let him come up. It was so cute. Mr. Chad got some really good pictures of all of us. The hugs and pictures did help for a minute. Nonetheless, I'm back here in the guest bedroom, still feeling alone. It wouldn't make sense to ask why I feel this way when I already have an idea. I just wish this feeling would go away. This sucks. I just want to cry all over again.

I called my friend Mia yesterday and asked her to sing to me. Specifically, "If Not For Your Grace" by Israel Houghton. Besides the fact that she sings so beautifully, I really needed to reach out to a true friend that would do that for me without asking questions. I'm glad she was willing. Lol. I didn't even ask her if she was busy, nor did she indicate that she was. She just did it. I appreciate that so much because it was so needed. That was my moment of fresh air. But now, I feel like there's a ton of bricks on me and I'm doing nothing to get it off of me…because of my own pride…I guess. I wish I didn't feel this way. Ok, now…I'm bout to cry. Goodbye…

November 23, 2007
Dear Diary,

Aww this is soooo cool. I was looking for a place to continue taking dance classes at in Tampa so I could stay active and continue learning technique. I asked Rollanda if there were any places she could recommend that I go and she told me there are a few places around Tampa, but until I found somewhere that I was welcome to come and train with them at Off Platforms Dance, Acrotumbling & Theatre Company for $40-$45 a month. This way, I'll be able to learn all the things they learn (drama, hip hop (which is optional), modern, lyrical, ballet technique, afro-caribbean, and acrotumbling). All that for $40 a month!?! Shut up! That's a great deal!

November 27, 2007
Dear Diary,

Oh my gosh I can't believe what I did. What we did. OMG why am I still here!??!? I am so confused and scared. Lord PLEASE don't let me die like this. Although I probably will never admit this to anyone, uh, I don't think I'm supposed to be in Tampa. But I don't want to be in Michigan! I feel like I'm being tossed around in my mind. I just wanna scream! There's so many things that I see that are wrong here...reasons I should leave NOW! But where will I go? Go back to feeling like I'm in bondage? Go back to nearly killing myself to meet the expectations of people? Uh, NO! I decided to break free from that and I don't plan to go back. Whatever. Lord...I beg of you. Please forgive me and help me get outta here! Wash me again. I never saw THIS coming...or....did I? I'm ashamed of my thoughts...but I can't stop them!

I'm so jacked up it's unbelievable. My mind is in total disagreement with what my body is doing. So let me back up to the day before Thanksgiving. I mean the day before we left to go to Atlanta. Yep. So Rollanda and I are lying on the couch watching a movie together, right? She's lying in front of me. I'm half sleep and I think she was, too. But all of the sudden, I felt her press on me. So, I took it from there and started kinda massaging her back, her side and her neck then I noticed she got aroused. Then she got up and said she has to go to bed. I said, ok. She asked me to wait for her while she fixed her tea before I went to my room and she went upstairs with Trish. Mr. Chad was asleep in their bedroom. I waited.

When she was done, I was sitting on the edge of the couch waiting for her. She met me at the bottom of the stairs and said "Goodnight mama. Come

34

give me a hug." I gave her a hug alright. I was already aroused, too. Big mistake. I started gently kissing her on her neck. That was it. No groping. No grinding. But the hug lasted like 10 minutes! She had a cup of hot tea in her hand the whole time. The she asked me "Do you still want to go all the way with me?" I said, "mmmhumm." She said "ok, let's go before I change my mind." After it was over...last thing I remember was her running from me, crawling on the floor. She got up, sat on the edge of the bed and said in a soft giddy voice, "I gotta go. I gotta go upstairs with my bestfriend." So she grabbed her tea and tip toed out my room, quietly closed the door and went to get in bed with Trish.

The next day, we left for Atlanta to be with Rollanda's family for Thanksgiving. Trish wasn't due to head for Ft. Lauderdale until either later that day or the next day. I forgot already. Anyway, I sat in the car and watched Trish and Rollanda do some lil gay kissy kissy smooch thing with each other for like 5 minutes while Mr. Chad loaded up the car with our bags. After all the goodbyes were done, Mr. Chad, Rollanda, Sparky (their dog) and I left. I sat in the back with the dog for like not even half the road trip. Rollanda and I were texting each other naughty things while she was in the front with her husband. I finally told her I want her to come back there with me. So she suggested to her husband that the dog come sit up in front with him and she come back there with me. He said ok, then she climbed over the seat to get in back with me and Sparky tried to jump in Mr. Chad's lap while driving. Anyway, she laid her head on my lap and covered herself with one of the throws from their house. I took advantage of it and started groping her. She welcomed it, so I continued. When we stopped for gas, she told me to come in with her to pay for the gas and get some stuff. As soon as we were away from Mr. Chad she asked me, super excitedly, "Where did you learn how to do that??? How? I wanna learn!" And she went on and on about it. She also expressed to me how my touch makes her weak. Shouldn't have told me that! Ha ha ha. But I would never do anything to her unless she initiated it. As weird as it sounds, I still have some amount of respect for her as a person.

So we stayed at her sister's house in Atlanta. Her house was so nice! I had so much fun there. I thought I would feel out of place as I normally do with people I don't know, but I was cool. They made me feel very welcome and at home. We went to the mountains, went to downtown Atlanta, toured the Dr. MLK church and another building across the street from there. We took the subway! That was a first! It was quite the experience! Lol. But everything was so fun. The food her sister cooked would make you wanna kick the dog. Man it was delicious!

35

All this stuff was during the day. But at night...aww man. That's a different story.

Rollanda and I were watching Talladega Nights in the den ....great movie! Nothing happend. Yay! But...out the clear things did start getting a lil heated. We ended up on the bedroom floor where Rollanda and Mr. Chad was sleeping. Mr. Chad was already sleep in the bed. Rollanda kinda instructed me on what to do to her and what not to do...so we just fondled each other for a while. Then I left the room. The next morning, Mr. Chad was out taking Sparky for a walk and Rollanda was lounging around in bed still. I asked if I could come in. She said yeah so I went in and we just held each other. Innocent right? WRONG!

Before I knew it, we were at it again. Touching each other. She told me not to...yeah... because if her husband came in she wouldn't be able to explain that to him. In my mind I was like "what?!?! did you just say that?" But I didn't let it show on my face.

Oh, I gotta skip to the dream I had the 2nd night I was there. I had to sleep in this huge bed with Rollanda's mom. It scared the living daylights outta me. I probably won't share this dream either! For more reasons than one. It does let me know where I am in my quickly fading walk with Christ.

Ok, here's the dream or what I remember:

I was in a weird place...everything was dark around me. I looked around this wall and saw two very tall, like 15ft tall beings talking. Just standing there whispering to each other. I tried to listen in closer so I could hear what they were saying. All of the sudden, I heard one say "I don't know what happened." The other said, "Yes, I know." Then they both looked at me and they said in unison "She forgot about GOD!!!!!!!!!" Their voices were so loud my entire body shook....in the dream.

Yes, but I woke up from the dream and it felt like the inside of my bones were trembling too! I was so so so so so so so sooooo scared! I just started crying. I jumped out the bed and onto the floor..on my face and started repenting to God. My heart was racing. I couldn't go back to sleep. I had no one to talk to. No one to tell.

The day we all left to head back to Tampa, Rollanda's mom prayed for us. I thought it was just for safe travels but she went off into the deep end! It was needed and I'm always grateful for prayer. However, all the while she was praying...in my heart, I was crying because of all the stuff that we did in her sister's house. Totally disrespected it. Nobody had a clue. No one but me and Rollanda. God saw it all...and I know He doesn't hate me, but if I were Him, I might not like me too much right now.

LOOKING BACK

This dream nearly scared the life out me! At that point, I knew God was right in telling me that I forgot about Him. Even before this trip to Atlanta even took place, I had forgotten about Him. I was full of lust and the desire was getting stronger by the day. I totally disregarded the truth of God's word because I wanted so badly to continue in my secret sin with Rollanda. This became an idol to me. This lust took the place of my love for God, my love for truth, righteousness and holiness.

For the record, lust is Satan's counterfeit of God's love. And during the time of this dream, I was burning with lustful desire for Rollanda. This was not God's plan for my life. This was not in His will. Nor was He pleased with me. Although I knew this, I did not care. My desire had to be fulfilled by any means necessary. I thank God for His grace! He could have taken His precious breath right out of my body that same night!

Deuteronomy 8:11 *"Beware that you do not forget the Lord your God by not keeping His commandments, His judgments, and His statutes which I command you today..."*

Psalm 50:22 *"Now consider this, you who forget God, Lest I tear you into pieces, and there be none to deliver..."*

November 29, 2007
Dear Diary,

Hummm…. Rollanda called me to come over last night. I know I should have stayed at Ms. Tonya's house. But I went, anyway. She said Trish wasn't back yet, Mr. Chad was sleep and she needed some company. I said ok and put a few things in an overnight back and drove over to her house. We watched a movie together on the couch in the living room until I got sleepy and went to bed in the guest bedroom. Rollanda knocked softly on the door, came in and got in the bed with me. Trish kept texting Rollanda while she was in the bed with me. I believe she told her she was laying with me, holding me or something because I was cold. Then, out the clear, Trish sends me a text and said "If you are bored then go over Mariell's". Basically she was telling me to leave the house. I didn't respond to it but I told Rollanda what she said to me and Rollanda got a little bothered by her remark to me and told her (via text) that she can't say that to me because it's not her house and it's not nice. After all the "melodrama", Rollanda suggested that we go in Trish's room and watch a movie. I was like, cool. So we went and got settled in the bed, put the movie on and just chilled. I was really enjoying the movie, it was good! But, um, I didn't get to see the rest of it because we ended up intertwining in lustful activities. Oops! Sorry Trish! I'm sooooo sure Rollanda didn't tell her we did stuff in her bed. She'd just die.

November 30, 2007
Dear Diary,

How about Trish came home yesterday...and I was still over Rollanda's house. Last night, I wish I was SLEEP!!! But instead I was interrupted by moaning coming from upstairs (right above the guest bedroom) and a bed lightly hitting the wall. I laid there, once again, in shock because of what I was hearing. This wasn't Mr. Chad and his wife because their bedroom is on the first floor of the house off the living room. No. This was Trish and Rollanda! O. M. G! I'm so sick. I'm soooo sick! When I heard it I cried myself to sleep. I had mixed emotions. I didn't know if it was because all of this was spiraling out of control? Is it because they didn't include me? Um, NO! This morning when I woke up, I didn't want to see either one of them. They just moseyed around the kitchen making themselves breakfast and tea as if nothing ever happened. I told Rollanda I heard them. She asked me what did I hear? Like I was trippin or something. I KNOW WHAT I HEARD!

I said I heard them two having sex. She said hummm. Then she laughed it off and told Trish I said that I heard them last night. But neither one of them looked too concerned. So we sat down at the table and discussed it briefly. She asked me how I felt. I was trembling inside because I thought God was going to kill me for sure. I felt so horrible. I didn't know how to feel. I didn't want to tell them what I was really thinking (that I came down here for one thing, but ended up in a house with a lying bisexual woman and her best-friend lover and her husband that knows nothing!) so I lied and said I was scared for their friendship. When stuff like this comes in to play, it often breaks relationships apart. So we basically left it at that. I went back in the guest bedroom and just sat there. I'm glad to be back at Ms. Tonya's. Dude this is insane! I need to leave. But my feet feel like cement! I want to tell my ma so bad but I'm too ashamed. All of this??? And I've only been here less than a month!

November 30, 2007
(Later in the day)

It's been one week since…you know. Man I feel so bad, confused, torn, shredded, unclean, backslidden-no wait, violently thrown back, messed up and all! Every day I wake up, I repent for what I've done and ask God to clean my mind, but at the same time, I feel like my prayers are in vain because I'm not doing what I should have done, which was leave! But I JUST got here! Dang! That sounds so stupid. I could JUST die today and I would JUST go to hell! Oh come on! In the back of my mind, I secretly hope it happens again. I'm so screwed. I could just cry right now because this has set me so far back. I gotta get my mind right. Starting today! God delivered me once, He can do it again. Earlier today, Rollanda texted me and asked me if I could come rub her head because she had a bad headache. I said sure and made my way over to her room. I came in and shut the door back. As I was massaging her head, I told her that I heard them last night. She was like, "What did you hear?" I told her straight up, I heard her and Trish having sex last night. I believe that was Trish moaning. I'm not sure. But the bed was squeaking. They were in the bedroom right above my head. She didn't say much at all about what I said. Never really admitted it. But I told her I was scared for them. I didn't say the real reason why, I just said I was scared because this would ruin their friendship. Then later in our conversation, I had told her we gotta pray and ask God to deliver us from the spirit of homosexuality. I shared with her, as I massaged her head, all the things I did before when I was running from this same spirit and lifestyle.

I changed my entire wardrobe, stopped wearing corn rolls (French braids straight back), started wearing earrings, everyday, changed my phone number, email address, closed my Myspace and Black Planet accounts, cut off old friends, just to name a few. I tried to tell her like, how hard this really was for me. And she said jokingly, "So what you saying? I gotta come out the closet now?" I had no real in depth response for that but I was thinking..UM, YES! While I'm on the subject, I promise she acted like she had never known there was a spirit of homosexuality. I had to repent for my thoughts after that conversation because I started getting mad like, how you gonna be an ORDAINED/LICENSED MINISTER and don't know about perversion, lust and homosexuality??? Whatever!

Oh yeah…and she had the nerve to tell me if I ever told anyone about this she would never speak to me again. Well, by that time, I had already told Pastor Odetta and Lenard. Wow. I had to tell. For my sake. I need accountability! Lord please; help me get out of this. Help her too. And Trish.

Deliver us all. And I feel super bad now because I realized I've slept with a married woman. I can't even look at Mr. Chad now. After I told Pastor Odetta what happened, she told me it would happen again. At first, I was like "Why would you say that!??!" Then later, I started hoping it would happen again. Man, I'm so screwed.

December 2, 2007
Dear Diary,

Aww man. It feels so good to be in the House again. The worship. Man I missed this! Just being in the House is refreshing. It's like, my goodness…this is where I belong. Not so much as here at this church, but in His house, this sanctuary. Oh, now that the word is being brought forth…um, this is soooooo not what I'm used to at home. Ugh. I miss my old church.

December 11, 2007
Dear Diary,

How about Rollanda told me the other day that she and her husband don't keep secrets from each other so she is going to tell him about what she and I did? At first, I was nervous. Then I came to the conclusion that um, yeah! That needs to happen. Good for her. I'm glad she's going to be honest with her husband. I don't know what she told him. But something told me she's not going to tell him about her and Trish. Anyway, I wasn't there when she told him, so I guess I'll never know. However, I KNOW she told him *something* because when we went to Wendy's the other day (me, Trish, Mr. Chad and Rollanda), Rollanda pulls out this make-up that someone donated to the dance company, opens it, and starts putting it on my face. Mr. Chad immediately started getting loud "Why are you doing that??!? Rollanda! Why are you touching her!?!? Don't do that!" The rest of us looked as shocked as I felt! She said something nonchalant and did a few more strokes on my face, then put the make-up away. I wonder what's going to happen, now? Later, I asked her what did she tell him. All she said was that she told him about the first time we did it. I was like, oh. Ok. Sooooo, now that I'm thinking about it, I guess she didn't tell him what happened in Atlanta…or, even what happened on the way to Atlanta. Or…what happened when we got back from Atlanta. Hmmmmm…..

From: Sierra
To: Pastor Odetta
Sent: December 13, 2007 11:29 am
Subject: Privacy

Pastor Odetta,

I was thinking...I have decided I don't ever want to tell my parents what I told you. This is my choice. Please, even if she brings it to you, don't tell her. That alone would crush her. I'm not asking you to lie. There are only two souls on earth that know. That's all I want to know. Please don't even tell Pastor James. I don't want him to know, either. I told you because there's a level of trust that I have with you that I don't have with many. Besides, I'm sure the Lord would show you anyway :0)

I'm handling it and today...I just realized something. I'm so grateful for God's mercy. Even in the midst of sin... He's still good. Um, yeah, but please don't share this. Never, ever, ever. Please don't discuss it ever in life. Not as an example, not even evasively. Please. Unless it's with me. I love you and thank you for interceding for me. I love you. Gotta go for now.

LOOKING BACK

I started out saying that I wanted and needed accountability. But as I continued to compromise daily, and refused to accept the fact that I was living in sin and once again engulfed in lust and homosexuality, somewhere along the way I decided I wanted to keep this under wraps for a while. I did regret telling Pastor Odetta. I wanted to keep it hidden so that I could continue to live in sin without interruptions.

Shame caused me to tell Pastor Odetta that I did not want her to share it with my parents. They knew that I used to deal with the very same thing in my past. For me to have gone back to it was extremely shameful to me. Not to mention that they did not agree with me moving down there in the first place. I was also ashamed because I was compromising the Gospel of Christ. I claimed that I was down there for ministry purposes, but truthfully, I wasn't. Everything I did for "ministry" was tainted because of my sin. And for this – yes, I was very ashamed.

Jeremiah 17:13 *"O Lord, the hope of Israel, all who forsake You shall be ashamed. Those who depart from Me shall be written in the earth, because they have forsaken the Lord, the fountain of living waters."*

I was completely wrong on all points. I was full of lust and I wanted to stay that way. Accountability is always needed! Put no confidence in your flesh. If you are struggling with something, I advise you to be honest with yourself right

41

where you are and ask God to deliver you. Today, I can say that not only have I shared it with my parents, but God has allowed me to share it with my church family and now, with the world. No more guilt and shame!

Revelation 12:11 *"And they overcame him by the blood of the Lamb and by the word of their testimony, and they did not love their lives to the death."*

Email conversation between Pastor Odetta and I
Sent: December 13, 2007 (*later in the day*)
Subject: Re: privacy

Pastor Odetta: Hi Sierra, I was very sorry to hear that you have made such a decision. It says a lot about your place. At any rate, you are correct. It is your decision. Love, Pastor Odetta

Sierra: Says a lot about my place? Por que?

Pastor Odetta: Proverbs 28:13

Sierra: Pastor Odetta.... I did confess. I confessed to you and Jesus. Is that not enough? Do I need to tell the world? I'm not trying to be sarcastic but I'm for real. At this point in time, no. I do not wish to discuss this with my parents. If I do, it will be when I'm ready. Right now I'm not.

 And I'm not covering it, I just don't want to tell them anything about it. I told you because I wanted to. I don't want to tell them.

Pastor Odetta: I have to say Sierra I am disappointed. I thought you were going to deal with this spirit that has been plaguing you all of these years. Instead you **are** covering it. No, you don't have to tell the world just the two people who love you and care about you. It will show Godly sorrow. You will be held accountable for your decisions. I think that is your greatest fear. Whether you realize it or not you are positioning yourself to fall again. You are allowing this spirit access to take over your life. I thought we had made a breakthrough.
 But you are taking it all back and regretting that you shared this with me. I am so sorry.

As always, no matter what, I love you.

~ Always, Pastor Odetta

LOOKING BACK

This statement, made by Pastor Odetta, is so true! I AM held accountable for MY decisions. What I attempted to do through the entire story was put the blame all on Rollanda, as if everything I went through, every single day was all her fault. But it wasn't! It was my fault! If I had followed the instructions given to me in the first place (not move to Florida, deal with the spirit of rejection in my life, get rid of the spirit of lust...etc.) then this story would have never been a part of my life. Instead, I chose not to take responsibility for my fault in the whole ordeal. I was scared to own up to it. I did not want to own up to the mess I created. I wanted to keep this hidden so I could continue to do dirt. I wished I hadn't told her even though I knew I was wrong.

However, now I can see how wrong I was. I decided in my heart to stay there and continue to live in sin. Nobody, not even Rollanda, made me do it. Often times, people try to play the blame game. They are looking for someone else to put the blame on so they won't be responsible for the consequences. That never helps the individual. The right thing to do is to take responsibility for your own actions, thoughts, and decisions. God will hold you accountable for what you do and say. I can't stand before Christ and blame everyone else in the world for why I didn't live for Him.

Matthew 12:36-37 *"But I say to you that for every idle word men may speak, they will give an account of it on the day of judgment. For by your words you will be justified, and by your words you will be condemned."*

Romans 14:12 *"So then each of us shall give account of himself to God."*

December 17, 2007
Dear Diary,
Although I haven't been over to Rollanda's in a while, I still feel trapped. It's like; I want to stop, I REALLY DO! I want to stop thinking about her, but I can't. I can barely look at her without thinking about sex. Even when we are in class, I can't really take her seriously. I can't take her praying for me seriously, either. None of it is real to me. All of the texts she sends me don't help either. "I love you, miss you, wanna hold you..." stuff she sends late at night...messes with my head. At the same time, I love the attention she gives me. It's weird. Like, she makes me feel needed by her. From a business aspect- she makes me feel appreciated and needed. Then at night, she flips the script. I don't know what to do! I can't be bisexual. That's not my desire. But, whether I will EVER admit it to anyone or not, at this point, I am...again. I'm in a relationship with Lenard, which is utterly horrible

because I'm doing him so dirty and he doesn't deserve this…and I'm also in a secret sexual whatever with my leader. This is soooooo jacked up.

December 22, 2007
Dear Diary,

It just got worse. Now I know I'll never speak of this because my mind is too gone. I don't even know how I got here! Rollanda took the dance ministry staff to a resort in Orlando as a token of her appreciation. It was very nice! We had a lot of fun there. There were 2 bedrooms (one with 2 beds and the master bedroom with a huge bed and Jacuzzi in it) and a pull-out bed in the living room. We went to Downtown Disney; we took pictures and just had fun laughing and talking about whatever! Oh, and we got a hand and foot paraffin. I've never had that before. My feet felt so silky smooth :0) Anyway, I'ma skip all the details because I don't feel like writing…my hand hurts and I'm sleepy. So, the first night we were there, we made our own sleeping arrangements. The second night, since so many people left, I slept with Rollanda in the master bedroom. It was just her and I. Everything was cool…until, when we, well, I was sleep, she turned over and mauled my shirt, ripped it…and… Yeah, so while this is going on, my phone is blowing up. It's like 2:30 in the morning. It's Lenard. Speaking the word of God to me. He was telling me he felt something was wrong, concerning me, in his spirit. He couldn't put his finger on it, but he knew it was something. I just turned my phone off because I couldn't bare to face the truth. I'm settling for an adulterous affair with this lady rather than give myself completely to this man that loves me. But, we are hundreds of miles away from each other! I'm not even sure what will become of us. I guess I'll accept anything that sounds good right now; just so I won't look at how bad this thing has become. In my heart, I know it's wrong. But on the outside, no one would be able to detect a single thing out of place in my life. I'm living a lie! But the lie seems so right…right now.

December 26, 2007
Dear Diary,

Ok, um, yeah, this is weird and I'm soooo not comfortable with this. I don't know 1 single person that doesn't celebrate Christmas. How about, Mr. Chad and Rollanda don't celebrate Christmas, like, at all. No exchanging gifts, no tree, I don't even think they acknowledge it. We did absolutely nothing the entire day! Ms. Tonya and Jessi went to Philadelphia to see their family. I had no money to go home to be with my mommy in Tulsa (I wish I did!!!). So I just stayed with Rollanda's household all day. The only thing they did was watch TV all day. I just sat in the guest bedroom wishing I was somewhere else. Not in Detroit, but not with people that don't celebrate Christmas. I know people that don't celebrate it; because it's said that it's a pagan holiday but rather celebrate the birth of Jesus. That's fine and dandy. I do both! Only in respect that it's the holiday, we celebrate the birth of Jesus. I'm not fond of trees and all that. But they didn't do nothing at all. Not even the story of the birth of Jesus was read. I found that to be quite odd. But whatever. Different strokes for different folks… I guess.

January 2, 2008
Dear Diary,

I can't believe this. I just had the worst New Year's, ever!!!! Mr. Chad, Rollanda, Trish & I went to Busch Gardens on New Year's Eve. I didn't have money to go to Tulsa or Detroit so I was stuck there. Rollanda gave me the ticket she bought for Ah'shely to go so I wouldn't have to pay. When we got there, everything was fine. I mean, for the most part. I was so happy to be there because I had never been before. I wanted to get on the roller coasters and laugh and have a great time looking at the fireworks and stuff. Man, not long after we got there, Rollanda and Mr. Chad tell me and Trish they don't want to ride anything, just look around and play the other games on ground level. I was like ok, thinking Trish and I would go get on stuff. Um, that didn't happen, either. We all ate a lil' something together, kept walking around until I felt like the two married people wanted to be alone. Obviously, Trish didn't want to leave Rollanda. Anyways, long story short, I ended up getting lost. I lost them in the crowd at the park. Ok, we're in Florida. It's freakin' New Year's Eve and we're in a tourist attraction park with literally thousands of people walking around. And I'm not from here. Why in the world wouldn't you be concerned that I'm lost or missing? I can't assume they didn't care. But whatever. It appeared to be that way. They wouldn't come look for me or help me find my way because they wanted to see the fireworks after the countdown (at 12am). I was totally lost! I couldn't believe they said that!!!

I ran halfway around the park looking for them. I texted all of them, well just Rollanda and Trish constantly because we couldn't hear each other on the phone because of the loud live band playing on stage and people yelling and screaming everywhere. I ended up on a park bench under a covering of trees with no side lights, crying on the phone with Lenard. I was so hurt and pissed because they just left me. They were sooooo selfish!!!

45

After the fireworks, I found them – they finally decided to look for me. The park closed at 1 or 2am. We met up by landmarks.

Once we met up, I was so upset, I didn't say a word. I was mad at Trish because she left me to go back and find Mr. Chad and Rollanda after we left them (together) the first time. I wanted to go on some rides instead of following Mr. Chad and Rollanda around doing nothing. Trish later apologized to me and sang to me until I cheered up. She made up a song just for me and screamed it to the top of her lungs as we walked through the park. It did make me laugh. It took a minute, but she always does stupid stuff that makes me laugh. I hope I never ever have another New Year's like this.

January 7, 2008
Plans after moving back to Detroit:
(I don't wanna go tho!)
(What "To-Do" while on lockdown~ because I know I will be!)
Spiritual connection w/God
Tags renewed- need insurance
Income tax
I want my kitten back :0(
Exercise daily
Read word daily
Attend church as much as possible
Get Pocahontas, Rema & Eden for church
Dance regularly
Get back to AIN Dance (asap!)
Pay off school tuition
Work on invention
Continue working on acrotumbling
Take salsa dance classes.

LOOKING BACK

I was making plans to move back to Detroit because I knew the Lord told me to "go back home" before I had ever got to Florida. But once again, I chose my will over His. If you are reading this and you are currently struggling between choosing your will versus the will of God, I pray that you will choose His perfect plan for your life. We often find ourselves in a rut because of our own decisions. Let's (continue to) allow the Lord to lead us, and not our flesh.

Proverbs 16:9 *A man's heart plans his way, but the Lord directs his steps.*

January 9, 2008
A word given to me by Rollanda:

You are going to walk through many doors with me that others will not get the opportunity to. Not friends, family or others close to me.

(This is what the Lord told Rollanda 2 months ago. She told me this is what He showed her concerning me.)

January 11, 2008
My thoughts:

From My Heart To The Pen~
Where there was once joy and laughter, there's now tears of sorrow. Uncertainty fills my days and I have restless nights. How can this pen express the fear that races through my heart? With each passing day my thoughts are ripping me apart. Feeling torn and unsure of my next step. My heart aches for love…but I have love. I am loved…by God. This pen can only do what I command being only a tool in my hand. My heart is forced to keep silent. Not even a pen can communicate the silent cries of my heart.

January 12, 2008
 Dear Diary,

I feel kinda bad because I can't afford to keep paying Rollanda for the dance classes she's allowing me to take. With everything I have to pay now...providing for myself with money I get from temporary jobs, paying Ms. Tonya to stay at her house, gas for my car, etc., with no job...I just can't afford any extra-curricular activities. I just told her that I didn't have the money to keep paying. But the good news is she's letting me stay. Yay for me! Honestly tho, I am feeling like this is a bit much for me. I mean, I can handle all that she's giving me but I don't think it's fair... Well, my ma in Detroit and my boyfriend keep saying she's taking advantage of me. I always disagree because I don't want to talk about it to them what's really going on. I'll explain. Rollanda never hounded me to pay her for classes which I appreciate... however... during the time I have been training with them, she's made me somewhat of an administrative assistant to the dance company to work for them in addition to paying for the classes I took. So I am responsible for collecting other student's payments, correspondence with company members (via text message, phone, email, class handouts, etc), local event research, making advertisement phone calls and more.

Now this I feel it's not worth it to train with them because I'm also doing a lot with The Dance Challenger. I'm currently the Executive Administrative Assistant for DC. To top that off, we're preparing for the tour in London next month so I've been over loaded with conference calls, 5am prayer every day, email correspondence with instructors in London, Bradford and Tampa... it's just too much. I'm feeling a bit overwhelmed. I can't deny tho, I am having a lot of fun and I'm learning a loooot of "stuff". But um when reality sets in, I still don't have a job with steady income. I only have enough to pay for my plane ticket and get a little bit of food. This job assignment I'm on is going to end the week we go to London. Booo… With all this going on, I feel like I don't even have time to have a real PAYING job!

January 17, 2008
Dear Diary,

Oh, I guess I spoke too soon. So, I am no longer the Executive Administrative Assistant. It's official. Rollanda just broke the news to me with no in-depth explanation. Of course, I want to know why! Instead, she's making me her personal assistant. I'm still mad about it and might be for a while. I can't believe she's actually going to PAY someone else to do what I have been doing for her for months. Granted, I probably don't have the skills to do some of the things this new assistant will be able to do, however, I just don't think it's fair to me. I'm pissed off right now and feel really taken advantage of. My family has been asking me for months now if she's paying me for all the things I've been doing for her. I just don't discuss it because I don't want to tell them "no". I already know they're gonna say she's using me and all that. They've said it before. But I look at it as I'm volunteering to do it. Just like everybody else on staff. Altho I have waaaaaaaaaaay more responsibilities than everyone else. So much so, I already have a hard time juggling this job I'm on (just a short assignment) and her phone calls and text messages that never cease to fill my phone! I'm so mad! This is so unfair!

January 22, 2008
Dear Diary,

I think I felt pressured to move back to Detroit because of the people. Because of Lenard, Pastor Odetta and ma. But now that I'm not talking to any of them on a regular basis, I don't feel pressured anymore. If that's the case, then I will be here in Florida for a while! And just say…if for any reason Lenard and I don't work out, moving back to Detroit is so out of the picture. I would have no reason to go back if we're not together. I'm sick of living to please people or live up to their expectations of me. No one is making me move tho. If I move back it will be a choice that I made to do so. I feel as though I have more spiritual support there. But I'm soooo stressed there! Ugh! God is still God regardless to where I live. Hummm....what I did was take what my ma said, Lenard said and what I heard Pastor Odetta say and took it as "God said". But did I hear it for myself? Nope! I have had dreams, scary ones. Indicating my spiritual state but none saying I need to leave here. So…why am I making plans to leave? What do YOU want to do, Sierra? *I'm sooo confused…*

February 6, 2008
Dear Diary,

The Lord never ceases to amaze me. Today, the lady I met at a conference in Vegas about 2 years ago called me today. We have stayed in contact off and on since we met. But since I've been here, she's been calling me, texting and emailing me a lot more. I'm not complaining, it's not bad at all.

For instance, when she texted me earlier today, she asked me to call her as soon as I could. Since I was at work, I had to wait til my lunch break to call her. Well, long story short, when I called her, she flat out said, "What are you doing?" I was like, huh? She asked what was I doing down there? She told me that she felt something was terribly wrong in her spirit, concerning me being in Florida, but the Lord did not reveal what it was. Needless to say, I did not fess up to anything.

She advised that I behave and do whatever I had to do to follow God. Before we got off the phone, she prayed for me. It sounded like she was about to call down all of heaven to save me. No joke! I appreciated it – even though I didn't take heed to what she said. That's so sad. And I KNOW it's God trying to get my attention. I could just kick myself! Ok, I'll deal with all of these emotions and stuff AFTER I get back from London.

LOOKING BACK
The word says that the Lord chastens those whom He loves. It also says that He draws us with loving-kindness. To me, this was yet another display of God's unfailing love for me. He had this first lady connect with me just months before I moved to Florida and stay in contact with me all this time. Even now, we still talk. She still calls just to check on me and pray for me. I thank GOD that He loves me enough to always send people my way to speak His truth and love into my life. He's constantly, gently and loving wooing me to Himself.

It's amazing that He's just so gracious! He knew that I would not heed the warning she gave me, just like I disregarded all the other lifelines He threw to me. But He never gave up on me. He never stopped pursing me. He could have taken back His grace and mercy. He could have allowed the enemy to have his way with me because I was indeed OUT of His will and uncovered. Yet and still, He kept me. God is soooooooooo goooooooooooooood! I am eternally thankful!

March 1, 2008
Dear Diary,

Alright… I have to write something about my trip to London. Even tho I'm still tired from non-stop running in Europe for 2 weeks straight and now I'm getting ready to fly to Michigan in a few days, this trip was full of mixed emotions. But for the most part, I had fun. I met some super awesome people over there. The pastors we stayed with were from Nigeria. They said I could go to Nigeria with them next time they go. Yaaay!!! I get to go to Africa! But anyway, we had prayer at like 5am every morning. It was cold in London every, single, solitary day. Our driver scared the living daylights outta me. I had never rode in those foreign cars with the steering wheel on the right side instead of the left. Man that was crazy. We ate good, everyday. I'm so glad Mariell was there. Oh, speaking of Mariell, God used that girl to save my life!

During the first week when we had some downtime, we went to tour London. We were near the shopping district that's close by Buckingham Palace. All 7 of us were getting ready to cross the street when my goofy self looks to the left for ONCOMING TRAFFIC (duh, we're not in America!) but their oncoming traffic was coming from the right side. It happened so fast. We were in the middle of the street on the crossing corner or whatever it's called, and I leaned forward to see if it was safe to cross, within seconds, Mariell pulled me back by my jacket just in the nick of time before I got hit by the double-decker bus that was charging towards me. I almost died!!!! What made it so scary was that Mariell wasn't even paying attention to me. She was looking at something behind her and happened to turn around and just grab me. Once we crossed the street and sat at the bus stop for the tour bus to come, I cried. I cried to myself because I was shaken by the fact that I almost got splattered over the streets of London (because I wasn't supposed to go in the first place. God truly spared my life.
That's all I wanna say about that trip.

Oh wait, no it's not. I will never forget one night after being at the church for hours; we piled up in the van to go back to the pastors' house. It had been a looooong day and everyone was tired. When me and Trish get sleepy, we get stupid. So, I don't remember how we started, all I know is me and Trish ended up saying every Spanish word we knew. Started off with "Buenos noches, Como te llamas…" Then we just got outrageous with it. It was SOOO funny! When we couldn't think of anything else to say, we just said "Que eeeh, uuuh, eeeeeh, eeeh, mucho, uno, uuuh, la playa en la casa, eeeeeh.." Oh my goodness. We laughed until we cried. Everyone was annoyed. Especially Mariell. She was bothered more so than anyone because she's Puerto Rican. We weren't making fun of the language, just saying every word we knew, or thought we knew. That was one of the best parts of the trip outside of the ministry stuff. Oh, and the last day of the conference in Bradford, Trish put on "Let The Redeemed of The Lord Say So" and her and I jumped around so wildly while screaming the song to the top of our lungs til we fell out in the floor. It was SOOO MUCH FUN! What a release! The other people that were still there from the conference and church staff joined us in our lil "screaming/dancing fit" moment.

Last thing, when we were in one of the tourists' souvenir stores in the shopping district, "Just Fine" by Mary J. Blige came on the store. Mariell and I must have forgotten where we were cause we broke out dancing and singing in the store, in our own little world. That was sooo fun! That's my bbsfac!!! Love her to pieces! I was so sad when she went back to the states. She only stayed 1 week while 4 of us stayed for 2 weeks. The rest of the time we were there was full of work; which wasn't all that bad. It was just the other stuff and TONS of freakin favoritism that got on my nerves.

For example, when it comes to us getting in trouble or whatever; Rollanda kept telling us to stay together, don't split up because we're in a foreign country and we don't know our way around. Why then, did Trish storm off across the street away from the group because she wanted to take some pictures of some statues or something RIGHT after being told not to do it? Granted, when we got back to the states, Rollanda claimed Trish could never go on another trip like that with the team again. But we'll see how long that will last.

Oh, and especially, when Greg took Rollanda, Trish and Ah'shely to Scotland and left Susan and I behind in Bradford, that was totally unfair. The excuse was that only 4 people could fit in Greg's car. Well if that were the case, no one should have went. So Susan and I were left in Bradford all day long while the other 4 went to enjoy their time in Scotland. To top that off, since I was mad about it, I did let it show. But I was blamed for being mean to Susan and ruining her trip, whatever. Ok, I know I could have been nicer, but dang. Everything is NOT my fault. I couldn't WAIT to go home at that point. What's interesting though, the entire time we were over there, I was expecting someone, pastor, prophet, minister, anyone, to call out the spirit of homosexuality in Rollanda or myself. Either one or both. Didn't have to say it was connected, but just call it out. Challenge us. Embarrass us. Discern it. Do something!!! Anything!!! But, to my dismay, it never happened.

Email conversation between Pastor Odetta and I
Sent: March 3, 2008
Subject: Thank u

Pastor Odetta: Hi Miss Sierra Rae. I want to say thank u for sending me the tea. What a sweet gesture. I am still waiting for your response to my last email. ~ Luv u, Pastor Odetta

Sierra: Hello Pastor Odetta. I'm glad that the tea reached you. I hope that the box wasn't too banged up. If it was, I apologize. I wanted it to be nice and pretty when it reached you. I really wanted to mail it to you from London but I didn't have enough time to send it. However, I'm just glad you got it. :0)
As for the last email, I didn't respond, not because I was trying to be funny or anything, but because I didn't really know what to say? What was I responding to? You asked what did I mean by "that". I only said thanks for checking up on me.
I meant nothing by that. Am I not understanding? Forgive me.

Love,
Me

Pastor Odetta: I was asking how r u? You said fine. I said what does that mean?

Sierra: Oh. Hummm... well that's changed. When I said fine, I meant I was doing ok. I wasn't sick, dying, or homeless. I was just fine. Today, I'm still getting over the flu and... that's all I have to say about that. Other than that, let's see... yeah, that's it. I'm ok. I know you are praying for me and I thank you so very much. I don't even need to say it. But I thank you.

Pastor Odetta: Sierra Larissa Shumaker the First,

You have to know that I am not asking about your health. You know me better than that.

Sierra: LOL!!! You're funny! I know you weren't speaking of my health. I don't know what to say without giving too many details which is what I'm trying to avoid here. I can't lie. I'm not a very good liar. :0)
So, um... I'll say I could be better!

Pastor Odetta: So why don't you just be honest and say," Pastor Odetta I'm not living right at this present time. I am in sin and this is where I choose to be for now." Why all the secrecy? I have taught you to be honest wherever u r.

Stop trippin'.
~ Pastor Odetta

Sierra: Because, that's what I want to say. If I don't believe that I'm living in sin then I won't say that. I don't see that I am. I have repented for what I did months ago and haven't returned to it. Why then would I say that I'm living in sin if I don't believe that I am? I'm not trying to be smart or sarcastic so I hope you don't take it as I am. But it is to my understanding that if I have fallen into sin, I repent to God and turn from the sin I was in, I'm good. I know I'm forgiven by Him. What is it that I'm doing now to make you say I'm "living" in sin? Yes, you have taught me to be honest, but there are certain things I choose not to discuss. Sometimes my honesty and bluntness can be taken or has been taken as disrespect. So I just don't go there.

Pastor Odetta: I know for a fact that you are in sin. You told me yourself that the Lord told you to come back to Detroit. There are a number of other things. You are so far away. But if you don't believe you are in sin, that's cool. Follow what you think you need to do. Just concerned about your soul.

~Luv ya, P. Odetta

LOOKING BACK
In this email conversation with Pastor Odetta, she was attempting to get me to be honest about my place at that time. But I refused. She did teach me to be honest about where I was, however, instead of doing so, I lied. Even though she called me on the carpet, I still refused. I did not want to admit that I was living in sin because it sounded so bad! I did not want that to be said of me. After all, I was still ministering in dance quite often with the dance ministry.

We just got finished feeding the homeless! We even took the conference to Europe and did a powerful piece! People's lives were changed! How can you say I'm living in sin when I'm doing so much good for the Kingdom? Oh, but it is VERY possible!

Matthew 7:22-23 *"Many will say to Me in that day, 'Lord, Lord, have we not prophesied in Your name, cast out demons in Your name, and done many wonders in Your name?' "And then I will declare to them, 'I never knew you; depart from Me, you who practice lawlessness!'"*

The truth is that, yes, I was living in sin. I did repent, but I was not delivered. And because of where my heart was, I never truly **repented** BECAUSE first of all – to repent means to turn. I didn't not turn. I stood where I was and spoke empty words. Secondly, everyday, during the day, I would repent with my mouth. But at night, I would hope for a phone call, a text message, a hint, or a signal from Rollanda.

Furthermore, I was still fornicating with Lenard. So yes, I was living in sin rather I wanted to admit it or not. Plus, just like people say all the time, "Well, God knows my heart." That is so true! He DOES know my heart. He knew it was filthy. He knew my heart was far from Him. He knew I repented with my mouth but my heart was saying something else. Man looks at the outward appearance. GOD looks at our hearts.

I also want to point out the fact that I was VERY disrespectful to Pastor Odetta in my response to her. There is a way to communicate your point without being disrespectful. I did not humble myself. Nor did I receive her words as caring or loving. She was only concerned about my soul.

Email conversation between Pastor Odetta and I
Sent: March 10, 2008
Subject: Hi

Pastor Odetta: Hello My Sweet. I hope you are having a good day. This is the glorious day that the Lord has made. He is faithful and just. I hope that I did not offend you. That, of course, is never my intent. But you didn't respond to my last email so I thought I should apologize just in case I did offend u. So, I extend my deepest regret if I did offend. The day will come when the scales will fall off. I have some requests stored up, Little Lady.
~ Love, Pastor Odetta

Sierra: Hellooooooooo Pastor Odetta- I did get your last email. I checked it from my phone and I thought I responded but I guess it didn't go through. Or maybe it wasn't that one I responded to. I don't recall. In either case, I apologize. And I accept your apology :0).

Requests??? What kind of requests?

Love u,
Sierra
Pastor Odetta:
Never mind. I am just sorry that I offended you.

Love & Prayers,
Pastor Odetta

LOOKING BACK

Sadly, the only thing I was concerned about in this conversation was the requests Pastor Odetta had for me. I thought she was going to ask me to dance somewhere. I totally ignored what was said before that. But what she said about the scales falling off was key! There was no way that I could receive what she was saying at that time because the scales on my eyes were so thick, I was blind to the truth. Acts 9:18 *"Instantly something like scales fell from Saul's eyes, and he regained his sight. Then he got up and was baptized."* (NLT)

This also goes to show that dance really WAS an idol for me. Instead of me being concerned about repenting of my sin, I was only concerned about dancing. Even after this conversation, I did continue to dance with the dance company. My ministry was tainted because of my sin. I cannot effectively minister to the lost when I, myself, need saving.

Later, I spoke with Pastor Odetta about her requests for me. I found out that her requests for me had nothing to dance. The requests were that I would totally surrender my life to Christ, repent of my sin and follow Him.

March 14, 2008
Dear Diary,

My trip to Detroit was surprisingly pleasant. My ma organized a dinner at some Wild Wings restaurant for me and my brother. Well, I was just in town visiting and my brother had just been released from jail, so this was a great time for a get together. I was so happy to see my cousins, friends and godchildren again. It's been so long since I've seen them. I'm glad Lenard came, too. He makes everything better for me. The overall visit was nice. No one argued. No attitudes. I felt awkward because I wondered if ma knew about what happened with me and Rollanda. I still think Pastor Odetta told her. But she said she didn't, so I can't pin that to her. I think she knows. Ma hasn't been on me about moving back to Detroit, lately. I'm super glad about that too. I know that if I needed her, I mean, her and my daddy would come get me in a heartbeat. I just don't want to come back to drama and stress. Then again, there is drama and stress in Florida, it's just hidden. No difference there. I'm enjoying myself too much to go anywhere else right now anyway. I already know I won't be in…wait, I didn't mean to write about this stuff. Lol. I just can't stop thinking about it. Hummm, I enjoyed my visit. My family is great. I love them and miss them a lot, but I'd rather be back in Florida for now.

March 23, 2008
Dear Diary

Happy birthday to me! Although we celebrated my birthday yesterday, today is my birthday and I wish I were with people that really loved me. Yesterday, Rollanda treated all the Dance Challenger staff whose birthday was in March to a lunch cruise. It started to rain a little bit, but you know, it was still fun! They made it a lot of fun. Plus, me and my loud mouth, made the birthday song even funnier. Me and 3 other staff members all celebrated birthdays in March. A few of the other DC staff members joined us on the cruise. The food was great. The drinks…oh, about that. There was a bar on the ship too. So shoot, Rollanda got an alcoholic frozen drink, so I got one, too. 'Cause since she got one, she can't talk about me getting one. Me, her and Trish had one. I think I had two. Lol. I don't remember now. We went on the top deck and took pictures while we were taken on a tour of the bay area. It was really nice! I had never been on a cruise before. But anyway, we all enjoyed ourselves. I just wish I had something to do today. My phone has been blowing up all day with birthday phone calls and text messages. I hid away from the world for a few hours today to cry my heart out. I don't want to feel this alone on my birthday ever again.

April 6, 2008
Dear Diary,

Wow. We just got back from Ft. Lauderdale visiting Trish's mom. Maaaaaan that lady can COOK! Reminds me of the way my family cooks in the mid-west. Of course, the best part of the entire trip for me was going to the beach!

Trish and her little brother taught me how to jump the waves. Her mom got in the water too. Rollanda didn't. She just stayed on the shore in the shade. Now I'm happy to announce that I swam in the Atlantic Ocean and the Gulf of Mexico. Ha ha ha! So much fun! Me, Rollanda and Trish went to the shopping district in Miami while we visited. We chilled on the side of this building which overlooked the ports for a few major cruise ships and some other sail boats. We even saw a few dolphins in the water. The whole visit was really just for fun cause Trish wanted to go visit her mom. I was happy Trish invited me for the trip! I'll never forget my time there.

April 9, 2008
Dear Diary,

I found this interesting. I promise, every time Rollanda politely tells me to keep my distance, I do. I struggle with it because I've grown accustom to her hugs and kisses…but whatever. My massage table was FINALLY delivered to Ms. Tonya's house after being lost by the airline. I brought it over to Mariell's with the rest of my things. Since I really didn't have space for it in the apartment, I was just going to keep it in my trunk. Yesterday, Rollanda asked me if I could come over to the house and give her a massage after class. I said "sure". So I brought the table and oils over, set it up and did the massage in the room next door to the office.

I set up a few candles, played some music, turned off the light and opened the blinds so the moonlight could shine in. Trish came in and sat on the floor during the massage. That was cool – at first. The only problem I had was that she wouldn't stop talking! My goodness! You see I'm trying to give this lady a RELAXING massage, right? Geesh! So, I kept giving hints that she needs to leave, until she finally got an attitude and left.

After a few minutes of Trish leaving the room, the massage did get a tad sensual, I must admit. But I didn't touch any private areas. When I was done with her back, she asked "Are you going to massage my front too?" I said…"uh sure?" I had never done that before. "So now if anyone ever asks if I've had a full body massage before, I can say "Yes"…" she said after turning over. I proceeded to massage the front of her body. As I continued with the now very sensual massage, she began to make noises. "Get on the floor" she said out the clear. I was like what? She repeated "get on the floor". So I stopped massaging her and got on the floor. She got off the table, left her towel on the table, got on top of me and proceeded to do things to me. Should I stay or should I run? My mind is telling me to leave. But my flesh is screaming a different tune. Talk about frustrated! How about, it's whatever!

57

Chapter 3
Illusions

April 12, 2008
Dear Diary,

Good news! Since we, the dance company, are no longer allowed to use the dance room at Rollanda's old church, we're going to start rehearsing, and I believe ministering in dance, at some church about 30 minutes away! That's great! I'm looking forward to it. Our first ministry event is coming up soon! We've been rehearsing like crazy!

On another note, I'm praying this is the beginning of a change in me and Rollanda's relationship – for the better. That way, I won't feel so bad about still being here!

Text message conversation between Rollanda and I
April 18, 2008

Rollanda- 4:28am I appreciate u so much. Thx u4 serving me wholeheartedly w/o reservation...thru my weakness and strength. U hav my hrt. I believe dat now.

Rollanda- 4:30am I celebrate u where u r and I look 4ward 2 ur success. U will do greater wks than I evr will. PTL.

Rollanda- 4:32am Im happy God put us 2gether in dis season. N I pray we make daddy proud. We've messed up. We took a wrong turn I pray dat G-d 4gives us n use us in spite of bc I love my Daddy. Lov workn4 Him. Lov wat He's called me2 do. Lov workn w u on dis job. 1day I hope I can pay u2 wk w me FT. N I hope my trust level w u gets bk2 where it was.

Sierra- 4:40am Im happy He placed us 2gether too. I am very sad about us fallin 2gthr. This is very hard4 me 2 jus get over.I want Him2 4giv us too.& its my pleasure 2 serve u.

Rollanda- 4:46am I'd lov2 hav u travel w me2serve. Be my r-hand woman. I'd lik dat. Only in G-ds timing & will tho. Bc He already showd me dat.I hope my sins didn't 4fit d prophetic destiny.

Rollanda- 4:48am U r wonderful 2wk w in d kingdom of G-d. I see (u) doing so much. G-d has so much 4u. Wish I cld tell u all I see in ur future...

Sierra- 4:50am What, like... what? Dancing?

Rollanda- 4:55am Naw. Dats not wats on my mind. U my lady is gettn ready2 entr a new season. G-d is callin u2 shadow me completely. So w all dat u r doing, whoa- best wishes.

April 26, 2008
Dear Diary,

 I just found the perfect ringtone for Rollanda. It's "East from the West". I think that's what it's called. It's one of her favorite songs. I don't know why it is... but I made it her ringtone because for 1, it's one of her favorite songs, and 2, once I listened to the lyrics, it pierced my heart. The chorus goes like this, "Jesus can you tell me just how far the east is from the west? Cause' I can't bear to see the man I've been, rising up in me again. In the arms of your mercy I find rest. Cause you know just how far the east is from the rest. From one scared hand to the other." Man, that song... is just what I'm sayin to Jesus! I don't wanna be like this or feel like this no more. I need His forgiveness and I have to forgive myself... I really want the Lord to forgive me for falling into this mess again. I feel so dirty inside. I wish I could tell someone....

Email conversation between Pastor Odetta and I
Sent: May 15, 2008
Subject: Hello

Pastor Odetta: Hi Sierra,

I haven't heard from you other than when you were being mean to me. When you wrote "So!!" on my wall. I didn't get it at first. And finally I figured it out. So what's going on with you? Are you okay? I try not to bother you because you seem like you don't want to be bothered. But I just want to say hi and I love u.

~ P. Odetta

Sierra: Pastor...Pastor....Pastor....

Wow. I wasn't *really* being mean. I said "so" because I saw a comment you made on someone else's wall and it kind of hurt. It was then that I felt like they had the place that I once held in your heart, I no longer have that place and it hurt. So my response was "SO!" Childish, I know. I had to laugh at it myself. I'm probably gonna delete my Facebook page soon. I have no desire to keep it. The only reason I would consider keeping it is if Nia wants me to. Otherwise, it's a done deal.

Nonetheless, I didn't realize I was giving the impression that I didn't want to be bothered. I don't know what to say about that. I am okay. I've been kind of busy, but what else is new?

Honestly, since the day you told me that you told my mother something I asked you not to repeat, I backed up. I felt that was a betrayal of my trust in you and it highly upset me. I mean no disrespect at all in saying that. But it's really how I felt. I do not wish to discuss certain things with my parents. Maybe later in life, or maybe not at all. And it's hard for me to express to you how I feel about you because I'm afraid that you'll just say "Ok Sierra. Forget it. Forget you." So, I just keep it to myself or talk to someone else that I confide in. I just wanted to be able to talk to you and believe that it goes no further than that. Not with Pastor James, not my mother, nor father, nobody but me, you and Jesus.

I still love you. I think about you a lot! I wanted to email you a few days ago. I wanted to call you and leave you a message. I miss you immensely! I'm just not sure where to go from here or what to say to you anymore. Not that I'm that mad at you (or mad at all), but it just feels like I disappoint you allllllllllllll the time and I don't wanna get caught up in trying to match up to your expectations of me again. That's how I feel. Again, I apologize if there was any disrespect in this email. It wasn't intentional. Thank you for taking a moment to think of me and email me. I appreciate you so much for that. I hope that you enjoyed your Mother's Day.
Love,
Sierra

LOOKING BACK

"I don't wanna get caught up in trying to match up to your expectations of me again."

Pastor Odetta never pressured me to live up to her expectations of me. She held me accountable with the Word of God. Since I confess to be a follower of Christ, then yes, she was right in correcting me with the Word – which is what she's always done. Because I was consumed with rejection, I was unable to receive the correction as love. Instead, I perceived it to be rejection by her and that she was against me. I know now that is NOT the case. The Lord says in His word that He chastens those whom He loves.

Pastor Odetta: Ms. Sierra,

I **NEVER** told your mother what you told me. I was encouraging you to tell her. Because you lead me to believe you wanted something different. Nevertheless I never told you that I told her that. I am not perfect, but I rarely go back on my word. I think you assumed that I would tell her. To this day, I have not shared that with your mother. If your mom knows, it's because the Lord told her or you told her thinking she already knew.

Secondly, I would never make a comment on anyone else's wall about you. What are you talking about? I do apologize if you thought I was talking about you. But it just wasn't so. What comment was it?

I am sorry that you misunderstood any of my communications. Everything works out for the best. You have found someone that you can trust. That's excellent. I am glad that your life is going the way that you want it. You only have one life to live. So enjoy it.

It's not that you are tired of disappointing me. Because you don't disappoint me. You are Sierra. And I know and understand that probably better than you. If you are truly honest, you would have to say that you disappointed yourself. Because basically you were trying to find yourself, as I told you before. You didn't know who you were. So you were trying to be what you thought everyone wanted. That will always get you in trouble. I just expect people to be real. Live what you say you are. Nothing more. Nothing less. If you are a sinner, be a sinner. If you are a Christian, be a Christian. I don't love what choices you make. I love you as a person. But it pleases me that you are doing okay. Glad to hear it. Love, P. Odetta

LOOKING BACK
"You didn't know who you were. So you were trying to be what you thought everyone wanted. "

Again, this is a true statement! Back then, there was no way I could receive this. Actually, I was offended by it! But now, I see that this statement was very true. It speaks to the reasons why I was so burned out all the time. Why I wanted to run away from home, even as a young adult. Why I got frustrated so easily when things weren't going my way. I tried to fit the mold of what everyone expected of me, except God. The only One I should live to be like is Christ. His plan for me is the only one I want to follow. As long as I am following Him, everything else will fall in place because there will be less of me and more of Him. My flesh will die daily. Through my relationship with Him, I am able to love purely. I am not easily offended. I know who I am and WHOSE I am.

May 25, 2008
Dear Diary,

Rollanda and all these dang emails are getting on my NERVES! All of our nerves! Geesh! The same thing we discuss on the conference call is the same thing we discussed in class and have notes on. Why do we need an email and text messages repeating the exact same thing? Lady! Get a grip! Lol. Whew. Now that I got that out, I am sorta looking forward to taking this trip to Miami. I hope we get to have fun after the flying trapeze class is over.

From: Rollanda
To: Samantha
Cc: OPDATC Members
Sent: May 27, 2008
Subject: Flying trapeze class- Miami

Samantha, how are you today? It's Rollanda. I love you. Hey, here are the details of the event for this weekend.

FRIDAY:
Depart for Miami, Friday, 2pm or 3pm...(Depending on when they get out of work)
Check into hotel between - 7 & 8 pm
DINNER - 8pm
Radio interview w/ DJ Piya and partner - 10:30 pm
SATURDAY:

Morning visit w/ DC friends - 11am
Hang out at swap shop or other ft. Lauderdale/Miami site - 2pm
Trapeze class Saturday - 4pm
Hangout at bayside after class - dancing, shopping, having fun, etc!!!
SUNDAY:
Ft. Lauderdale inter-coastal boat ride w/ Senator Alex Row - Sunday, 9am
Lunch - 1 pm
Depart for Tampa - mid or late afternoon - 2 or 3 pm-ish

From: Rollanda
To: Pastor LaShaunda
Sent: June 2, 2008
Subject: Help!

Hello again P. LaShaunda, it's me! Again!!! Sorry. I know you are busy and
I'm sending you 3 long e-mails. So sorry. But I didn't like the last e-mail I
sent you. This one is a bit more explanatory.

As mentioned before, I would like for you to come speak to Off Platforms
Dance, Acrotumbling and Theatre Company about the impact they COULD,
WOULD make in this community by serving the community. It will be just
us tho... a private chat. I would LOVE VERY MUCH if you came and spoke
to us!!! If yes, when is a good time for you to come please? I really NEED
seasoned Christian people to pour into our lives. We meet on Mon, Tues,
Thur from 5-9pm. you can come ANY of those days at any time you like.
Please just like me know and I'll rearrange the schedule for you. The general
topic would be serving, servant hood....that sort of thing. But some points I
would like you to touch on are:

a) Personally serving the community (Not just be sending offerings but
getting our hands dirty too)
b) Armorbearoring/serving your leader. Explain what that even means
c) Respecting your leader (Oh, this is a big one right now. Got to nip it on the
bud! FAST!!)
d) Last BUT not least. Serving each other. They get selfish w/ each other too
much.

This group is tough *Pastor LaShaunda*!!!!! As you know, they are fairly
young people and new in the L-rd (most of them are). They
are stubborn AND selfish w/ me and with each other too; AND at times
disrespect as well (not all of them). This is a first for me. I'd never had to

deal w/ such stubborn people. OMG!!! They love the L-rd w/ all their hearts tho. Wonderful wonderful younger ladies, love me, love each other, loves the L-rd...but Jesus help their attitudes and stubbornness 😷.

ANNNDDDDDDD, they love to have their OWN way. My goodness! Even after our lonnnnnnnngggg word or worship session they come right out of that and want they own way!!! What the heck!!! Not all of them are like that but enough of them are. I've been praying on how to handle them (definitely don't want to give up on them because everyone else did!! plus people like you didn't give up on me and G-d didn't give up on me when I was a stupid, bigger mess (than I am now) in the beginning of my Christian walk. PTL!!!) I just can't do that. I won't give up! But how do I teach them to be more respectful (without slapping the devil out of em 😡 because I want to at times). How do I best teach them to be selfless and to have a BIGGER heart to serve in a greater way!!! If we all serve more our impact would be so much greater on this community!!!! Please HELP!!! Please let me know. Ok. It would be so appreciated. Thanks in advance.

Ohhhhh, and please let me know how much time you will need for your talk please. You can just flow. Thanks.

June 3, 2008
Dear Diary,

We all carpooled between Trish's car and Rollanda's car and pitched in on gas. We all met up at a well known church in Tampa on a Friday afternoon. LeChelle, Samantha and I parked our cars and hopped in one of theirs. The ride down to Miami was fun. I rode with Trish and Samantha. When we got to our hotel, it seemed like everyone was pretty much in a mellow mood. I was quiet. Just waiting to see what we were going to next. We decided to just chill for the evening. The first night we were there, I remember so clearly the things that took place. LeChelle and Samantha slept in one bed, while me, Trish and Rollanda slept in the other, with Rollanda n the middle. Her and I rubbed on each other all thru the night until we finally fell asleep. The next day, we were supposed to go to the Flying Trapeze class, but we ended up not going because of the cost and come to find out, Trish didn't have any money. We were supposed to get some kind of deal- bring 2 people 1 gets in free. However, it didn't work out like that.

LeChelle was embarrassed and ready to go home because she said it wasn't professional of US to book a spot with these people then arrive and refuse to pay. Trish got upset because of something dumb and stormed off as Rollanda chased her down on foot. Samantha and I were like ooook, it's whatever because we came down here for this, we're here, so let's do it. But…we didn't do anything. So we all walked around the outdoor mall and had fun looking around and doing a little shopping.

Back at the hotel, after getting settled in from a frustrating day, we all decided to get cleaned up and just chill. LeChelle went, and then Rollanda jumped in the shower. Rollanda called me in the bathroom for something…I think she asked me to bring her something. Then after she got out the shower, it was my turn to go in. I was about to get undressed then I heard a knock at the door. It was Rollanda. She slightly opened the door then let herself in and locked the door behind her. She came right over to me, pressed her body against mine and embraced me and motioned for me to kiss her (body). No words were exchanged, only body talk. I answered the call…with gentle kisses and nibbles on her moist skin. A few moments later, we released each other and she proceeded to walk out of the restroom saying "..and that's all I have to say about that!" and closed the door. I stood there for a minute…amazed at what just happened…and turned on at the same time. That night, was a replay of the night before. We fondled until we fell asleep. None of the teammates saw anything. I'm sure they were curious to know what the reason was for our semi-strange behavior during that trip. One other thing I'll never forget. Even though me and Rollanda know what we did, it was never mentioned. But Rollanda wrote all of us apology notes for the way the weekend turned out and prayed that God would bless us and something else. I laughed at the note. I felt if anything, she should expose our inappropriate behavior that took place behind closed doors. And we're a Christian company? That's laughable. I bet she didn't tell her pastor friends about that! She could have kept that note to me. If you're gonna apologize, apologize about something that really happened, something that matters!
This is what the card said:

Sierra,

From the bottom of my heart I apologize for this weekend. Sorry that it wasn't what it was meant to be. I take full responsibility for-
　　1) The failure
　　2) My attitude
　　3) Any other attitude that I may have allowed
I pray that you were not hurt in the process. I promise this will be fixed by His Spirit as G-d spoke to my "<3" and showed me what to do & how. I speak peace into your life…into your <3 in Jesus name. Amen!

I love you. Ms. Rollanda   Col 3:23

June 22, 2008
Dear Diary,

Lenard just came down to Florida to visit me! Yay! He got in town
yesterday. I'm so happy he is here! I figure, since we're all planning to go to
dinner, it would be a good idea to invite Rollanda so her and Lenard can
meet. All the roommates were at the apartment, Mariell's friend, Clark was
there too. It seemed like everyone was kinda taking their time getting ready,
lounging around and just chit chatting. When Mariell gets a text from
Rollanda asking where we were because she had been sitting in the parking
lot of the restaurant for 10 minutes already. Apparently we lost track of time,
or weren't too concerned about getting there by the time we set. Lenard and
I get in the car and I started speeding over to the restaurant, less than 10
minutes from the apartment. Ok, tell me why when we pulled up, Rollanda
grimmed me then sped off? Ok, she didn't speak to Lenard, nor me. She
could have stayed. It wasn't necessary to get upset at me. For what? Then
Rollanda said to me that if I really wanted her to meet Lenard then I would
have made time for it to happen. Lady, please. You got me messed up. It's
not like I care THAT MUCH for you to meet him anyway.

June 28, 2008
Dear Diary,

Man I will be SO GLAD when this teaching session stuff is over. I feel like
(and I'm not the only one). Rollanda is only having us go through this
teaching so we can learn how to respect her and serve her. Granted, she *does*
do things for us, she teaches us a lot, but at the same time, the leader should
also respect the people serving him or her because we don't have to do it. If
we volunteer to help her, that doesn't give her the right to treat us like dogs. I
mean, maybe it's just me. Maybe. Trish is her "suck-up friend" so I'm sure
even if she gets "rebuked" (I guess) in front of us, I know when they go
home, it's gonna be a different story and her corrective actions for her never
stick. Anyway, I'm not concerned about her in this case.

The session with Dr. Ruiz and her husband stood out to me the most because
they preach deliverance. Once again, I was EXPECTING them to, I was
praying that God would reveal/call out the spirit of homosexuality in me and
Rollanda or at least detect a foul spirit operating in one of us. Something!
Jesus! But, it didn't happen. Sucks. Ugh! They did have us to go to anyone
we may have offended within the team and apologize, talk it thru and all that.

It was like a prayer session going on, or like, an altar call in the classroom. They had us come up, whoever wanted prayer. They prayed for us…then, Rollanda came and gave me a hug and said "I'm sorry". I busted out crying so hard I thought I would collapse. She was still holding on to me and I saw the expression on her face as she said, "Oh my God." It wasn't like, oh I really hurt you, but moreso like dang, she's dramatic. The thing is, she never said what the heck she was apologizing for! I know tho. Well, I think I do. But for real, I'll be glad when this is over. I feel it's pointless. I'm open to learn from the people she brings in, but until this huge issue with corrupt leadership is addressed, I'ma have a hard time receiving anything from any of these people, especially her.

July 30, 2008
Dear Diary,

How about, I'm so glad this month is over! Rollanda has worked us to death! I'm glad we did get a chance to dance after being "sat down" for so long. I'm really only happy about the acrotumbling class because it's my favorite– but as for the teachings, I think that's near a close.
A few weeks ago, the dance company celebrated its 1st year anniversary. In the process, we lost a company member (luck you), and two others were released. So that only left 3 company members, me – the apprentice, and Rollanda. We worked so hard to build the set for the concert, get all of our garments together, took group pictures at the university, and still went home with sore hips and ankles every night from dancing on hard cement floor. Lord knows that woman worked me, above all! Let's see, not only was I working from never-ending To-Do Lists from Rollanda, but also making calls to parents for the camp she attempted to put on, walking around her community with Trish to pass out flyers for our concert, helping her keep the team in order, etc., etc.

My mind is all over the place right now because I'm so tired and mentally drained. And I'm frustrated! Now, I'm being faced with moving, once again. I'm trying to find my own apartment so I can give Mariell her room back. I think this will be a good move for me if everything works out. I pray I find something affordable – and quick!

August 3, 2008
Dear Diary,

I'm glad that Rollanda and I have been staying away from each other. This is really good for us. It's been tough; beyond tough, extremely hard to talk to her, go through the mentoring program and dance class with her – knowing we aren't delivered. I know I should really be concerned about myself, but I can't help but LOOK AT HER. She and Trish recently asked me why I don't hang out with them anymore. I don't really have an answer for that. I do miss Rollanda. And she misses me too. Her kisses and deep hugs ruin me. Just when I had these thoughts somewhat under control…dang. But we agreed it's best if we stay away from each other for a while or at least not be alone with each other. I want to keep doing it because I know it's for the best. But it's hard. I miss her. I wish she didn't miss me back or didn't tell me she loves me 50x a day. That makes it worse.

August 12, 2008
Dear Diary,

Rollanda and I just got back from this huge dance conference in Atlanta. Rollanda was teaching and since I'm her assistant…I got to tag along. Always up for a free trip! Lol! I had to work the merchandise table for DC, but that was fine with me. While Rollanda was busy teaching her workshops, I was at the merchandise table teaching the kids how to do cartwheels with 2 streamers. Oh yeah, Samantha was there too. She went with her friends. I was SOOOO glad to see her. We had fun together in an empty ballroom with cathedral ceilings, tossing up our streamers, doing front roll-overs, flips or some fancy modern dance move and catching the streamer before it hit the ground. I didn't say we were successful! LOL. But it sure was funny to watch. One of my friends from Michigan came down with some people from her church, too. Man that was awesome. It was almost like a big ol' dancing family reunion! Lol! Anyway, I didn't get to attend any of the dance classes because I didn't register. Plus, I was there to assist Rollanda. And I did. Endlessly. I was tired from running back and forth from her workshops back to the merchandise table, or to our hotel room to get her a small blanket to cover up with because she was cold…but I did it without complaining. The whole trip was fine to me. But my friend Jas had pointed out something that upset her concerning Rollanda. When I was at the merchandise table, I was socializing with the potential customers and Jas. I forgot what happened…if anything at all. But I guess I wasn't as attentive to the table as Rollanda may have wanted. She called my name and gave me a really mean look, as if to say "Get behind that table!" Jas was highly upset after she saw that. But I didn't say anything. I just went behind the table, waited til she went in the main ballroom, and did whatever I was doing before. It's not like I left the table. I was standing in front of it. That was dumb.

August 19, 2008
Dear Diary,

Ok, um, yeah... I gotta change Rollanda's ringtone because I feel so seriously bad, everytime it goes off because I know it's only HER texting me at 2:00 a.m. (asking me what am I doing and that she misses me and all that). It's never Lenard because he is in bed by 9 pm cause he has to get up so early for work. Oh my gosh. Until I get my own place, I have to be considerate of Mariell because she's trying to sleep! And so am I! At 2 or 3 o'clock in the morning, what else would I be doing besides sleeping? Um...trying to go back to sleep? Lol. Anyways, my phone has been driving Mariell crazy cause it goes off constantly in the wee hours of the morning and I know she knows it is Rollanda. Even tho she never says anything. I would turn it off but I need my alarm to wake me up in the morning. But oh! The reason why I'm writing this entry even tho my hand hurts from writing so much... is because I'm starting to feel torn inside and a little bit upset cause I'm being toyed with. Earlier this year, Rollanda and I agreed not to mess around anymore and not to be close to one another or be alone with one another. It hurt when she said it at first, but of course I understood why, and it was needed! We both need to get ourselves right with God! But since then, she's been coming on to me! In Miami, at the hotel with OP, she approached me in the bathroom when I was about to get in the shower. She texts me at all types of crazy hours of the night. I do respond, cause if she initiates, I just follow thru. Stupid me. But I do! She texts me and says, Trish and Mr. Chad are asleep and she needs someone to hold her and that I should come over. So... I get out the bed at 2:30 in the morning, grab a few things, get in my car and drive 12 minutes to her house. For what? Just to hold her on the couch and watch a movie til she gets sleepy then she goes to bed and I go to the guest bedroom. Then Mr. Chad and Trish would wake up the next morning like... "When did you get here?" It's never a suspicious thing, but I always feel odd and just...not right. This has got to stop. Man I need help! Jesus!!! We didn't have sex or anything...but I can't deny the fact that I was thinking about it!

August 21, 2008
Dear Diary,

So, apparently, Rollanda has been working to get Off Platforms to be entered into some kind of dance competition at college we've been rehearsing at. Ok, great! I know lately she's been talking to us a lot about making an impact in the community and whatnot. I guess this is a start, in addition to us dancing at the church every month. During class today, she explained to us that this competition is not a Christian competition, which is even better because we'll be able to bring Jesus to the college students through dance. Ok, sounds good so far. Right? Well, next she tells us the songs we'll be doing there. We have 2 so far, and another one we're going to start working on soon is a popular skit somebody found on YouTube.

This is the part that made me mad. She made Mariell the gambler, Trish is the spirit of suicide – I think, Rollanda is playing the image role, I forgot Krissy and Samantha's character, but she made me the lesbian. Why? She said to me, "I think you'll make a good lesbian." She said that IN CLASS! Are you kidding me? Not only was I embarrassed, but I was highly upset! Needless to say, I can't wait till this is over.

From: Rollanda Robertson-Anchorage
To: Sierra
Sent: Fri, 12 Sep 2008 11:38 am
Subject: Re: My One Month Goals

ROLLANDA'S RESPONSE IN BOLD

My one month goals
September 9- October 9, 2008

- Purchase a bed - **We'll start looking on sat after the cruise**
- Get my computer and 2-in-1 printer and scanner
- Purchase a computer desk (Big Lots- already priced), bookshelf and file cabinet - **Check with AG. She got a really good one for a GOOD price at Sam's club recently.**
- Have obtained (approved) student loan $6000 - **Please keep me posted and let me know what I can do**
- Sell promise ring - **Try the flyer and try the one company with the ad that comes on TV about selling your old broken jewelry as well. please keep me posted and let me know what I can do**
- Employment
- Design garment for lady in Minnesota
- Purchase nice lamp, waste basket, laundry basket for bedroom
- Know what I'm doing regarding school (when do I start? what school?)
- -In the next month or so... get money from my student loan so that I can do the following:
  a. Get FL tags and insurance; pay ticket
  b. Pay tuition at Kapaer and HCC

c. Get my car fixed (pump and belt and detailed)
d. I would like to get Ms Rollanda's car detailed as well (where? BC she has leather interior**)** **- Yea!!! Thank you**
- Send both brothers in jail money - **Awesome**
- Organize DC, OPDA&TC and Ms. Rollanda's stuff (in file cabinet) - **Yea!!! Thank you**

-Rollanda Robertson-Anchorage

From: Sierra
To: Rollanda
Sent: September 13, 2008
Subject: Update Re: my one month goals

I sold the ring. I took it to a pawn shop a few days ago. I was told that it only retails at $60. I wasn't really looking for the amount of money I could get, but rather get rid of a piece of my past. I completed the app for the student loan with my parents info as cosigners and it was declined. Now I'm back at square one for the moment. What can you do? If you know of any other way I could get a grant or something, please let me know... I know of a few websites; Financial Aid, Sallie Mae, FastWeb that deals with student loans, scholarships and grants. There are many more. But I have a unique situation. I'm not a student at the moment so I don't know how this would go. I need to make some phone calls. I need some advice. Please help.

September 22, 2008
Dear Diary,

I am so...very...upset and alone right now! Oh my goodness. It's like almost 11 o'clock. I'm sitting in front of Rollanda's house. Her husband isn't home yet. I don't have a key yet because the first set they made for me didn't work. And Rollanda and Trish are not here yet. We got out of class at 9 pm. That was almost 2 hours ago! I've been sitting in my car since about 9:20. I don't want to call Mariell because I feel like I'm invading her space. I'm always over there. I know she doesn't mind, but I'm not sure. Rollanda isn't answering her phone! Ugh! I hate this! I wish moving into her house wasn't my last resort. I wish I could have just moved into my own place and I wouldn't have to go through this! Why is it that I have a room I'm paying rent for and can't even get in the house? I'm tired and sweaty from class. They just texted me and said they aren't rushing home. They are out. Are you kidding me?!?! I might just drive to the beach, park in front of one of those clothing stores in the parking lot and sleep in my car. I'd rather do that than stay here tonight.

September 27, 2008
Dear Diary,

Wow! I have new news! OP actually WON 1st place in the dance competition! Oh my goodness. This means, we're going to be dancing at homecoming! I have to admit, I am a little nervous. This is one of the largest colleges in the state of Florida! Oh Lord. I'm too tired to think about this right now. Lol. We only have a few weeks to prepare. I pray that God is still able to use us, even tho we're all pretty messed up. I'll speak for myself. Um, I'm not too excited about playing the part of a lesbian in the skit. I mean, granted, basically I am one right now in real life, but I don't want to publicly portray that part. Oh well! Since she gave it to me, I'm going to do it and it's gonna be convincing! One of my concerns is after the skit is over; will those that watched it question my Christianity because I played that role just a little too good? We'll see....

September 29, 2008
Dear Diary,

Here's the dumbest thing ever. Rollanda MADE Mariell move into her house for one month. It was for mentoring purposes. I don't even know why she did it!!!! I guess it's that whole honor your leader thing. She still had her own apartment and rent to pay. Crazy! In either case, I was glad she was there with me! Lol. Rollanda said that she was trying to teach Mariell some life lessons in how to clean and how to take care of her home. I guess Rollanda doesn't understand that Mariell is a busy young lady. She goes to work at 4:30am every morning, she's focusing on finishing her degree, she teaches dance, dances with this company and she has a busy social life. Needless to say, she doesn't always have time to make sure her room and car are squeaky clean. She's busy! So since she's been here, Rollanda washed and folded all of Mariell's clothes and put them away in drawers and hung some up in the closet. She gave Mariell chores to do in the house also. Her chore is to clean the bathroom that her, Trish and I share and also clean Rollanda and Mr. Chad's bathroom. Mariell looked at this as Rollanda is attempting to teach her how to clean by having her move into her house and clean her house for her.

What's funny is me and Mariell talk all the time. I know how she hates being at Rollanda's house. I completely understand. It's bad enough while in class, all we hear is "All of you are selfish and rebellious. You don't know how to honor your leader!" Blah blah blah, be quiet! It's such a huge inconvenience gas wise too because her job is like almost 45 minutes away from her own home, so now she has to leave even earlier to go to work, drive further to and from and she doesn't even make that much money. I mean, gas is like almost $4 a gallon! Ain't nobody contributing to her gas! I think this is so unfair to her. But it will be over in a month. I know she will be so glad. I will too, for her sake. But while she's here, we stick by each other and keep each other company.

October 4, 2008
Dear Diary,

Today, I did something I've never done before…I went, HORSEBACK RIDING!!! It was so much fun! I feel bad tho because my daddy had been telling me for years that he wants to take me horseback riding. And now when he finds out I went without him, his feelings might be hurt. I wish we could have went together but it's been like 3 years since he's been telling me he wants to take me and the opportunity presented itself to me to go and I hopped on it! I hope he takes it gently. Me, Trish, Rollanda and Mr. Chad went to meet Krissy at her family's horse stable. I had been close to horses before but never this close! Lol. I took a few pictures to show my family of my horse riding adventures. Lol. Krissy let us pick our horses to ride, brush them, and walk them over to the huge fenced in area where we would ride them. There were 2 horses to choose from, one of them had a saddle, the other one didn't. I was scared I would fall off so of course I got on the one with the saddle first. Trish rode the one without the saddle. Mr. Chad didn't ride because of his condition, I guess, I'm not sure. But he took a few pictures for me while we rode. I felt a little daring, so I decided to get on the one without a saddle, as long as the horse didn't run. Man, why did they wait til I got on the horse to tell me that this saddle-less horse was mixed with mustang? That would explain why it refused to just "walk". That horse wanted to run as soon as I got on it. Talk about being scared! Lol. But it was a lot of fun. I hope I get to come with them and do it again.

October 14, 2008
Dear Diary,

I'm just a little lost for words right now! The homecoming carnival is over. Now I can rest. Lol. No, but for real, today was amazing. The carnival was pretty big – and the stage we dance on was pretty high. Lol. We didn't have a lot of space to work with (depth wise) but we made it work (without falling

74

off the stage). I don't think I'll ever forget that moment when it was my turn to seduce Trish, who was playing the role of the girl that once had a close relationship with Jesus. I had on Rollanda's knee high brown and beige lace-up boots, some bright pink tights, this short (and I do mean short) beige pleated skirt, a short sleeve pink shirt with hearts all over it and my braids were down, I walked with a bounce in my step as I approached her, went around her once time, dropped down (in a squat) behind her to give the illusion of something happening), then gave her a kiss on the cheek and walked away.

I heard the crowd making all kinds of crazy noises. I was confident in playing my part tho. Shoot. If I'ma do it, I may as well do it full out! Lord, help me! Lol. But once the guy playing Jesus stepped back on the scene, the crowd went wild! Aww man, it was amazing! Once we were done, we kind of went back into the crowd to watch the other acts coming on after us. We heard so much feedback from that piece we did. A lot of people were crying, I heard that there were some ladies that were watching that got convicted when I did my part because they too were living in the homosexual lifestyle or playing with it. I even heard somebody or a few people gave their lives to Christ!

Now, I can say all the mess we had to deal with, all the extra rehearsals, being frustrated, hungry, tired and in pain was all worth it. Amen. Goodnight!

October 19, 2008
Dear Diary,

Oh I'm so bored! I need a steady job. This assignment will be over in a few weeks. All I do is stay in my room, every day before class and after class. I talk on the phone to Lenard as long as possible until he falls asleep on the phone. There's so much going through my mind, but I refuse to write it because I know someone will find it. This isn't right. I feel like I'm going numb, to everything. I just don't care anymore. But I don't want to feel this way. This is so dumb! Ugh!

October 24, 2008
Dear Diary,

At first, I thought it was cute. But now it's just downright annoying. Rollanda man, like, everyday, she sings the cuppy cake song to Trish or plays the ringtone on her phone for her. That's stupid to me. Why wouldn't she do that for her husband, instead? I rarely ever see her do stuff like that for him. It's moreso she's hugged up with Trish, sleeping with Trish, going out with Trish, working in bed with Trish, eating in bed with Trish, watching movies in bed with Trish, going for long drives with Trish…the list goes on and on. I'm sooooo seriously not jealous. Not this time. I also see that she does certain things like this and tells me places or things her and Trish are about to do, with the implication that I am not invited, just to play us against each other. Oh, I see that one plainly. I was falling for it, at first. But since I'm paying attention now, I know better. I have better things to focus on than some crazy junk like that. Get real. (o_0) Annoyed!

October 31, 2008
Dream

This is all I remember…aww man… Key points: *Another house, not Rollanda's current home. Large rooms. Dr. Mela Ruiz stayed overnight. Lotion/body scrub given to us from someone, demonic, (4) free tickets to Hawaii, Trish's bags packed before I ever found out about the tickets, excitements, door slammed in my face (Rollanda invited me in Trish's room as they packed, then Trish slammed her door in my face). I hit the door out of anger and pain. Dr. Ruiz prays in the spirit upon waking up. Picks up the lotion bottle. Demonic. Also Trish's packed bag. (Hawaii tickets; Rollanda told me not to get my ticket to the Bahamas because she was given 4 free tickets to Hawaii at the beginning of November. But I was never invited to go).*

November 2, 2008
Dear Diary,

Today…was just one of those days where I wish I could get in my car and just drive away from here and never come back. I would literally drop everything. I mean, walk out of rehearsal or off the set, not say a word, get in my car, go get some of my things and leave without saying a single word. I can't say that I was actually looking forward to this day. Kinda because I hate dancing hip hop. Love to watch it. Hate to do it. I seriously suck at it. And I feel like I was being forced to. Ugh. Anyway, the first part of the day was busy, busy, busy- which is typical for this dance company. But it was more pressure for me because I was the main one helping Rollanda get everything in order and make sure everyone was prepared and where they needed to be.

I hate when Rollanda gives Trish stuff to do (things that AREN'T projects) and when she doesn't do them, it comes back to me to do. Booo that. So everyone's getting their makeup done by the MK ladies. All the dancers are gathering their clothes for the different shoots we were set to do that day, complaints are quietly spreading about how they don't like their makeup, bla bla bla. All this is going on while I'm rushing around making sure the pool area is set for us to come shoot the video. The sound guy is ready to go, I still gotta get my makeup done. Gave up my only case of bottled water because no one bought any for us to drink while we were out, deal with attitudes and still wear a smile. Altho I was a lil frustrated to begin, I just stuck by my friend as much as possible and I was ok. The first part of the day was actually fun. While we were shooting the hip hop DVD under the gazebo, there was a slight breeze, it wasn't that hot outside yet, the music was blasting...it was cool. I made sure to stay in the back of the other 3 ladies so I wouldn't be seen doing my horrible version of the hip hop piece. All the drama didn't start til we went downtown.

Omgosh. I was beyond frustrated. It just...happened. I kinda blanked out. No, wait. I got upset, because out the clear, while watching two of the dancers do some dance they either made up or saw on some show (and I must admit, these girls can dance for real), Rollanda said that if she could, she would send them to NYC to study dance, because they are really serious dancers and they can make it because they don't give up every time they mess up. They keep going." I took that personal because I was the ONLY one in the group that would wanna give up easily whenever I mess up. But that was during the time I was beginning to lose my mind because I was sick of her talking down to me all the time. Sick of her mean glares and smart comments...yet claiming to "help me"? HOW!??! And still claiming to do all that you do for Christ? When at the end of the day, we all know who you'll be snuggled up with and it ain't your husband!!! So don't come at me with that "Let's pray" bullcrap until you get yourself together and stop being a hypocrite for the sake of public popularity! After that, I kinda spaced out. I felt my eye twitchin...LOL. Naw, but I was really upset at that moment! I thought, "How dare you!?!?"

When the camera lady was ready, we all moved to another spot near a bridge for them to take pictures. I had the company camera and was responsible for taking pictures while the camera lady was filming. Rollanda was steady barking out orders for me. At one point, I didn't move. I just stood there, staring. Then Trish blurted out "Sierra! Where are you?!" And I snapped out of it. Then Rollanda came over and snatched the camera from me and said I'm dismissed for the day. I didn't say a word, just turned around and left. I was happy to leave. I called Lenard immediately and rambled on to him about this great injustice that has been served to me. He helped me to stay

77

calm. After about an hour of them dancing their hip-hop piece by the river, I guess it was time to go to another location. So, Rollanda asked me "Where's the money?!?" I pulled it out of my pocket, she snatched it from me. Then told me "Just give it to Christina!" So I handed her the case of MY water, the garments and whatever else was in the jeep.

And on top of that, I had to drive Andrew home. I took him back to the pastor's house down the street from Rollanda to take the music equipment back, and then dropped him off at a bus stop in Mr. Chad's jeep. I was pissed beyond belief. Come to find out, after doing a few more hours of film time in different locations, they had a freaking party for the DVD and didn't even tell me, nor was I invited. BUT I was the one who had to email the video people and contact another lady about DVD cases, do research on prices for all this stuff, find out dates and set appointments for the MK ladies to come, plus a whole lot more. I had to do all that, but I don't get invited to the party? Did I not work hard enough? I wasn't even notified about it. It's not even that I wanted to go at all...because I didn't. It's just the point of it all. Why am I even here?!!!! I'm so sick of being treated like a dog.

November 10, 2008
Dear Diary,

I had a ball over the weekend! Oh wow. I went to Detroit for Lenard's birthday. Nessa called me on Monday to ask me to come to his surprise birthday party...on Thursday. I was like...WHAT?!?!?! Today is Monday! Lol. I don't even have any money?!?! But long story short, I made it happen. I bought a 1-way ticket that Wednesday morning and caught a plane to Detroit Thursday morning. Nessa picked me up from the airport, told me the plan for the evening and kept me hidden until time for his birthday dinner. I waited outside on the side of the house until it was time. A few minutes passed, and finally, they gave me the signal to come in. Melodies of "Spend My Life With You" by Tamia and Erik Bennett, played on Nessa's cell phone as she hushed everyone so he could hear the song. As the female verse was sang, that was my cue to walk in. I quietly walked around the corner of the dining room where he was seated in front of his annual birthday lasagna...he looked so sad. When he saw me, he slouched down in the chair, buried his head in his hands and sighed. His demeanor totally changed from that point. He was all smiles. We embraced each other and he dropped a few tears of joy as his family also joined in tears, smiles and cheers. I love this man!

November 18, 2008
Dear Diary,

Sadness has consumed me. Frustration is no longer an issue. Well, not at this point. I really think I'm getting numb to all this sin, compromise, deceitfulness and other junk I care not to even write. I just want to scream until my lungs collapse. I can't believe this is happening. Shortly after I came back from Detroit, some weird stuff started happening. Ok like, last week while I was fixing myself something to eat in the kitchen, I got a text from Pastor Odetta. All she said was "I love you." I looked at that and burst into tears. I felt that love text message drop kick my heart like BAAAM! Take that! Rollanda and Trish came in the kitchen just as I was reaching for my phone. I hadn't said anything to them except good morning. When Rollanda saw me crying, she asked what was wrong. I said "Nothing is wrong. My former pastor just sent me a text saying she loves me. That's all." And she said "Well move back to Detroit then!" That wasn't in a joking manner, she just said it like, "I don't want you here anyway, so go back to where you came from." I said nothing in response, just meditated on the text. I cried because I KNOW that love is GENUINE. It's pure! And she would never hurt me. I know that she only wants what's best for me, which is NOT to be HERE! I know it! And I'm steady killing myself by staying here like a retard! Ugh!

OH! And let's not forget the slap. Yes, Rollanda just hauled off and slapped me. Not the same day, but a few days ago. I was standing in front of her, we were just chatting about something not important and she just slapped me across the face for no reason, then laughed! And I stood there and took it. I didn't flinch. Yes it hurt. Instead of hitting her back, I said "Because I respect you, I'm not going to hit you back." I just left it at that. I didn't tell anyone she hit me because I'm ashamed, I feel stupid and....omg. What else is there to say? I am stupid for staying here and letting this happen.

November 20, 2008
Dear Diary,

I'm so mad! I can't stand these people. The ONLY reason why I'm even here right now is because...well, I don't know, but I don't have another place to go, otherwise, I'd move out of here today! I guess I'm just frustrated because of their stupidity. Trish texted me and asked if I was going to be in Tampa for Thanksgiving because if not, they need to get a sitter for the dog. Ok, first of all, you are already 3 hours away with your family. If you were so concerned, you would have handled it before you left. That is not my dog, nor is he my responsibility. Rollanda finds out that Trish is asking me over and over again about where I'll be and I didn't respond to her. Why? BECAUSE I DON'T HAVE TO! That's why! Plus, at the time, I still didn't know for sure if I was going to be in town or not. But that's none of her concern. Since I didn't answer, Rollanda and Trish start panicking and they had to make some phone calls to see who could come get their dog. Blah bla bla. So what. If I were there, I would have taken care of him. That whole situation was blown out of proportion.

I can't wait to get out of here. When it comes down to it, I see Rollanda is all for self- not others. I say her and not really Trish because Trish, from what I see, is simply following in Rollanda's footsteps. She doesn't even know who she is. Her identity has been lost in Rollanda's shadow.
I can't wait to go to Tulsa in a few days. I'm glad me and Kay started talking again. I can't wait to see her and the kids. It's been years since I've seen them.

November 30, 2008
Dear Diary,

I'm visiting my family in Tulsa for the holiday. I am sooo glad I got away from Florida! I can't have a repeat of last year. Since I can't stop thinking about this mess, I'ma just write it out. In early spring of this year, my friend had a slight family emergency and asked me to do her a huge favor, which consisted of me NOT getting my own apartment. At the time, I was searching for a reasonable apartment in Tampa. Under $500 if possible. After a while, I found a nice one! I recall the day I went to take my application and app fee to the leasing office.

Right as I was getting ready to hand my application to the lady, my phone rang. It was my friend. "Where are you?" she asked with a sense of urgency in her voice. "At the leasing office" I replied. "NO WAIT!!! DONT GIVE IT TO HER YET! PLEASE!!! Just wait a minute" she yelled. Laughing, yet confused, I was like uh, why? She explained to me that she has to move out to go help her mother for a few months and she needed me to move in her apartment and take over her rent for her. So, like any good friend, I did. I spoke to Lenard about it and he was a little leery about the idea of me moving in her place but we both concluded his was good for now. Plus I'd be helping my friend handle a family emergency. All the while, I'm thinking to myself, I don't really want to sign a year lease and be stuck there.

Every other week or so I'd remind myself that my time here (in TPA) is very short. I know I have to go back to Detroit. I'm just fighting it. Anyway, I never fully attached myself to the reality of me living in FL. the 4 month stay at her apartment (4bdrm dorm suite style) was very nice and peaceful. $489 rent, everything included plus full size washer and dryer, wireless internet, cable TV, fitness center, computer lab with printer, huge pool...did I mention the computer lab? Heck yeah! I'll take that!

My new roommates - Juda, Kashmier and Porshe, were all very kind to me. We, as well as Mariell, all had a sister type relationship. Everyone was from a different country or state, which made it even more interesting. All these different languages and accents flying at each other every day. Lol. Especially when we got upset with someone (on the phone mainly), then it really came out. Lol! We had typical sister behavior; borrowing each other's clothes/shoes/hair products, make-up/jewelry (and sometimes not returning it), cooking meals together, dancing in the living room, all night studies (all nighters- not me, but they did!), fighting over who left the dishes in the sink, who moved my clothes out the washer/dryer, Beyonce' experiences, going to church together, helping with choreography (all of us were dancers), taking care of each other when sick, doing each other's hair, etc. There was almost never a dull moment in that apartment. I would mostly stay in the room whenever I was there without Mariell, that is, until I got adjusted to being there. Four months came and went so fast! Toward the end of July, I started to pay more attention to all of the phone calls or text messages I'd get from Rollanda asking why I don't hang out with them anymore and I should come over or I should join them for dinner after class. I'd end up just saying ok and going over her house.

Well, not every time. But for the most part, yeah. While I was living at Mariell's, I only saw Rollanda and Trish at dance or at church, occasionally. Other than that, I didn't press to hang out with them. I was content with that. I was at peace over Mariell's. If I wasn't at dance or at work, I'd spend the majority of my time on the phone with Lenard. Towards the beginning of July was when I realized I needed to make some major decisions regarding where I would live. I didn't have a stable job at the time. So I began collecting unemployment. I pretty much figured I couldn't get an apartment with that income. As a last resort, I asked Mariell if I could stay for 1 more month until I figured out where I was going to move because I had no place to go yet. She said yes, without hesitation. We agreed to split the rent for the next month.

The whole month of August was great! We bonded like real sisters. It's easy to say during the summer, but especially during these 4-5 months, we became the best of friends. One day, Mariell was telling me about a room Rollanda was offering for rent at her new 6 bedroom house. She told Ms. Tonya and her daughter they could rent a room(s) and the offer was also extended to Ah'shely- another longtime friend of Rollanda's. When I heard this, I was greatly disturbed because Rollanda knew that I didn't have a place to stay yet and didn't even bother to ask me about it nor offer me a room. What kind of friend is that?!? Seriously!? I would never do that to any friend of mine. Part of me made an excuse for it: Perhaps she's not extending the offer to me because of our history?? Then those thoughts were overruled by more realistic ones, mixed with anger: I'm about to be homeless and you as my so-called mentor/director/friend doesn't even have the decency to look out for me? If it were the case that it wasn't offered because of what her and I did, then Trish shouldn't stay either because they had sex just two days after she came on to me! Not only that, she knows I have no family here so it's not like I really have options.

I thought about these things for a few short weeks and hesitantly (out of desperation) broke down and asked Rollanda if I could rent a room from them for about 6 months. It hurt to ask because I wish I could have just stayed with the roommates at the Lodge. All of them were okay with me being there but it wouldn't have been fair to them because by one extra person living there, everyone's utility fee's would have been affected. So I needed to go. Once Rollanda and Mr. Chad said it was ok for me to stay at their home, a meeting was set up within the next week for Mr. Chad, Rollanda and I to discuss the terms of my stay and lease agreement. In this meeting, I stated that I only wanted to stay for 6 months at the most. I didn't have a stable job, but I was pretty confident I would be able to pay the rent. Mr. Chad said "Well how about 1 year?" I hesitantly said "uuuh, ok…?" So the lease agreement was printed up saying my term is for 1 year at $500 a month with a $5 a day late fee. Full access to the house and pool in backyard. Only off limit areas were their personal bedroom and bathroom, Trish and Ah'shely's bedrooms and the office. I would always ask if I could use their computer before going in there. Never would I just barge in and use what does not belong to me.

Rollanda and I sat on the couch and she read the lease to me and explained everything in its entirety so I would have an understanding before signing. I agreed to everything. So, before I moved in, I had to give them $1,000. That was $500 for first month rent and $500 deposit. I had money sent to me via PayPal from my moma, money put on my Green Dot card from Lenard, and however much I got from unemployment all equaled $1,000. I remember the first week I was there. I felt so out of place and uncomfortable. I had my spacious bedroom with a beautiful view of the stars at night. Mr. Chad made me a key to the house within a few days of me being there. Normally after coming in from class or wherever I was, I would say "hello" to everyone, then head upstairs to my room and shut the door. After the first few days of doing this, Rollanda said to me "One rule of the house is everyone must hug the lady of the house when you come in." I had the most confused look on my face after she said that and all kind of crazy thoughts started running through my mind like "who the heck do you think you are?". But I simply replied "ok". Gave her a loose hug and proceeded upstairs. I stayed to myself a lot while there. Often times I would read a book, try to read my word, pray, talk on the phone, or just sit in silence and think about what a mess I've made of my life. After all, I had no computer, no TV, no bed, and nothing else to do.

After I was there for about 2 weeks, Rollanda and Trish would come knock on my door, asking what I was doing and I should come hang out with them. Hanging out with them usually consisted of them hugging all on each other on the couch and me sitting on the love seat by myself, or us having tea in Rollanda's bed, then a movie- which resulted in them hugging all on each other- OR- all of us sitting on the couch watching a movie or anything on TV with the end result being…you guessed it! Them hugged up on each other and I'm just sitting there. This went on for about 2 months until I got fed up with feeling like the third wheel. As soon as they would start cuddling, I would leave the room or go to my room because I was highly uncomfortable. I remember one time I got up to leave and one of them asked where I was going. I said I'm going to bed. I got so tired of that. Then another time while riding in the car to class I got on my phone because I was in the backseat bored from listening to their conversation between each other. Then they had the nerve to tell me I was being rude because I got on the phone while we were in the car. I said "excuse me?!? It's not like ya'll are talking to me anyway." So I stayed on the phone. They literally had a conversation for about 15-20 minutes without including me so yes I sure did get on the phone. Had we all been conversing, I wouldn't have done so. That's so stupid. Perhaps they don't know what "rude" means because they are rude to me every day!

Shalom Off Platforms , how are you? Per our meeting tonight, here are the probationary guidelines:

Merit and demerit system (this section will include probation)
*Probation period for bad behavior or disrespecting any team member or leaders – 2 warning after which you get 4 weeks on probation
*Probation period for bad repeated tardiness – 3 verbal warning after which you get 2 weeks on probation
*Probation period for lack of good being a team player, not caring – 1 warning, 8 weeks probation

Probation Guidelines:
* A verbal apology to team asking permission to stay on the team. Members might vote
*Must send written apology to entire team explaining your behavior and what the bible has to says about said offense/behavior
*Must perform community services hours with DC or a ministry assignment by Rollanda Robertson-Anchorage . Five hours per week in said office
*Will not be allow to minister on stage during probation period
*Will be in charge of all clean up and set-up for entire company (within reason) during probation period
*Must do a research/study, and complete a written report on said offense or related offense…and teach a 30-minute workshop on the topic using research notes as handouts.
*Must take a class of said offense at own expense
*Two (2) of the same offense or any three (3) probation is cause for expulsion from Off Platforms

The result of the probation should be:
*A learning and growing tool.
*Not to repeat the same offense in the company within 12 months
*To be able to teach what the bible says about the topic…said offense
*For leader to establish consequence for members actions
*For the growth of the entire company

From: Rollanda Robertson-Anchorage
To: Rollanda; Sierra@DanceChallenger.org; Sierra (personal email)
Sent: Saturday, December 06, 2008 1:50 PM
Subject: SIERRA TO DO LIST Dec 1st - Dec 15th

One of the MANY weekly (added to daily) To Do Lists from Rollanda
(Her requests are in bold. My responses in italics)

How is it coming with the tasks below?

SIERRA TO DO LIST: Dec1st – Dec 15th, 2008

Sierra, how are you today? I know you are busy looking for a job. Here is a
list of what I need your help with in order of priority

1) Please check your inbox daily. Let's meet every other day. Say Monday,
Wednesday, Friday **deadline now**

2) PLEASE. PLEASE. PLEASE follow up with the IRS thing. Let me give
you info NOW

3) update with the Data entry due **Nov. 10th** *{Rollanda, I am still working on
it}* **(WHAT NOW!!!)**

4) STILL need a ballet / modern instructor and tumbling instructor, AND
leaps and lift - for OPDA&TC for nov / dec. You will be in charge of paying
them for me

5) PLEASE book us for 10 (or did I say 5) community events before the end
of Dec. this could include The local Walks in Tampa   *{Rollanda, I'm almost
finished with this}* **(WHAT NOW!!!)**

6)) Schedule a conference meeting with the ENTIRE Europe team. I'm
looking at late Dec. or early January. OK. That is the 6 people here, Greg's
entire support team and the support team in The Netherlands (they don't have
all their stuff together yet tho ☹. Pray.) **Monday 6pm**

7) Call MMP protégés and give assignments

☐   AG - eblast for Europe

85

    ☐   PG – in charge of Nique and Mariell;s grad party at the retreat

    ☐   PG – constant contact eblast to all address in 2 DC email boxes (Rollanda & info)

    ☐   CB – all of MP classes recording on DVD by Dec. 20th and in my office

    ☐   ?? – find location for WEY 2009

    ☐   TH – follow up with bookings from 2008/2007

    ☐   VA – help clean out e-mail box

    ☐   JR – help clean out e-mail

    ☐   TM – make copy of PowerPoint on DVD for Sunday

    ☐   CB – activate DC status

8) Please follow up with OPDA&TC regarding the 3 lines for the prayer

9) Follow up with OPDA&TC goals

10*)* Ann (friend of Kim) re: curriculum **WHAT'S THE UPDATE HERE???**

11) Follow up with Julie Marie – Tennessee

127) Mia Michels or Mandy Moore, Tabitha and Napoleon ???– anytime??? 2009 **WHAT'S THE UPDATE HERE??? PLEASE DON'T DROP THIS. THANKS**

From: Rollanda
To: Sierra
Sent: December 7, 2008
Subject: Addition to the "To-Do List"

Sierra would you please do the following for me?

-Would you please email Honey my teaching from red light, green light as well as my teaching from the 1st week of semester 2.
-Test sunbiz so that you are super-duper familiar with it before tomorrow's class.
-Set your yahoo calendar to alert everyone re: the board of directors meeting. The following groups needs to be informed: OPDA&TC, BOD (S.H, P.C, p. Netta), MNP, WEY (Greg, Ronia, Tam and Tonya too) & SG2K volunteers and staff. See the previous e-mail for the list. I just sent out a reminder but I want weekly reminder from you from now on. Do you have everyone's e-address??? Please let me know.

Rollanda Robertson-Anchorage

From: Sierra
To: Rollanda
Sent: December 16, 2008
Subject: Clarity

Rollanda, I need to let you know something. I'm not sure why you're taking away these things you asked me to do for you, but my reason for saying I couldn't do the constitution is not because I don't want to do it, it's because I already have quite a few things that I'm doing and I know I can't focus on that right now. I don't want to add anything else that requires time to my list of things I'm already working on. That's all. And everything else that I do in a course of a day, besides looking for a job or going to work is for you. What I'm doing for you isn't stressing me out. Also, you did tell us before if we feel we have too much on our plate to let you know. I don't think I've ever said it before. But I just don't want to add anything else to what I have right now. That's all.

From: Sierra
To: Pastor Odetta
Sent: December 17, 2008
Subject: Hi Pastor Odetta.....

Here I go again. Wait, before you respond to this email, please respond to the other one. I have to let her know what you say. Ok, so, hummmm... I wanna talk (or rather email) but I don't know what to say or where to begin. Thank you for praying for me and loving me still. It's funny...I still have every text message you sent me. I know I'm not where I should be...I'm on my way. I haven't totally let go. Yes, I have been discouraged lately. Too much. But I tell myself, even if I have to crawl, I'm not gonna stop going after Jesus. I can't. Or else I'll die. I just gotta keep moving forward.

Oh my gosh Pastor. Oh my goooooooooosssssssshhhhh. I have so many things I just want to tell you...but it's not the easiest thing to do. Like, I wanna tell you how I know I've fallen off. I'm just being real. I can't even tell you when I first felt the change in me. I wanna tell you how I've been discouraged in dance (although it's something I love to do and I KNOW it's a tool He's given me to worship Him with...). I have actually contacted my former dance teacher from Michigan regarding that. We just haven't connected yet.

I wanna tell you about what the Lord was telling me and showing me about ME while I was at a huge creative arts conference in Atlanta in August. It was regarding me taking things for granted and how the enemy would love for me to become indecisive and confused so that I would lose sight of my purpose and destiny.

Lately, He's been showing me things, giving me dreams and its almost as if I can hear people's thoughts. It's weird. Like, I could hear something (neither a dream, nor actual conversation) regarding someone, and then it comes to pass the very same day. I know that's dealing with the prophetic (something I'm still kinda running from but can't). I wanna tell you about the season I'm in. At first I didn't know what the heck was going on in my life, sometimes I still don't. I believe God is trying to get me to the place where I trust Him completely. Not just with my words but my life will testify... that I totally trust God. My faith is shaky. This sucks!

There's more. Lots.

A lot of stuff I deal with I can relate it back to when I used to serve you. Something would click inside of me and I would say "Omg. That's what she meant by that!!! Awww man! I gotta go through this again!?!?!?!"

I know this email is all over the place. Please forgive me. I'm really sleepy but I have too much on my mind to go to sleep. Plus I need to do some studying before I go to bed. And by the way, my cell phone is cut off so you can't call me. But I can receive text messages.

I'm going to end this here email because I'm getting deep in my thoughts now and I may begin to type out what I'm thinking. Not good. I love you. Thank you for reading this. I appreciate you.
Sierra

From: Rollanda & The Dance Challenger, Inc
To: Sierra
Sent: December 17, 2008 12:28 am
Subject: Re: List of things I was working on.

Sierra, thank you for sending me this list. You are now relieved from these duties. I'm not taking it because you are busy...or feel that you plate is too full. Will send you my reasons in writing. Later though....
As for now, you new and only assignment is to: Contact all of OPDA&TC members and 5 leaders (see below), none of which are related to you...and explain to them your rebellious act and your reason for it...then report back to me exactly what they say (because I may be calling them as well).
Leaders to contact:

PC, P. Netta, P. Mela Ruiz, your former pastor and a staff member of your choice from your church (I guess that would be the church you currently visit in Tampa) after I've heard back from you. We'll talk.

From: Sierra
To: Various people
Sent: December 17, 2008 2:15 am
Subject: From Sierra. Please read (and reply) if you have a moment.

Good evening,

I am sending you this email as a result of rebellion on my part. I was instructed by Ms. Rollanda Robertson-Anchorage to contact you and let you know what I've done and my reason for it. After you read what I have said, please, by all means, give me feedback. I appreciate your time.

I have a few things I'd like to share with you. Earlier in the spring of this year, I left town without informing Ms. Rollanda. By the time she found out, I had already reached my destination. My reason for doing so was because I wanted to take a weekend get away. So, I left without thinking to tell her. Yes I admit, that was totally out of order. But apparently I didn't learn from that because a few months later, I did it again. This time, I did it to surprise someone for their birthday (out of state). I was also a little stressed and felt I needed to get away. This time I did tell her I was leaving town, but I didn't say where I was going. I'm not sure if I told her exactly what day I was leaving either. So, same as before, I didn't properly inform Ms. Rollanda about what was going on with me. This is also due to my thinking (at the time) that me leaving town would not interfere with any of my responsibilities therefore it was ok for me to leave when I did. The things I had to work on, I took them with me.

Just recently, a member of the dance company (and one of my closest friends) graduated from college. Initially, me and my friend were planning to spend the entire weekend together celebrating for her graduation. This was planned months in advance. The day before graduation, I received a text message from Ms. Rollanda saying for us to wear our company t-shirts because that's what we agreed on. I said to myself, I didn't agree to that...I don't think I was in class that day because I don't recall hearing that before. Long story short, I didn't wear the shirt. Flat out rebellion.

The above accounts could have been Sierra just being Sierra or acting out of anger without thinking clearly. I do see where I have went wrong here in not properly communicating with my leadership, not being a team player, not submitting to my leadership and my actions did not exemplify respect. Since these things have taken place, I have done a self-examination and am praying about the things I know I have to do from this point. Please believe me when I say, God is showing me, me. Please, please give me feedback as soon as possible (please) on what I stated above.

Thank you again for your time.

With love,
Sierra

Responses:

From: Pastor Netta
To: Sierra
Sent: December 17, 2008 8:28 am
Subject: Re: From Sierra. Please read (and reply) if you have a moment.
Sierra:
Did you have to just send this to my husband and myself? To the whole leadership team? To everyone who is part of DCM?

First of all, could you let me know the nature of your job description with Ms. Rollanda. Are you on call 24/7 or do you have set hours of service? If you have set hours of availability do are you required by the guidelines set to keep Ms. Rollanda informed of what you are doing on your off hours? What is your agreement? That will help me to respond correctly. Do you get paid for your responsibilities or are you in a servant "mentor" relationship?

I am just not sure the type of relationship God has called you to serve in so it is hard to respond.
P. Netta

From: Sierra
To: Pastor Netta
Sent: Wed, December 17, 2008 9:53 am
Subject: Re: From Sierra. Please read (and reply) if you have a moment.

Good morning Pastor Netta,

Ms. Rollanda instructed me to send this email to you, my former pastor, a staff member at the church I currently visit in Tampa, every member of OPDATC, Dr. Mela Ruiz and Ms. Paula C. Not to the staff of The Dance Challenger per say, just to those she specifically named.

I am currently serving as Ms. Rollanda's personal assistant. It seems as tho I am on call 24/7 in serving/assisting her. There may be days we work together late or I receive text messages about work related issues, etc. There are no set hours. We usually meet face to face on Mondays, Wednesdays and Thursdays for updates. This just started about a month ago. I have no set hours of availabillity to her. I told her she can come to me whenever she needed to. There were no guidelines nor agreement set in place stating that I nee to inform her of what I am doing during my off hours. Last but not least, no, I do not get paid for my responsibilities as a personal assistant nor administrative assistant. I apologize for not clarifying this beforehand.

Sierra

From: Pastor Netta
To: Sierra
Sent: December 17, 2008 12:28 pm
Subject: Re: From Sierra. Please read (and reply) if you have a moment.

Sierra,

First of all, if you have offered yourself as a servant assistant, the hours you have available need to be set in writing so you know when your off hours are clarifying when your work hours and personal time begins and ends. Of course, we all have emergencies and you stand ready during those times for change. The way you know when you have a personal rest in your spirit that things are well done and you can make plans without being concerned about interruptions (of course as I said unless there is an emergency or a special big event).
Everyone should have a sabbath at least one day a week that is agreed upon by your leadership for your own personal protection from burn-out. Whether

a job is paid or unpaid, it is best to have a written agreement so that all parties involved know what is expected and it is agreed upon so that when things like this occur, you have something to refer to in the evaluation process. Since you are coming from a "servant lay person" position there are two ways this can be handled professionally for clarification and to protect your friendship because Ms. Rollanda is a wonderful friend.

Possibility one is you write down your own job description of what it is you are able and willing to offer based upon your time and energy available. Then you sit down with Ms. Rollanda and get her feedback and agreement on the terms set. Both of you sign and date it. Another possibility is you can ask Ms. Rollanda to write down what it is she needs in a personal assistant as a job description and then you decide if you can or cannot agree to these terms based upon your present life schedule (job, ministry, family, etc). If you agree then sign that you agree and then that becomes your reference as to what is expected. Pray and ask God if you have bit off more than you can chew or if this is a training ground for what you need to learn for what He has for you in the future. Once you agree, then you know that breaking that agreement has consequences.

Ministry is definitely NOT a 9 to 5 job and you have to be flexible to a point, but even pastors need to set a day off that no interruptions are allowed for their own personal sanity and that of their family (once again, excluding those emergencies that occur). There is also vacation time agreed upon for health, rest and refreshment.
Ms. Rollanda is a dear friend and it appears to me that there just needs to be some defining roles and agreements or disagreements settled on what is expected. If you find what is needed is more than you can handle with your other responsibilities, it is best to find out now so that a friendship can be saved. Miscommunications happen when job descriptions are not laid out and I have decided that friendships that can last a lifetime are a lot more important to salvage because they come from the heart than a business relationship.

These are just some suggestions based on the information I have at present. It appears to my husband and I that since there is not a clear job description (whoever writes it), there is miscommunication. This is just one of those awesome opportunities to learn something new about each other. Amen!

Sierra, I am going to give you a sandwich (good - bad- good). The first thing is that at least you are up writing to me in regards to the matter, so that means that you are thinking about it and feeling convicted. <u>That is a good thing.</u> The fact that you are looking for input and wanting to discover the real YOU, lets me know that God is working and that is where He usually takes all of us. The bad: **Yes, that is rebellion.** Even if it means wearing a T-shirt, something as simple as that, is really a TEST from God Himself to see where you are. The motives of the heart. When He asked Adam "where are you?" or Cain, "Where is your brother, Abel?" those are to test the heart or expose the heart (a mirror on the person).... You can act a certain way towards your leader, but God always knows the heart. He knows that you are murmuring or complaining, resenting.. your leader. Sometimes the flesh kicks in and we just want to do what we want, that is normal but we still have to have a spirit of power, love and sound mind (self-control)... Self-control is the fruit of the Holy Spirit. If you let the flesh conquer, it will conquer in other areas as well. What about when your husband says you can't go somewhere or spend a certain amount of money? How will you react? Are you ready to totally surrender to that authority? The key with you Sierra; is having to submit to ANY authority. I know that it comes from your background and your authority figures not quite being who they had to be (not so good of examples for you). You must set the trend for yourself and then for your future generations to come.

Now to finish the Sandwich: You must talk with Rollanda and admit your sins. Repent from the heart and work hard at staying focused because there is true reward in that (blessings). You can melt the heart of God. I thank you for confiding in me and for being the young lady that you are. I think God is definitely molding you and the fact that you are letting Him, is key. I know that you will make it. It may take a few scrapes and blows, but you will become better and better in the Potter's Wheel. Yes, it's painful to die to self,

but it's all worth it!!! Love you much and please stay in touch. P. Mela

From: Trish
To: Sierra
Date: December 18, 2008
Subject: Re: From Sierra. Please read (and reply) if you have a moment.

Sounds like something I would've done. I don't think that I'm someone that should be giving you feedback because God is still "showing me, me" as well. Good thing is that you realized you were wrong and you are trying to make it right. Amen.

From: Samantha
To: Sierra
Date: December 18, 2008
Subject: Re: From Sierra. Please read (and reply) if you have a moment.

I think we can all agree that you could have done things differently and there seems to be a big lack of communication in this company. Not just from you. It is something we all need to work on. But yes, you rebelled. You're human. Ask for forgiveness from God and those you affected by this act and let's all move on. I honestly didn't think twice about any of it. When you went on the trip though it would have been nice to know where you were but again, not much harm was done. Really just the point. I love you. Samantha.

From: Lenard
To: Sierra
Date: December 18, 2008
Subject: Re: From Sierra. Please read (and reply) if you have a moment.

I read this and it sounds more like you are beating yourself up for your faults only...don't get me wrong I think it's great that you are able to acknowledge your mishaps and realize that there is some growing that needs to take place. At the same time, I feel an in-depth speaking of your personal issues plays a great role in your defiance. Baby, the emotional break away from your loved ones and the transition of your living arrangements with the battle of containing a secure job are things that had you distracted. I understand those things are a part of life but they also shouldn't be neglected. Sweetie you're striving for a spirit of perfection but you're not perfect and I don't believe the few bad choices outweigh the assignments you accomplished in being an assistant for Rollanda. Please hear me, I'm not saying your disobedient acts are acceptable but the fact that you acknowledge them and are ready to move

94

forward should count for something. I love you and I'm going to respond to you a little more later…Gotta get to work. Kisses for your day honey!!!!!!

From: Pastor Odetta
To: Sierra
Date: December 19, 2008
Subject: Re: From Sierra. Please read (and reply) if you have a moment.

Hi Sierra,

I hear what you are saying but have Rollanda give me a call. You have my phone number. Ask her to call me either today or tomorrow. I will be tied up the rest of the week. Love & prayers, P. Odetta

DECEMBER 22, 2008
Dear Diary,

I am so upset! We finally got settled and everything at the resort for the staff retreat. Despite our hectic beginning, the meeting went over well. At least, I thought it did. Sure, sure. Everyone was late getting there, the dinner that was supposed to be cooked or whatever didn't happen because of whatever reason. So Rollanda and her husband had to take us all out to eat at Olive Garden. While we were all waiting to be seated, we sat outside of the front doors of the restaurant on some benches in an open area. I couldn't help but notice Rollanda and Paula (one of the board of directors) talking. I had a hunch they were talking about me.

I mean, who wouldn't make that assumption? If two individuals are STARING at you while talking to each other, wouldn't you assume the same? I wonder what Rollanda is telling Paula about me? I know it had something to do with the email she had me send out to all these "important people" and await their feedback so that I could be further humiliated. Well, hummm, I wonder if Rollanda said anything along the lines of…"I wonder if she's acting out like this as a result of us having sex?" or possibly, "I wonder if we never would have had sex would she still respect me as her leader? Or ummm maaaaaybe "I bet I know why she doesn't seem to care anymore! It's because I took advantage of her in a weak moment in her life and seduced her into having sex with me and lied to my husband about it in his face!" Oh…wait… silly me. That would almost be too much like right! Surely she wouldn't say that. So then I wonder what kind of things she's filling her head with about me. How I'm such a slacker and I'm so disobedient and

95

rebellious. Paaaaaahhhhleeeeeeze. Why in the world would I want to obey someone who's not even submitted to anyone? Not even her own husband? Why should I care about what she thinks of me, what she tells others of me, or even says about me to my face? Her words do not define me. She's not my Lord or my God. She didn't die on the cross for me. I owe her nothing. I don't care about Paula. She apparently doesn't like me anyways. I felt that from jump street. But hey, since when did I care about that either? Oh well. I enjoyed my free meal for the evening.

I'm proud of myself though. Despite how I was feeling, I played it cool. When Rollanda asked for her money so they could pay for dinner, I politely came and kneeled at their side to give them their funds. Whatever was excess, she gave back to me to hold. Guess I could say I was a "yes girl" tonight. I didn't have anything to say to anybody. I was fuming! Yes, heated! Because I know I was going to be blamed for everything that happened earlier that day. This is how it all went down:

Ah'shely and I were instructed to do a lot of stuff for the retreat that weekend. The bulk of it was given to me as a result of a large portion of Ah'shely's load being taken away from her by the head hauncho because she said Ah'shely moves too slowly. I just said yes and ok to everything and did all that I could do to get it all done. The night before the we all left to go to the retreat, me, Rollanda and Norfintrollface were in the living room packing up stuff that was needed for the meeting and whatnot. I decided that night that I was going to ride with Rollanda. That way, I could make sure I got there on time, I could help her unpack and set up…I could drive her car to pick up Val and Buttkiss when they arrived. Everything would be gravy. Rollanda packed her car up that night. Later that night, I got a text from Mariell asking if I could come over to her apartment. She still wasn't feeling well. She was afraid of taking the medication the doctors gave her because it was so strong and asked if I would stay the night and ride with her to Orlando. I said "sure thing mi amiga!", and went right over. The next morning, Mariell and I got up early to get ready for the drive to Orlando. I think I forgot something at the house and had to drive back to get it. Then I went back to Mariell's, parked my car and proceeded to get ready. We had everything mapped out. What time we were leaving and when we would arrive in time for the meeting. I had to be there like 2 hours before everyone else, so we had to leave even earlier. While we were getting dressed, Ah'shely calls Mariell and asked if she could ride with her.

Mariell and I talked it over and asked Ah'shely if she was ready to go and told her what time we'd be there to pick her up. Ah'shely said she was ready and she lives right off the freeway. We said ok. About an hour and a half later, we left Mariell's apartment, on schedule, headed for Ah'shely. We called Ah'shely when we got off the freeway on her exit and asked her how to get to her house. How about, we drove down about 50 blocks before we got to her sister's house….30 MINUTES FROM THE FREEWAY! Oooh we were pissed. To top that off, when we got to her sister's house, she wasn't even ready. Ah'shely had to take stuff out of the back of her sister's car and take it back into the house. Her clothes weren't even packed in a bag. They were on hangers. Since we didn't have space in the trunk and minimal space in the backseat, she had to stuff the boxes of things she was bringing for food and her clothes in the backseat with her. On our way to Orlando, Ah'shely and I silently shed a few tears. I cried because I was so pissed off because I knew all of this would fall on my head and plus this would be the end of me being her assistant for sure. I have no idea why she cried. We didn't talk about it. All three of us was like, we don't even wanna go! We would prefer to just stay home but oh well. It's whatever.

When we got there, when I tell you this lady was mad, oh she was fuming at us! My pants and uniform shirt wasn't dry so I had to run and find a dryer to throw it in so it could be dry before the meeting started. Ah'shely hadn't put any of the bags together for our guests so she started doing that in the foyer of the resort. Rollanda was so close to screaming at her telling her not to do it, just forget it cause it should have been done before she got there. She was also going off on me saying that her husband went to go pick up the two mentees from the airport since I couldn't make it in time and that he would just pay to take everyone out to eat that night since none of the food was set up. She called him crying…and she said "My Chad would never let me look like a fool in front of all these people." Hummm…I felt a tiny bit bad. But it was beyond my control. It wasn't like I could have driven my own car. I couldn't drive it because for 1, I had no money for gas and 2, because my tags have already been expired for 4 months. And she knew it! But yet and still, Rollanda asked me, "Why didn't you ask me for gas money and drive your own car? You had all of the money for our weekend in Orlando, so why didn't you ask?" she says. Are you for real?!? She was so mean to me the entire time we were there. Icy glares, to barking orders, to just being plain cold.

Not to mention that my moma is the one that made it possible for us to even get that resort. She let us use her pass or whatever so we could get the resort for like $99 a night. It was soooo beautiful! Everyone loved it except…the Grinch. She complained about it the whole time, in my hearing. She said she would never come there again. She wishes we would have gone somewhere

97

else or where we were last year…bla bla bla. Ungrateful! That upset me even more! Oh oh, not to mention that she said none of the dance company members could stay the night because this retreat was for staff members and mentees only. But guess who got to come anyway? The next day, Rollanda tells us that Norfintrollface was whining to Mr. Chad that she's bored and she misses Rollanda and whatever, so she decided to let her come and spend the rest of the weekend with us EVEN THO she stressed no one can come unless they are staff or mentees. She was neither! Favoritism! I was glad she was there once I got over my anger because she always makes me laugh, but that's beside the point. If you're gonna do it for her, do it for all.

Lastly, on the last day of the trip, I was supposed to go to the mountains with them for the Christmas holiday. So, while standing in the kitchen, I asked Rollanda a question about something and her response was "When WE get back from the mountains, then I'll talk to you." That "we" did not include me. So she basically let me know I wasn't welcome to go with them anymore. That would leave me by myself for Christmas. With no family, all my friends in Tampa are with their families and I'm left alone. Wow.

December 26, 2008
Dear Diary,

I'm so happy to be in Detroit right now, I can't even lie. I'm glad Mariell let me spend Christmas day with her and her friends because Cruella decided she didn't care about what I did for the holiday and uninvited me from spending it with them in the mountains. And she had the nerve to send me text messages while she was there talkin bout "Sierra, it's so beautiful up here. I can touch the clouds." "Oh, it's so lovely. I think I can see Jesus." "Trish & I just got out the hot tub in our cabin. You would love it here." Ok, why you gotta rub it in my face. I hate her for that. Instead, I spent the last week in the house by myself, me and the dog. I'm trying to figure out how I'm going to eat. I had no money. My unemployment ran out. I put a post on my Myspace page crying out for financial help. I got 2 responses but no follow thru. My moma always sends me money when she can. Lenard started sending me a $50 allowance every week which is helping me out so much. I even called one of my cousins, whom I NEVER ask for anything from. Nothing! I asked her if she could help me by sending me at least $30 or anything so I could get some food. After her run around the block and back, she basically told me no because of whatever. I was so upset. So hurt. So alone. So, I do feel bad about this, but I did what I had to do. I took some money from the envelope containing funds the team was saving for our London tour next year. I had no money to eat with, no gas money in my car,

98

couldn't pay my rent and I had no help. I took a little at a time until I realized all of it was gone! It was about $200 total. I had to explain to Lenard what I did and beg him to help me pay it back because the person that was giving it to me to hold needed it back because her lights was about to get cut off. I did it in desperation. Man.

I feel like such a low-life. And I've even been considering stripping just to get the money to pay rent before they get back in town. I'm too scared to do it though.

Chapter 4
Something Has To Give

January 1, 2009
Dear Diary,

Well, it's the New Year. I have to make so many decisions it's not even funny. I looked backed at the first thing I did in the New Year. I won't even write it in this journal because I know someday someone will read it. So there! MYOB! Anyway, I feel like a year of my life was spent learning "things", how to do this better, how to do that better, but not growing spiritually...but rather dying. Location DOES matter. It's not always about happiness. The decisions I have to make this year will be tough. Very. But I gotta do it.

January 2, 2009
Dear Diary,

(Continuing from yesterday) Even if I have to move back to Detroit, I need to. My spirit is suffering. I'm having fun in Florida; meeting new people, traveling more and more. But all of that has come to a screeching halt. Oh yeah, as of December 13, 2008, I am no longer Rollanda's assistant. Ok. That's fine. I'm hurt, but not crushed. I shall bounce back. I'm not sure how much of that I will express in here, but it is what it is. I need to run to Christ with all I've got though and not look back. I was asked about if I ever cared about this certain dance company. I do, but I don't. I'd rather leave before I'm kicked off. If that happens, it most likely will be my fault (for lack of caring!). I never got over this whole rejection thing anyway. Sucks pretty bad. Ohh booo hooo...Cry me a river! Besides, how could I "minister" to anyone while living a deceitful life?!? Oh, cause my "leader" is??!!? Um...NO! I've got to get outta here!!!

January 6, 2009
Dear Diary,

Wow! Well, right now, as it stands today, I am crushed. Once again, my heart is hurting due to a relationship. I haven't even been hurt by men like this. The greatest pain I have experienced has come from the women closest to me in my life. Why? The place I'm at now, not spiritually, but geographically, I no longer want to be here. My feelings are beyond hurt. By someone that's supposed to be my friend. Man, for a minute, I honestly felt like me being here, the whole ordeal was a huge mistake. But I ONLY say that because my heart hurts. It would be easier for me to cut off the one who hurt me rather than to deal with it.

I feel like this person may love me with her mouth, but we BOTH can be very spiteful. We have the capability to conjure up really mean things about another person. Difference is, I never do it. She doesn't put an action behind the words. Just words, icy glares, purposely doing things she knows I like to do and not inviting me, an intimidating look…whatever. Example, her and Trish were planning to go horseback riding again. Trish mentioned that they were going in front of Rollanda. Rollanda gave Trish this look and said "You weren't supposed to say anything." It was because she just wanted them two to go. Although, a few weeks ago, I asked Rollanda to ask Skye if we could come back and ride the horses again. But OMG. I wish I had the finances to get a truck and some help and I would bust up tomorrow. No need to run, just walk away. I don't have a reason to stay. My family is important to me and although we get on each other's nerves, we got each other's back. At the end of the day, there's no way in hell we would let something happen to the other. We love unconditionally.

We may not always see eye to eye or whatever, but you know… I love my family and I freakin' miss my friends in Detroit. The poverty level may be high there, but hey, love is there. And it's the real kind of love. It's not flaky. And the love of my life is there- Lenard. I love to give him taco flavored kisses. My point is, I have never had a "friend" to insult me and my entire family by calling all of us poor. NO. That's not a friend. And a friend wouldn't tell me I act like I need freaking counseling everyday! And if that were true, my FRIEND would help me through it and not make me feel like crap! I wanna curse; I'm so freaking hurt and fed up. Wait, not fed up yet. But I gotta bounce. Please help me Lord.

January 7, 2009
Dear Diary,

(Continuation from yesterday) I'm so pissed off I don't know what to do. I haven't been doing anything but crying. I can't even believe I'm in this mess. How in the world did I allow this to happen? How did it get this far? I wasn't even able to write about the phone conversation me and Rollanda had after prayer a few days ago. Ok, so, after 5 am prayer, she tells me she wants me to call her as soon as prayer was over. So I called her. That's when she demanded that I get my behind back down there because I don't have a dollar to support myself with and my family doesn't have a dime to support me with either, so I need to get myself back down there NOW! I know I made Lenard mad when I called him and told him what she said. He didn't want to, but he got me a ticket back down to Tampa. When I left Tampa, I told Mariell I didn't know when I'd be back....if I'd come back. So, I left it up in the air. I told Lenard the last time I left Detroit to make sure that was the last time I was leaving him. He tried to keep his promise, but I messed it up. When I got off the phone with Rollanda at 6:18am, I went in the living room, hugged my ma and just balled my eyes out. She had no idea what was going on. But I just needed a hug from someone who loved me. I wish I could have told her everything. I should have told her. But shame kept my mouth shut. I hate the way I feel. I hate this whole situation. I hate it! I hate it!!! I can't take too much more of this!!!

January 11, 2009
Dear Diary,

I have never in my lifetime met an adult this crazy. I mean, a grown lady crazier than my favorite cousin, RCP. Woooooowza! This lady, I'm talkin bout Rollanda- She had a huge kiddy party for her birthday. She said she's turning 26- which is how old Trish and I are. Strange...to say the least. She refuses to tell her real age to anybody. But whatever. The party was so much fun. Me and Trish stayed up almost all night the other day working on signs and making kiddy pictures and putting them up all over the house. The majority of them were like kid creations – pictures of Rollanda with hearts around it, "I love you Rollanda" pictures...etc. We put up at least 40 different pictures and signs. Trish and I still had to figure out what we were going to wear. Trish had a bright idea- for me and her to be twins! Rollanda wasn't feeling that at all. She suggested that Trish should pick something else. I wonder why... hmmmm. So Trish decided to dress up as a baby and I went into the costume closet in the garage and threw some stuff together. Needless to say, it was a hot mess! Lol. On the day of the party, Rollanda had a big

103

bounce house put in the front yard, a petting zoo in the back by the pool, bobbing for apples, face painting, games, hot dogs, chips, cookies and juice to eat, and everybody had to dress up like a kid in order to get in. Quite a few people came. It was so much fun! She depended on me and Trish to kinda be the "life" of the party since we were down-right GOOFY! We even had one of the guest bedrooms decorated as a little club- it was complete with black lights, shredded newspaper thrown all over the room, a mic and a spotlight for whoever dared to take the "stage" and a stereo, blasting loud. Oh my goodness. Trish and I had sooo much fun in this room. She sang her own version of "Happy Birthday", rock star style, on the mic. That junk was hilarious! We had other kids come in there and we threw newspaper up in the ceiling fan and made it rain. Lol!

Instead of singing "Happy Birthday", she had us sing the Toys R Us theme song. I screamed it to the top of my lungs, off beat and out of tune, on purpose. Lol. I was determined to enjoy myself. Lol. Oh, last thing, I threw a cup of water on Mariell while she was getting her face painted....how about this chick chased me all the way down the street (and I was running with some black glitter Dorthy shoes on) and back into the house, screaming to the top of her lungs "Sierra! You better get over here!!! OOOOOHHHH!!!!" I couldn't help but to laugh! Which made her even more mad. I ran back in the house and upstairs to my room. Lol. She was right behind me! She came in there screaming and ranting...both of us out of breath! Lol! Tooo funny! That was the highlight of my day.

From: Sierra
To: Lenard
Sent: January 21, 2009
Subject: Here's the email I was gonna send. I'm just gonna leave it alone

I don't feel that this probation period is just. According to what is written in the bylaws, or the OPDA&TC Handbook, the longest probation period is 8 weeks based upon the offense. My issue with this is not going through the process. My issue is that I feel this is a special case created just for me. 4 months probation? For what? And my offense wasn't clearly stated. Based upon the probation guidelines that you put together, I should only be on probation for 2 weeks, 4 weeks, or 8 weeks. Not 4 months. That isn't fair. It's not fair to me and it's not fair to the team. I feel like you're trying to make an example of me. I would like clarity. What is my offense classified as? Any why is it that the probation period is longer than what is stated in the book? My point is, stand on your word. You stated that you wrote the probation guidelines. Yet you choose to put me on a 4 month probation period. Let's take a class vote on the matter. I'm sure others would agree.

Its bad enough that I want to quit the company but I feel like I'm not growing like I want to. I'm not growing spiritually or in dance. I was at one point, but I feel like I'm at a standstill now. Anyway......its whatever.

January 25, 2009
Dear Diary,

I have decided, as of right now today, that I will begin journaling on my computer vs. in my journals. Why? Because it takes less time for me to type than it does to write and I love to hear my fingers ratta-tap tap on my keyboard. Let's just see how this goes. Because as it stands right now, I don't have a computer stand for my computer, still. And I honestly don't use my computer, everyday. But we shall see. Anyway, Thursday, I lost a friend. We went to high school together. I remember her so well. Kay and I befriended her so she wouldn't feel so alone. She was such a sweet person. It was very tragic to hear about how she died. I still don't know 100% why she did it. She drowned her 17 month old baby girl, and then she drowned herself in the Little Green River, by my moma's old job. I cried so hard the day Kay broke the news to me. Then I cried the next day. And I cried the next day, too. A lot. Today is Sunday and I haven't cried yet. But whenever I think about her, or swimming, rivers, water, ocean, bridges, drive over bridges, anything like that..or even just thinking about my FRIENDS, I cry.

We weren't the best of friends, but I knew her and I loved her. Just because she was a part of my life. It doesn't even matter that I haven't spoken to her since we graduated (that I can recall anyway), but I still knew her, and her existence in life meant something to me. Even now it's hard to think about it. I woke up this morning, she didn't. She now how has a 10 year old daughter that doesn't have a mother nor a little sister, anymore. That hurts my heart. I know this is random, but so what. I'm also a little pissed because when Rollanda was mourning the loss of her former mentee's brother (or whoever she is to her), I was there for her. I checked up on her when she stayed in her bed for hours, crying. I was there to comfort her or just sit in the room (on the floor) with her just to keep her company.

I even went to the funeral in Miami. But now a week later, my friend died, and hmmm, it's like "well get over it." No compassion. Nothing. She looks at me like "why are you crying?" I don't understand this selfishness. You want people to be compassionate toward you when you're sick or going thru

105

something, but when it comes to other people, you act as if you don't care. Or, you'll just pray. Got it. Whatever. If it's not her beloved Trish or Chad then they don't matter as much.

Next subject. I will soon begin studying the dreaded Statistics!!! Dun dun duuuuuuuun!!!!! LOL! Yes, I have a test on Wednesday and I gotta be ready!!! Ok, enough of that. Years later, maybe I'll be able to say "Yeah, I remember the days I used to hate math. Now I can help other people conquer their fears of math".

I miss my Lenard. I love this man so much. But in getting to know more about him, there are some things that concern me and I just pray that what I feel is wrong. I fear that he will one day leave me. I pray that he doesn't. For whatever reason. I pray that I will be a faithful wife to him and that only my breasts will satisfy him. We are so compatible. Gosh, we have so much in common. I love him completely. I love the way he loves his family, how takes care of his son, sisters and his mom. I love the way he loves his niece. He's a man that takes care of his responsibilities. He's very comical, intelligent, good-lookin, God fearing and full of love for me.

I love Rollanda too. Although she hurt my feelings really bad and made me cry more than once. It's weird. Maybe God is doing this thang and answering my prayers. I asked Him to help me forgive. I don't want to be bitter towards her. I still love to be with her. Just for her. When she's not wearing any hats and she's just Rollanda. I miss her so much. (Yeah, I'm still living in Lotz at the Robertson-Anchorage residence). I miss spending time with her, holding her, laughing together and just being in her presence when she's chilling. I love that woman so much. And I'm grateful to have her in my life. I thank God she's my mentor. I love you Rollanda!!! If for any reason you read this, which you shouldn't, but in the event that you do, I LOVE YOU SO MUCH and I wish that I could give you the biggest hug I can muster up with all the strength that's within me and give you a huge WET kiss. Thank you for every minute you've invested in my life. I love you with all of my ability to love. I miss my Uncle Charles ya'll. LOL.

I pray that my event is successful. I don't feel like I'm doing enough. Like I'm waiting for something to happen. I need not wait till the last minute to put this together. It's just that everything takes finances. I set a date, April 18th, but I can't pay for the facility yet.

I'm done for now. I'm on the phone with my boo-nan, bout to eat an orange and then going to wash my car.

106

LOOKING BACK

Everything I stated in the paragraph about loving Rollanda was completely off. Lust and rejection caused me to crave being with this woman. Furthermore, for the very same reasons, I was not able to love her with a pure, Godly love. The love I spoke of at that time was simply lust. I can now say that I love her with the love of Christ, but I have no desire whatsoever to be with her in any shape, form or fashion. The description that I gave of me wanting to be with her was lustful and unnatural. The only One that I love with all of my ability to love is God, then my husband. God was nowhere in that, at all.

January 29, 2009
Dear Diary,

I can't believe that Rollanda had the nerve to have a discussion on root issues and understanding the prophetic as a dancer/ as a calling. No wait, this is what the email said for our next mentoring conference call session. It's dealing with identifying the root issues in our lives:

"In order to live in the fullness of who G-d has created you to be...you must be completely whole. Sometimes that takes deliverance. Take an self inventory, notice any destructive behavior patterns? DEAL WITH IT!!! You will not move forward...you will NOT be success for long if you have root issue that you are unwilling to deal with. YOU CANNOT escape the results of destructive behavior until you face them. There is a root issue. Find out what it is...and deal with it NOW!!!"

Hmmm, there is much to be said about this one. How can we, or, how can I possibly focus on talking about prophetic dance considering what we JUST did the other day? Are you serious? And she's making it mandatory that I participate. Unbelievable. Apparently she has me on the agenda to give a testimony. I don't know what I can say to a group of dancers from all over the USA about how this mentoring program has impacted my life in a positive way – considering – I've slept with our mentor. I mean, really? I'll have to write down what we did in a few days. Still trying to process this huge mess I put myself in...and how to get OUT!

From: Pastor Odetta
To: Sierra
Sent: January 30, 2009
Subject: Dream Interpretation

Hi Sierra,

I sent your dream out to several prophets (without your name attached, of course). Here are their interpretations of the dream. I have put dividers between each response. If you have questions for me, please ask.

Love & prayers,
Pastor Odetta

THE DREAM: **(from December 24, 2008)**

OK, this is my dream. I believe it took place in Tulsa. Not 100% sure of this. But the house resembled my old home. My cousins on my daddy's side were in it. I remember seeing Teesha specifically. We went inside of the house and looked around. There were spider webs here and there. I went upstairs to my old room. (That's where everything was happening.) I opened the door and saw my pink walls and a few things left in the room on the floor. The room did have a musty stench to it. I proceeded to the window from where the light was shinning in. I slowly pulled back the curtains (I remember blinds too, but now I don't know which one it was for sure) and as expected, there were some thick spider webs and spider eggs in the window. As I looked up the corners of the window, I continued to pull the curtains back and then I saw a huge thing that resembled a turtle. I'm not talking about a snapping turtle either. I mean one of those 100 year old tortoises that live in the sea. The really, really huge ones that look like they are still lingering from the dinosaur age. So, it had a shell like a turtle, I remember seeing some orange substance from under the shell. It didn't have a bottom enclosing/protecting shell, just on top. I don't know what was causing it to stay stuck to the wall, but it was up there. Once I got a glimpse of this thing, I ran out the room and got my cousin and whoever else was with us. We all went upstairs and the thing was starting to come down off the wall, like, slide down...on purpose. As if we disturbed it and now it's time to get us out. I do remember it looking at us. At this point, I have to skip ahead because I don't remember everything well enough. Next thing I recall was us there being discussion about not killing it but take it and dump it in the ocean. Or maybe it wasn't a discussion about not killing it. That wouldn't make sense. We

wanted it dead. So I said let's throw it in the ocean. So they or we wrapped it in a huge sheet and took it out back to the sea and threw it in. The thing gained its life back and morphed into something even huger than what we saw. The shell was just to protect the brain of this thing. It ended up looking like some kind of mutant squid/octopus/turtle. It swam away.
The end.

I believe that was a foul spirit. I know it was.

THE INTERPRETATIONS:
Well to keep it simple, we know it's something from her past, unresolved or something trying to resurrect again. It also involves People whom she's very familiar with (father, and cousin, Teesha). I believe it's safe to say this person was comfortable enough to go into the house and go into her room. This would bring her into her past. She was drawn to the window (revealing), something was going to be revealed.

The spider webs and musty stench represent an Undisturbed area in her life. There is some Deception as she expected thick spiders webs & eggs. But unexpected, a huge thing appeared that looked like a turtle. Self examination/she needs to ask questions?
There is something still there that has grown over a period of time-she thought it was something else. She rec'd some deliverance-but the strong man was never up rooted-here it is now showing up after all this time. She recognized it as something harmful. It could be something she got delivered from and the enemy is trying to bring it back up.
The part I have a question about is why they didn't kill it, but they took the time to wrap it up-and throw it in the ocean. The thing came to life and grew larger than what it was before-it also changed into something seemly different. It's still not dead (its alive)!

~~~

The first thing that got my attention was the old turtle like thing.... it just dropped in my mind as a old strong hold that has been in the family for at least a 100 years... Usually, a house represents the person that is having the dream. What were the few things left in the room? Was this something that should have been taken care of before the move? There is something operating in her life "on the daddy's side". A family curse?

Spiders are usually symbolic of a female. Spiders know their power. There are/were some things left in its embryonic stage that did not reach its full potential. A room in the house could represent a part of the soul that needs to be dealt with (the thinking, will or emotional), since it was the bedroom, this

109

is the place of rest and intimacy with one's self... I believe the window represents a portal or an opening that the light is shining through but there is something sitting at the gate of the opening which is probably hindering or being a barrier to the full illumination light (wisdom, insight, opportunity) that is God's Highest and BEST for her... she needs to do some inner searching, in fact, it is probably something that she has literally pushed aside.

"I remember seeing some orange substance from > under the shell. It didn't have a bottom enclosing/protecting shell, just on top" I looked up the color and got this: Orange denotes hope, friendliness, courtesy, lively, sociability, and an out-going nature. This spirit may be very friendly and sociable. I believe the fact that the turtle did not have a shell (protection) all around is sign of her ability to destroy this thing's influence once and for all in her life. " I said let's throw it in the ocean. So they or we, wrapped it in a huge sheet and took it out back to the sea and threw it in" WHY in the world would you handle an enemy like that? Is something going on or has gone on that might offend?.... I believe it came back worse and to live in its mutant state is because they should have killed it and threw in the sea--- I think all along, whatever has been plaguing this person and or the family has been dealt with as something precious and haphazardly thrown into the sea (spirit) but not cutting this thing off at the head--- IT IS TIME! Meaning deal with it!

~~~

First of all it sounds like it will fall on the line of one of the things Father spoke of concerning this year, which was restoration of the family. What came to my heart was unresolved issues in the family that are still lying dormant, but need to be addressed. Sometimes in things being uncovered, they get worse before they get better. The discussions among themselves were very typical, when trying to decide if we need to deal with something or just sleeping dogs lie. I encourage this person to not let sleeping dogs lie, because the end of the thing is victory, even if it doesn't look like it. It seems like whatever the issues are, they produce much anxiety, fear and concern. But there was enough courage to attack it and deal with it, in spite of the fears and concerns. The house, the room the cobwebs mean it's nothing recent. It's an old spirit and it is not a big a secret as she might think, that's what half the shell seems to signify. It was not totally protected from exposure. It was oozing. Again I encourage this person to pray and allow God to reveal, expose, and dispose of..... Whatever it is.

~~~

There seems to be a lot going on with this person. There are a lot of old unresolved issues. There also appears to be generational curses; but there is one specific stronghold that the person doesn't seem to want to kill. God is trying to get her attention. He wants her to finally deal with the thing once and for all. Because demons come back 7 times worse than before. And she hasn't dealt with it as God would have her. It might appear to swim away, but it has the authority to return unless you kill it.

February 2, 2009
Dear Diary,

This is so funny! Rollanda just announced to the company that the London tour has been cancelled for this year. Why am I not surprised? I am SO glad it's cancelled. Although, I would have jumped at another opportunity to go to London or Bradford, no, um, we were going to Amsterdam this time. Thank you Jesus for hearing my prayer and canceling this tour! We don't need to go! I know I sound crazy. Lol.

February 8, 2009
Dear Diary,

I'm so tired of Rollanda trying to make me jealous of her and Trish. I know that's what she's doing. She won't spend any time with me or do things with me that I ask her to, not even watch a movie with me or come sit with me. Instead, she'd say no to me and go do it with Trish. For example, wait, this is an example of trying to make me jealous, not something I wanted to do. For the past few days when I leave the house, I just leave. I make sure I get up early enough so I don't have to see any of them. I know what time Mr. Chad leaves out to walk the dog and what time he leaves for the day (for the most part). I know that Trish and Rollanda don't get out the bed til almost noon, everyday. So, I get up, get my stuff, whatever I need for the day, and make a bee line for the front door, get in my car and drive off. Then later, I'd get a text asking "Hey ma'ma. I miss you. Where are you?" I'd either make up something or just give a vague answer. When I leave at night, they get upset when I don't tell them where I'm going because I guess they feel like they are my family or something? Yeah, I think NOT.

So, the other day, Trish and Rollanda decides to leave at like 1am. I was up. I asked where they were going and I got no reply. While they were gone, Rollanda texts me and says they are going to look at the stars together. I didn't even respond. Wow... really? You and Trish are going stargazing? Who does that? Best friends don't do that. Couples do that. People in relationships do that. She texted me a few more times and made comments on how beautiful the stars were. Bla bla bla. And even when they were in the Carolina's in the cabin! She did it then too! She texted me, knowing that I

111

wanted to be with them, but because she uninvited me the day before they left, I couldn't go. She texted me and commented on the hot tub her and Trish were in, I would love it there, and how when they walked outside the cabin, she felt like she could touch God or the clouds, or something like that. I'm like WHY ARE YOU EVEN TALKING TO ME!?!?!? Ugh!

February 13, 2009
Dear Diary,

I have so many things on my heart right now. So much on my mind. I wish I could just spill it all. To a listening and understanding ear. I wish Jesus could be here in the flesh with me so that He could comfort me because only He knows how I feel right now. Only He knows how I'm crying inside more times than I'd like to. I STILL feel lonely even in the midst of crowds of people, just like I did years ago when I wrote that poem "Lonely". It's not even a laughing matter. This is the kind of things people commit suicide over. Not saying that I am thinking about committing suicide or anything. It's just, I don't know. I should do something for people that feel alone. Why? I'm glad you asked! :0)

Because I don't want anyone to feel the way that I have felt for so long. It's a really crappy feeling. I cry tears that no one sees and scream silent screams that no one can hear, but God. No one understands it (Isn't that the story of everyone's life???). But no, for real. People try to figure me out, only God knows why, and they get upset because they can't figure me out. Ok, right now, I just felt like Lenard. Like, the very thing that irritates me that he does to me, I find myself doing it to others. Why??? I don't like that. We would be okay all day long, then out the clear, towards the end of the day (or any given time of the day), he'd flip on me and come out with all these concerns, fears and doubts about our relationship. All the while I'm wondering what the heck he's talking about. I know within myself the things I have done to cause damage to this relationship. Maybe he's feeling in his spirit the horrible things I've done and he's feeling uneasy. If I were him, I would, too. I love my Lenard. I really, really do. I have never loved any man like I love him and I really do want to be with him for the rest of my life. I love him. This is the man that I choose. Despite all the flak we are receiving from outside parties, we still love each other.

To be honest, I'm a little leery about the stability of our relationship. I don't know how much longer he's going to be willing to wait for me. EVEN THOUGH he told me if he had to wait another 5 years, he would wait because we have the rest of our lives to be together. Let's see.. What if I

112

don't move back to Michigan? Then what? Will he move here? Will he pack up his life and relocate for the woman he desires to spend the rest of his life with? Will we relocate together? What will become of us?

Next concern. My best friend Kay. She's the bestest friend I have ever had on earth. Amanda K.W. was my first best friend. Kay rocked it out!!! LOL! But yeah, I don't know what's going on with us. Are we not supposed to be friends? I mean, after what just happened... I don't know what to say. I was disappointed that she wasn't able to help me with my event. I can express how I feel if I want. Shoot. I'm human. And she's entitled to her opinion and can respond however she wants in response to my disappointment towards her. I can't force someone to get up that doesn't wanna go anywhere. That's just that. But anyway, she says that I'm an interesting person. I do agree. Now, she brings up 3 instances where I stopped talking to her. The FIRST one is when she was gay, she said I stopped talking to her.

Next, when she couldn't come get me from the airport, and now this. Ok, yes, the gay thing. Because I had just received Christ and I had to let some people go because I wanted to focus on Christ and not be sucked back into what I was trying to run away from. When she couldn't come get me from the airport, I was very disappointed because I was looking forward to seeing my best friend that I hadn't seen in YEARS! Ok, naturally, one might be just a TAD bit hurt by that. But I got over that quick because I still wanted to see her asap.

Now this? Oh, this. I was upset. Now I'm fine. I even contacted her and told her the reason for my silence. That's a big step for me. Shoot. Normally I wouldn't even bother with it. Obviously I cared enough to say something. But anyway, now I feel like she's avoiding me even though she said I didn't hurt her, nor is she upset with me. I called her twice today and texted her so many times and only rec'd like, 1 response. She said she was going to bed. Whatever Kay. Whatever!

Next thing. I need a hug. I need to be held and just attended to. Gosh. I really do. I miss that! Sure, I'm one to gravitate to where I can get it. Sorry. That's how I roll. Now that you know, WHAT YOU GON DO ABOUT IT? What? Sue me because I love affection and attention? Because I crave it? So. My kids will get it all! They will never have to wonder if mommy loves them. When I have a bad dream, I want someone to come hold me, pray with or for me, stay up with me, talk to me, sing, something! Shoot. I just..man, this.. Ahhhhhh I wanna scream! What if someone finds this later in life? What if something actually happens to me and they find this on my computer

113

afterwards and say, oh, she talked of suicide. Bull. LOL. No boo. This is me being hurt, lonely, a lil upset, neglected, affection deprived, needing to be hugged and attended to. Not in a lustful way, but just like babies need to be held, cuddled, nurtured, kissed, loved..I feel that it should never stop. Continue the love forever.

Now here's the jacked up part that I really need deliverance on. I want Rollanda to come into my room and help me relive my dream. A dream, a simple fantasy that I wish was reality, that she'd come knocking at my door and we'd relive this dream once more.
That is SOOO bad!!! Ohhhh! Yea, I know. I so desire to be free from the chains the enemy has bound me with. Whom the Son sets free is free indeed. I can be free ~ As long as I don't go running back to put the chains on once He has set me free from the bondage of sin and death. Chains. I wanna be free for real.

I need the Lord to heal my bleeding heart. Correct every wrong. Every bit of confusion, make it all clear for me. I can't see through the fog that's in front of me. It's causing my vision to be blurry. I need my heart to smile. Where is the smile that used to reside in my heart and the laugh that would speak volumes of the joy bubbling over in my heart??? Where did it go??? I need to be freed from myself. I know God is able. I just feel like dancing. Forget about a technique. I want to dance for Jesus. That's it. That's it. That's it. I want to dance what I feel in my heart. I want to dance freely. Just dance. Be free to love, to laugh, to just be...me.

Enough of this entry, for now. I do need deliverance from this, but I still wish that she would come and lay with me for a while. I just miss her. As OFF as that sounds, yeah, I know. But, whatever. It is what it is, until I change it.

LOOKING BACK
"Sure, I'm one to gravitate to where I can get it." "Sue me because I love affection and attention? Because I crave it?"

I thank GOD I'm free from that stinking thinking! Crave is such a strong word. It means to long for; want greatly; desire eagerly, desire intensely, to beg for. This is clearly rejection at work. Yes, rejection. Why would I need to beg someone for attention? Why did I feel this strong desire to be with, talk to, lay with, go out with or just be around any particular person? Christ is the only One I should yearn for. And to say that my children will get it all - referring to attention and affection, that may sound good, but not with the spirit in which it was said. I spoke from

114

rejection. There will be balance in my home. I will put none above Christ, my husband next, then my children. They will receive love from both parents, and we will love them with the love of the Lord, always.

"Enough of this entry, for now. I do need deliverance from this, but I still wish that she would come and lay with me for a while. I just miss her. As OFF as that sounds, yeah, I know. But, whatever. It is what it is, until I change it."

To say, "I do need deliverance from this" was right! The words to follow that showed where my heart was; still full of lust. I did not simply desire her company because she was a "good friend", lust had a stronghold on me and it drew me to her. It kept my mind on her 24/7. The last part of this entry says that it's going to stay that way until I change it, which was also right. I would have stayed in that same spiritually dead state, had I not *decided* to get up and run for Christ with all I had. It wasn't easy, by any stretch of the imagination. But it was well worth it. I had to want to be delivered. It wasn't enough to just say it, I had to put action behind that. The scripture always requires us to participate. We must "act" on it. The Word of God will work, if we work it. Faith (that I would be delivered) without works (moving toward the things of God, repenting, turning from sin, changing my sinful lifestyle to be pleasing to Him) is dead (James 2:26).

In order for us to receive salvation, Romans 10:9 says,"*IF you confess with your mouth the Lord Jesus AND believe in your heart that God raised Him from the dead, (THEN) you will be saved.*"It starts with our obedience to the Word. We can't even receive Christ if we don't FIRST confess Him with our own mouth. The same requirements apply for deliverance. We must first obey the Word of God! The scriptures tells us to guard the doors of our mouth, watch our ear gate and our eye gate, avoid evil, put away sin. So God won't just take it away from us, we must do what He said and "put" it away. He even gave us a remedy for managing our thoughts in Philippians 4:8!

From: Rollanda
To: Dance Challenger Staff
CC: Board of Directors
Sent: February 21, 2009
 Subject: Revamping the company

Hello Wonderful People, how are you today? I love you sincerely,

This e-mail comes for two (2) reasons. 1) Re: DC email accounts 2) Re: New Staff or re-positioning or releasing of current staff members.

I love you. I sincerely do. You are like family to me. If you are getting this e-mail its because in my heart of hearts I feel that you are apart of the Dance Challenger family - ***my family!!!*** And I want to keep it that way. There are a few things we need to work out though...we need to grow family...and we can do that together. Will you do it with me?

1) As you know we have been experiencing problems with our Dance Challenger e-mail accounts for a while. They fix it...it breaks. They fix it...then something else goes wrong!!! 🐌 Man, we've tried!!!! We've been working with I- Power (that's our internet host company) for the past 6 months or so, to fixed this problem of e-mail blockage and larger storage capacity. It's been one thing after another. Sadly, I've paid them 5 years in advance (yea) so I don't want to lose all that money... Soooo much for being a good customer. It's not all on them though. Some of the problems are on my end -e.g.: too much e-mail for storage.

2) Concerning The Dance Challenger and moving forward for REAL!!! This is a serious time for me. A time of training HOW TO BECOME MORE EXCELLENT. I'm tired of the same old, same old stuff, mistakes, excuses, etc. With everything that is in me...I am moving to the next level. Some of you will come with me. Some of you will not. That's a fact of life. That's ok though. As with Abraham and Lot both couldn't go forward together successful! Had they stayed together both would have failed. There came a time for them to go their separate ways. I love you with all my heart but I will not carry you into failure. I love you too much, I fear G-d too much to allow you or me to stay in the stay place. We have got to MOVE, GROW, EXCELL!!! Let's do it together. In 2009, we can no longer afford to carry dead weigh though...or do things just because...or have people in positions just because. No. No. No. G-d is calling all of us to a high standard. A higher place in Him. I'm looking for people with heart/passion in whatever is done in this company. Those who have NOT become complacent with this responsibility to G-d...those who have NOT become too comfortable with me...those who are NOT lazy with their gift. In these hard times, I'm looking for hardworking focused people (do you know that's how people are surviving in the work force today?)...Those willing to go above and beyond.

Those willing to give of themselves to the nations and not expect anything from me in return, but rather from the Almighty G-d Himself according to Eph 6:8.

I've individually met with most of you; heard your heart and shared my heart, etc. And as you know by now we ARE moving FORWARD!!! The question is ARE YOU COMING with us? You are invited to come. Those who will stay will be those who are sold out 100% to the vision AND the visionary (that's me) because you need to be happy serving here.

As we go forward and revamp the company, reposition people and hire new ones, I feel that this is a good time to revamp e-mail on our end. As of Sunday night, Feb 22nd, the following accounts will be deleted...

Christina@DanceChallenger.org
Mariell@DanceChallenger.org
Ah'shely@DanceChallenger.org
Trish@DanceChallenger.org
Sierra@DanceChallenger.org

All others will remain intact unless otherwise stated. Don't be discouraged though you are still family. You still have a place in the company, if you wish. We are just repositioning people at this time. We need you. We need "people" to move this VISION forward. Please agree in prayer with me that I find passionate, hardworking, obedient, "make it happen folks" to help carry us to the next level. If that is YOU then you are on the team. If not, I ask G-d to weed you out so that NONE of us lag behind. The enemy is busy and he is NOT lazy. This time around e-mails will be given out as needed rather than just because.
 If you are interested in MOVING FORWARD with The Dance Challenger's volunteer team, Chad and I have scheduled an open meeting for Sunday, March 1st 1:30pm - 3:30 pm. Meeting will be held at our home or at Lutz River Fern Library. Location to be confirmed. You are welcome to attend. ***You must RSVP before coming. I will not assume that any of you will if I don't hear from you.*** One reminder will be sent via text. Your attendance will show that you wish to continue with the company.

Again, know that I love, respect and honor you for who you are in my life. Be blessed Loving G-d, Serving YOU. Rollanda

March 2, 2009
Dear Diary,

So the meeting yesterday…yeah, about that. I don't care. I don't care to be a part of this anymore. But I won't say it because I want to be a part of it. I mean, if I'm here, and I'm not doing anything with the group, it would be so weird. However, like I said before, I don't care. I showed up to the meeting, listened, and yeah, that was it. I have been over Mariell's for the last month off and on trying to stay away from Rollanda and Trish. Ever since the threesome, I can't stand to be around them. I thought Rollanda would get the hint by now; I OBVIOUSLY don't want to be around YOU! She sends me text messages after class asking why I don't come hang with them anymore. She even made a statement along the lines of I don't love her anymore or some junk like that because once dance class is over, I grab my stuff and leave. I verbally say BYE, but I don't hug anybody. I just leave. Why? Because this is fake to me. I'm tired of living a lie. I'm tired of trying to please her all the dang time. I'm sick of being around both of them. Mainly her. Trish is just trapped and doesn't know it. But how can I help her when I need help too?

So, I thought after the threesome that I would never tell a soul about this and I'd take it to my grave. But once I decided to be honest with myself, I came to the conclusion that I would tell. I don't know who, but I would. I can't die with this on my heart. I know Trish and Rollanda will never tell. Even if I don't tell anybody, I'ma write it down. Maybe someone will find this and read it. I don't care.

This happened super bowl weekend. It started by Trish sending me a text message a few nights before the super bowl, giving me a hypothetical situation about what if somebody wanted to do something. I forgot. I should have written it down before I deleted it. Dangit. I deleted it because she asked me to so that Rollanda wouldn't see it because she would get angry at Trish if she ever found out. So, I was like, just tell me what you're saying. So Trish texted back that she's always wondered what it would be like to kiss me and asked me to please not look at her no different. I was in bed laughing at that message! I said "Sure, I won't look at you any different. Bring it on." After a few minutes, Trish came to my door, knocked softly and cracked it. I opened it and she came in and sat on the edge of my bed. We kissed…giggled, then she left. When she got back to her room she texted me and said I could have gave more of a kiss than that. So I replied, come back then! She did. We kissed again, laughed some more –as quiet as we could so Rollanda wouldn't hear us, and that was that. The next day, she kept staring at me. I stared back with goofy faces. I was fine…I thought nothing of it. But she just kept looking at me all day.

The next day, I don't know what she told Rollanda, but I believe she discussed our little conversation about having a threesome. We met Rollanda at the library where she was doing some work on the computer. Me and Trish was a little giggly, so was Rollanda. But she kinda played it cool. She knew what was going on. Rollanda told me that if I shaved then she'd do me too. That night, it was a done deal. After Chad, Trish, Rollanda and I left the clubhouse from watching the super bowl, we went back to the house. Mr. Chad went to bed early as usual. But Trish, Rollanda and I stayed up in the living room watching movies. I couldn't even watch the movie because Trish and Rollanda was on the couch, under the cover, mauling each other. I was so distracted, upset, left out, and I had enough. I left and went to bed. After about 30 minutes, I hear a light tap at my door. It's both of em. They came in and laid across my bed. I'm like, …uh ok? What's up?

Rollanda starts taking control of the ordeal. She told Trish to go ahead and stop being scared. We'll help her. So Trish and I started kissing while Rollanda watched. I'm not sure when the clothes came off, but everyone's did. I remember Rollanda telling Trish to pleasure me. We all did each other. But the thing that got me, was at some point I was basically pushed out my own bed. I stood on the side of the bed and watched with my own eyes, Rollanda going to town on Trish like there was no tomorrow. Then at that moment, no lie, I promise, Rollanda's words came back to me "I didn't say it's never happened to me, I said I've never did it to anyone back before." LIAR! As I stood there, my heart sank to my feet and I said to myself, "I'm going to regret this for the rest

of my life. This is it. This is it! I can't do this one more day!!!"
I remember the next day, they were both so cool about it.
Everyone was downstairs preparing their breakfast as usual. Mr.
Chad was still oblivious to what his wife, Trish and I did the night
before . I asked Trish what made her do it and she wouldn't tell
me. Only thing she kept saying was "You don't know what
happened before we came upstairs. You just don't know." On the
outside, everything was fine. AS USUAL!

Later on that day, I asked both of them straight up, if anyone was
to ask them if they were gay, considering what we JUST did, what
would they say? Both of them said, "No." I said, so you don't
think what we did was gay? Again, they said no. Rollanda said
she was experimenting or some junk. Dude, are you serious?!?

It was over the top gay! And oh, last month, Rollanda
and Trish had another petty argument and stopped talking to each
other for a few weeks until Mr. Chad stepped in and demanded
them to fix the problem. Anyway, one day while the 3 of us was
sitting on the couch in the living room, Rollanda asked me do I
get jealous when my best friend spends more time with someone
else rather than with me. I said NO! She's a grown woman. She
has a life and so do I. Then she grabs Trish, strokes her arm,
kisses her face and said "I do." Out of nowhere, I said, "You don't
own her!" She said "Yes, I do. This is MY Trish. Mine." Trish
said nothing but smiled sheepishly. I had to get up and leave the
room. That's insane! I can't do this. I have to stay away from
them or this will never end.

March 8, 2009
Dear Diary,

I had so much fun with Mariell and Samantha yesterday! We went
to Planet Beach Spa and then out to Olive Garden for lunch. We
all had certificates for 1 free session at the spa. I had never been to
a spa before, let alone a spa where no one massages you, it's just
spa treatments by machines...I guess. I got in the hydro massage
thing where you undress and get in this huge capsule-like bed that
has steam and some kind of UV lights inside, complete with XM
Radio so you can listen to whatever you want and a fan to keep
your face cool while you're relaxing. It almost put me to sleep, but
I was too excited about the experience so I wouldn't allow myself

to fall asleep! I talked Mariell into getting in the hydro massage after me. Oh my goodness...why did she almost have a panic attack? It was tooooo funny! Right as I was getting settled in my next massage room, I hear "SIERRA!!! SIERRA!!!!" I'm like, who in the world?!?!? It was Mariell. Screaming for me to come help her. I was too busy laughing to focus on what she needed. She was saying the steam was too hot and they were trying to kill her. Lol!!! That was the best part of the whole day for me. Ha ha ha ha ha! After that little episode, I watched Mariell and Samantha get aroma treatments with the plugs up their noses, inhaling different aromas. I'm so glad we got pictures of that experience. These pictures are priceless! Oh, and I got a spray tan! Ha! It was free, so hey, why not? What an experience!

When we went to lunch, we decided we were going to write this off on our taxes (if we could) because we were going to give out our business cards and a sample of cosmetics to the first woman we saw! Lol! Anyway, I told them about why I was so sad that day. Long story kinda short, it was because after I got hurt in class, everyday so far, my body has been in more and more pain. I took a hot bath while no one was home to help ease the pain. While I was in the tub, Rollanda and Trish came home. Rollanda was looking for me and started calling my name. I yelled "I'm in the tub!" So, she runs upstairs, knocks on the door and asks if she can come in. I said sure. So she comes and sits on the stool and asks why don't I have any candles lit and said that I don't know how to take a relaxing bath or some mess like that. I said "because I don't own any." She then asked if she can bring me some. I said I don't care. All the while, Trish is standing by the door telling Rollanda to get out and let me take my bath.

A few minutes later, Rollanda comes back with like 5 candles, lit them and placed them around the bathroom. Then she stands there and just stares at me for a minute. Then we had a little conversation about my body hurting. I made a comment saying I wish I had a hot tub to get in or could go to a hotel and use one because my body hurts soooo bad. Rollanda said if I wanted to use theirs just ask. Later that night, I texted her and "just asked" if I could use their hot tub. I didn't get an immediate response. A little while later, she responded and said she had to ask Mr. Chad. Of course, I was a little surprised, but was like, Ok. The next day, I texted her and asked if she ever asked him. She said yes and his response was no because he didn't want people in their tub or something like that. Later on that same day, after they came back from picking up Mr. Chad from the airport (he was on a business trip in the Bahamas), I came out of my bedroom and was shocked to see Trish and Rollanda going into Rollanda and Mr. Chad's bedroom with her bath towel about to get in their tub because Trish said she didn't want to take a bath in OUR tub. WHAT!!??!!?

So Trish and Rollanda got in the hot tub together while Mr. Chad was in the office doing work. In my face!!! When I talked to Rollanda about it and how my feelings were hurt and stuff, she instantly got angry and told me not to ever compare my relationship with Rollanda to the relationship they have with Trish. Totally shut me down and hurt me even more. I don't understand how you can claim to have all this love for me, but yet when you know I'm in obvious pain to the point I can't even lay in my own bed because the soft mattress hurts my back, won't even do what you can to help me? For real?!?!?! And then she wonders why I've been so distant from her lately. That's all I can write. I'm mad all over again and I don't want to cry anymore.

March 10, 2009
Dear Diary,

For the record, my body (which is healed in Jesus name) has been in pain for the last 6 days for reasons I cannot explain. I tried going to the hospital yesterday. I went to Tampa General, waited for 2.75 hours and was never seen (that's one bill avoided! LoL). But this morning, my hips and shoulders feel so much better. I sat up for 5:30am prayer this morning for 15 minutes and my lower back hurt SO BAAAAD!!! Oh, Samantha prayed for my Jesus to heal me today. :0) Yaaay friend!

March 15, 2009
Dear Diary,

This medication has me so messed up. Dude! Omgosh…since apparently I can't operate a vehicle, I may as well write. Not much though! This muscle relaxer will put me out in about ehhh…5 minutes. Just wanna make a note about another lil dumb something I did simply because I just don't care about too much of nothing right now pertaining to anything. So…after me, Samantha and Mariell left from having lunch at Perkins…oh wait. Let me back up because I didn't wanna go out to eat to begin with. I looked a mess. Physically felt like worse than a mess. Just filled all my prescriptions with all the money I had left…save, a dollar, and Mariell calls me (as I was on my way back to that lady's house to get cleaned up and hide in my room for the rest of the day) and begs me to come eat with them. I said no at first and gave every excuse I could but then decided…hey, why not? Glad I went tho! After our food was served, the elderly couple sitting across from us politely asked if they could pay for our meals! ALL of us! Oh God were we grateful! We said we knew things like this happened but normally we only saw it on TV! We thanked them repetitively as they left.

After we left, as I laid in the backseat of Mariell's car with pain rushing down my spine and through my hips, I said "Hey, let's go to that tattoo place. I wanna get my navel pierced. I'm high on pain meds so I won't feel it anyway." They laughed at me but we went. It was a funny experience. I'll never forget it. Samantha recorded it on her phone and Mariell held my hand. Lol. Maybe I'll regret this later too. I had a fun day yesterday…in spite of the pain. Thanks to Samantha and Mariell. Oh, now I'm stuck over Mariell's. Can't drive because of the meds. They propped my legs up on their couch and got me laying flat. All I can do is eat…and well, just sleep. Hurts to crawl, sit up, lift my arms, and lay on my side. Hurts to move at all. I barely have strength to pick up the phone. Meds kicking in. Nite nite.

March 16, 2009
Dear Diary,

I've been down for 2 days now. 3 days since I went to the hospital. This sucks big time. I'm in so much pain. I can't move at all. The only thing I can do is take this pain medicine, sleep, and lay on my back with my feet elevated. That's it! The bad part is, even though I'm in pain, I'm soooooooooooooooooooo glad I have a real reason not to be in class today. I don't want to be there. I know I should just quit but that would be awkward with me still living with that lady. I'm so irritated with the whole concept of THAT company for more reasons than 1!
I want to dance. But not this bad.

On another note, I'm upset and the anger is growing more with each passing day. Reason being is because since all I can do is sit here, I've been doing a lot of thinking. I remember about a month ago when Rollanda and Trish had the flu at the same time (because they were always all over each other so one got the other one sick). I went out to the store and bought them whatever they wanted because they were sick. I called and asked Trish what she needed and she said Thera-Flu. So I said ok, I'll get that and you both a box of tissue. I told her to ask Rollanda if she needed anything, and she said she wants a grande cup of Tazo tea from Starbucks. So…what did I do? I went to Starbucks and got her some tea. I spent money I needed to eat with for the week to go buy them things that would help them get better. On top of that, when I got to the house, I made their Thera-Flu for them, set up their cups, boxes of tissue and Rollanda's tea so they wouldn't have to get out of bed.

But now that I'm injured, I don't get a phone call, a text message, nothing. A get well card from the dollar store? Not even a "let me come pray with you". Nothing. You do all these things on the outside so they can see your good works, but you pick and choose who you will care for in your own house???!?!? UGH!

March 20, 2009
Dear Diary,

This is so funny. Not really. But I just thought about this. I've been an apprentice with the company for 1 year and 3 months, right. The purpose of an apprentice is to train with the company (everything they learned), pay a monthly fee, then after a year the apprentice is given the opportunity to audition for the company. Well in my case, I paid the monthly fee til I couldn't afford it anymore, I slaved for her, then was still denied an opportunity to audition because I was on "so-called" probation. Once 1 year was up, I didn't even want to be affiliated with them at all! I'm speechless... I didn't pay attention to the ones that truly love me from the jump when they told me this lady was using me and I'm being taken advantage of for so many reasons. She never pays her staff for the work she requires...no...demands them to do. It's insane. Not to mention I was doing more than everyone. I did all my stuff with more crap being piled on DAILY, PLUS I had to help the other staff members/ dancers get their assignments from her completed (for whatever reason). Did I complain? NO! I just did it. I put myself in this situation. Now I gotta get outta here.... For real this time!

Chapter 5
Running For My Life

CHAIN*OF*EVENTS 2009
(The short version)

- 3/22 Lenard flies down to TPA and surprises me
- 3/23 Birthday
- 3/25 Lenard proposes~ I accept
- 3/26 Lenard flys back to Detroit.
- -I was released from OPDATC, MNP, DC and anything else regarding her
- 3/29 Kicked out of house
- 3/30 Meeting with counselor, accompanied by Mariell. Storage purchased and I began to move my things
- 3/31 Payment was demanded for rent and right to my belongings were denied
- -Police were contacted and escorted me to get my things
- -Keys to house were returned
- 4/1 Anxiety attack (Had me down from 4/1-4/5)
- 4/6 I called emergency meeting with Dr. Ruiz.
- -Rollanda and Trish confronted by Dr. Ruiz
- 4/7 Meeting with Pastors L and Mela Ruiz , Rollanda & myself (Rollanda said her husband couldn't make it)
- -Rollanda left a note on my car after the meeting demanding payment in full before I left town that weekend
- 4/8 Rollanda called
- 4/9 Rollanda called
- 4/10 Rollanda called
- 4/11 Rollanda called

- -Rollanda saw me & spoke to me very harshly at the Total Shout Showcase
- 4/12 Flew to Tulsa (relocated there)
- 4/13 Rollanda called
- 4/19 Rollanda called
- 4/23 Lawyer contacted for my legal defense

From: Sierra
To: Rollanda
Sent: Fri, March 27, 2009 7:27 AM
Subject: Read this when you have time

This email is a result of our conversation last night after the OPDAT&C interest meeting. After you gave me your decision regarding releasing me from pretty much everything concerning you, you said it's like I really don't care. It's sad that you get that impression. But just like you said at the end, it is what it is. If that's the decision you made, what choice do I have but to accept it? I'm not going to fight for it. I'm not going to cry about it. Yes, it does affect me. Yes, I do wonder about the things that you told me regarding something the Lord told you that we are supposed to do together. I wonder since you're giving up on me, are you letting that go, too? It's amazing that you have a very low tolerance for the things I do or have chosen to do in my life...because of how it looks on the ministry- not even wanting to give me another chance you say? Wow. You said that you are releasing me from your mentorship and being your leader and you don't want to be anymore. I'm wondering where that came from. Hummm, that's all I have to say about that. I heard you say you have nothing against me. But my heart tells me otherwise. Just like you can discern when things change in a relationship, so can I. And I know my heart is not deceiving me in this.

This is just funny to me.... how all of this happened after I got engaged. You said last night that you want to be happy for me and our engagement because I'm happy. Well, sad to say, I'm not expecting you to. Not once did you offer any "congratulations". Not even a verbal "Happy Birthday." You said you were releasing me because I'm "defiant." Ok, your opinion is your opinion. I know that I can be stubborn when it comes to getting my way sometimes. Or when it comes to my personal life, I will do what I want the majority of the time. Why? Because it's my life. In the end, I have decisions to make that no one else can make for me. I expect my leaders, whoever they may be, to give me advice, wise counsel and choices. Not demands, but choices. God gives me choices. It's my decision to make. Therefore I expect the same from whoever is leading me. Let me make the decision to do whatever. I'm not this god-awful person that goes around ruining other people's lives. So then I don't understand why I get the treatment that I do. Sorry that you didn't find out about the engagement the way you felt you should have or that Lenard didn't come to you and tell you his plans before hand. I'll leave that alone.

When I first got to know you, it was a privilege to be in your space. I was honored to do anything for you. I would go above and beyond, go out of my way every single day to do things for you. My life was already busy before I met you. But doing things for DC was a pleasure for me. It was a joy. It wasn't about you. I saw the God given vision of the company and ran with it. Everything was all good then. To be honest, my respect level, trust, and reverence for you as a leader began to slowly diminish the first day you came on to me. My spirit was telling me to run! Run with all my might in the other direction. But I didn't. I figured after a while, things would change. But because I'm not like some that would come and pour out my guts to you, you don't know a lot about me nor how I felt about that whole ordeal. It affected my spiritual walk, my ministry, my testimony, everything...greatly. More than I'm stating in this email. That one night opened maaaaaaaaaannnnny doors that had been destroyed for years. I pray this never happens to you again or anyone else you come in close contact with. Just because you may be over something doesn't mean the other person is. When I tell you that this spirit is nothing to play with, I'm sooooooo serious. It's very, very, very strong. It can come in many different ways. Uses anyone who is willing, even your best friend. It doesn't matter. And even if you think you're over it mentally, the spirit can still be there... for years! Just laying dormant, waiting for the opportunity to arise again. That must have been the case with us. I can't speak for you because I don't know your spiritual state. But that night gave the spirit of homosexuality and lust leeway back into my life. I don't blame you as a person. I'm just telling you what I saw and now see.

What helped me get through this was much, much prayer. I prayed earnestly to be delivered from it. I didn't look at a female for a long time. Like, if I saw someone in a swimsuit, even just to say oooh that swimsuit is cute. Anything the devil can use, he will. The pictures would stay in my head. I had to guard myself with what movies I would watch. Who I hung around was also vital. I had a LOT of strong people around me to hold me accountable. I read scriptures about homosexuality in the Bible every single day. I studied it. Tore it apart. I read other books on it as well. So I now know that even tho I acted as a bisexual person according to the worlds standards, I was a straight up homosexual according to the Bible. According to Romans 1:26. Women doing things with women that are unnatural and I also know the penalty for it. It's also in Leviticus. So this is nothing new to me. I studied the spirits associated with it so I could know what to call out of myself when I prayed. I was very careful about the way I hugged anyone. Not just women. But especially women. I didn't cuddle with annnnnnyone for yyyyyeeeeaaaarrrrssss. And that hurt me so bad because I'm a highly affectionate person that craves to be held and loved. I changed the way I dressed. Just to make sure it wasn't appealing to the homosexual crowd. I stopped wearing braids for a long time. I changed my phone number. I changed my email address. I went down to the altar every chance I got for prayer against lust. I changed a lot! I'm not saying anyone has to do all of this to get delivered. This is what I did because it was necessary for my life. I don't know all there is to know about this subject, never claim to. I'm just sad that I have to deal with this once again and even sadder about how it happened.

Regarding Off Platforms : I was unhappy in Off Platforms for quite some time. I wish that I were in the first "pow-wow" meeting so that I too could have stated what was on my mind. This is something that was needed a lllllooooooooooooong time ago. As a matter of fact, ya'll should do this on a monthly or quarterly basis. It's needed! Because everyone feels a certain way about things going on within the company. There's a lot of misunderstanding, miscommunication, negative feelings, disappointments, etc. Don't get me wrong, what this ministry is called to do requires hard work and people that are committed to the process. But in the midst of it, no one should be wounded, left offended, left wondering if they can come talk to you as a leader because instead of listening, you'll just respond and take action.

There were more good times than bad for me in Off Platforms . Yes I'll miss it, but at the same time, I believe my time was up a while ago.

Regarding The Dance Challenger: I love DC. I enjoyed being a part of the company. Going to miss all the staff...well, past staff members. Going to miss the conferences and everything that came with being a part of the ministry.

Regarding your mentorship: This is the part that I don't understand why you are releasing me totally. I'm not sure if I'll ever have another mentor. I'm tired of being hurt. This is shocking to me. In a way, I feel that you are doing exactly what (you said) Pastor Odetta subliminally suggested to you - that you give up on me and send me back to Detroit. I feel that since I got engaged and you didn't know it was coming, you found out when everyone else did, and whatever else, you decided to release me. It's as if this was building from something else for a while and I'm not sure what. If it's regarding my personal life, I'm sorry. That's where I draw the line. It's hard to have someone that is so many things to me and still be able to come talk to you as a person and expect you NOT to take action. Like, I couldn't come talk to you, Rollanda the person, it was always Rollanda the leader. Eh, nevermind that. Perhaps one day I'll have a mentor that will not give up on me, no matter what. It's just not clear to me why you're releasing me from your mentorship. When I started being mentored by you, yes, I did tell you a lot of what was going on in my life. But I didn't tell you everything. I never told you everything. Is that a requirement of being mentored by you? I don't understand this at all. I really don't. And I'm sorry, if you can't deal with me and my so called drama, then ok. I feel you may consider it drama because you yourself have never experienced it. That's just my opinion. I don't know that to be factual. But if you say you accept me for who I am, you have to be willing to accept that also. But I thank you for your mentorship. I thank you for pushing me. For pouring in to me. For giving me a part of your life.

Regarding my physical condition: It's funny to me how you seem to be bothered by the fact that I stayed with friends during my time of recuperation from my injury. I gravitated to those that cared. Sorry if that offends you. I will explain. You did come in

131

my room and pray for me and drink tea with me. But I notice things... I guess some things I just can't mention because you may consider it comparing relationships and I'm not trying to go through that with you again. Not now, not ever. I just feel that when it comes to me being sick or hurt, I would be left to myself. With my back being strained, it affected everything that I did. There were days I just cried because my back would stiffen up to the point I couldn't really move. I couldn't sit down for more than 10 minutes before pain shot through my lower back and hips. It has been intense for 2 weeks straight. It's just now getting better to the point I can sit longer than 30 minutes. All you know is that I'm injured and I'm choosing to stay away from "home". I couldn't even sleep in my own bed because it hurt so badly. I have been sleeping on the couch for 2 weeks because its firm and the pillows kept my neck and legs propped up so my back could be straight while I slept. This wasn't just a vacation or I just chose to stay over Mariell's because I wanted to be away from the house. Instead of assuming, you could have asked me. If you cared to know...you could have asked.

True, I could have called you and talked to you about it. But I suppose I expected too much from you (regarding this), as my leader, as my mentor, as a person in my life. And regarding the "family" of Off Platforms , my family wouldn't treat me that way either. 2 1/2 out of 4 showed they truly cared and were concerned about my well being. One didn't ask about me while I was in the hospital, after I got out, when I was in dance class on the floor crying, Not one time. That's not showing the love of a family member, nor the love of Christ. I don't do that to people. When people around me are sick or injured I make sure I go see about them. Even if it's an inconvenience. I do it. Because I love them and I want them to know it. In sickness and in health, whether we're at odds or cool with each other. I'm still there.

Regarding my living in your house: There was quite a few times where I felt unwelcome. It's okay that you and Trish are friends. But I felt shut out. Ya'll would go in the room, whether it be your bedroom or hers, work from the bed, eat breakfast in bed, watch movies in bed, have tea or whatever you do, and the door would be shut to me. I was not invited. So it's like...ok, how am I supposed to feel welcome with this going on every single day? That's why I just stay in my room. At first it bothered me, but then

I just got used to it. That's just how ya'll are. This is not to compare relationships at all. But you mentioned things about me being disconnected in the house. When things like this are done repeatedly, when doors are shut in my face, when I am not included, I will back up. It only makes sense. I pay rent there. It never stated in the lease that I would always feel warm and welcome. I still feel like there's an urgency with you to get me out of your house. I don't know why. But I have felt like this for a while now. Even with what you said last night "I don't know why I keep thinking May. Maybe that's because that's what I wanted it to be." Now, if you didn't want me out, then why would you say this? I appreciate you and Mr. Chad allowing me to stay in your home. You didn't have to. I know it is a huge favor. This is why I respect your space. I don't bother anyone's things, I don't barge into your room unannounced, I don't use your things, I stay out of ya'll way, I clean up behind myself and I'm pretty much quiet. So again, I thank you for allowing me to stay as long as I have thus far.

Regarding you as a person: I will always love you just the same. I love you as a person. I loved you as a leader first, and then as I began to know more about you, I loved you even more. I completely accept you for who you are. Flaws and all. And I mean that from the bottom of my heart.

Please remove me from every email and text message distribution list you have. Thank you.

P.S.
I didn't appreciate you calling my fiancé a loser. You may not recall the conversation, but I do. I didn't say anything in response then, but I never forgot it. It was offensive and you shouldn't say things about people you don't know. You do not know Lenard. He is not a loser but he is a very good man. A very respectable man, very hard working, supportive, loyal, trustworthy, compassionate and more.

March 28, 2009
Dear Diary,

OmG! I've only been engaged for 2 whole days and he's already considering calling it off!!!!?!!? It's all my fault! Lord WHAT

HAVE I DONE??! He doesn't deserve to be treated this way and I am such a horrible person to hurt someone who is so dedicated to loving me. Omg. Omg Omg. I can't stop crying! Even tho... ok, let me start from the beginning of today's mess. I went outside to sit in my car so I could have a private conversation with Lenard, just to talk like I normally would. (ask him if he remembers what we talked about first) He asked me if there's anything else I needed to tell him. I said yes. I could hear the pain in his voice as he asked me what else happened and tell him everything. I cried as I told him of the different sexual encounters Rollanda and I had, then the bombshell...the threesome. I've been keeping this from him for 3 months now...and it's been killing me. But I guess not enough to blurt it out before now! How could I have? I mean...ugh! It sounded as if his heart literally broke and I could not only hear it, but feel it through the phone. There was a long pause before he said another word. He said honestly, I'm considering calling this engagement off. I dropped the phone on the floor while screaming "NO, NO, NO!!! I'M SO SORRY I'M SO SORRY!!!" I cried and cried until I had no more breath in me and I thought my head would explode. He was still on the phone...calling my name...pleading with me to calm down.

A few minutes passed before I could regain partial composure. He said that he was thinking about postponing it, but he's not. But he reassured me that I hurt his heart very badly. I started crying again. How could I have been so careless? Here, I have the love of my life...hurting...because of me. Because I chose to be stupid and mess around with this devil lady that I could care less about. It's not even worth it! I have got to get out of this god forsaken place! I wonder if he will ever forgive me? Well, he already told me before we got off the phone that he forgave me. So the real question is, will I ever forgive myself? I don't deserve him. I'm even more crushed because this is a fine demonstration of how I've done God too! He yet loves me while I'm off skipping to my lue, doing my own thing, totally ignoring the fact that He's waiting for me to come back to Him...with arms wide open. What the hell am I doing!!! I'm so lost! I'm so deep in this crap I gotta dig up just to see the bottom! JESUS I NEED YOU!!! Please, please, please, pppppplllllllleeeeeeeaaaaaaaasssssssseeeeeeeeeee rescue me! I just can't do this without You!

From: Rollanda
To: Sierra
Sent: March 30, 2009
Subject: Re: Read this when you have time

Sierra, I wasn't going to reply to this because I know that e-mails are monitored online and can never be erased...but I thought she thinks I don't care. And I know G-d is able!

I read your letter. Thank you for finally opening up to me and sharing your heart. Too bad it was now and most that came out was not good. But it's good to hear what's in there. All I can say is that I am sorry, I am sorry, I am sorry. For everything! You are right. You are right. You are right. I got to get back to holiness TODAY!!! Trust me I know and (no need to discuss w/ you. its private). anyways, please forgive me for everything - opening an evil door to you (I didn't and don't know how strong it was or is), for hurting you, for being rude to you, for being a bad leader to you and the others as you claim, for not including you, for not caring about you and the others, for being a dictator leader, for messing up your life, for not being a good mentor, a good listener, a good communicator, for causing you to lose respect for me, for not being there for you when you were in the hospital (...didn't know you were "in" the hospital") but sorry. And sorry for everything else. You are right. I've messed up. I'm moving on from here. I was wrong in many times as you so kindly pointed out...I'll now look at myself in the mirror. I encourage you to do the same and maybe you'll see why the same thing is repeated in your life. Oh, and sorry for calling Lenard a loser. That was so wrong of me. Seriously, I wouldn't want anyone to talk about my Chad like that. I think he's cute and strong. So I'm sorry.

You know I did congratulate on your engagement when you text me. Even though I don't rejoice w/ you, i did congrats you. Trish was there as my witness. I mentioned it to her and she watched me text you back "congrats" Sierra on your engagement". Your birthday - surely you got my message Sierra. No time for games. Surely you did. I text you when I remembered. I called you to wish you happy b-day and ask what you wanted...I even got you a cake. So maybe on both ends we didn't communicate. See that's why I celebrate myself on my b-day because I can't rely on people to celebrate me. I just see me getting all the blame -

135

engagement, birthday, bad leaders, the works...I'll take it. You know why because I feel personally responsible for all of this. Trust me I feel personally responsible. I've never been here before. But I know that one thing. Am not staying here. I started all this mess, that why I'm ending it Sierra. It ended for me! Hope you'll do the same. There's so much I didn't because you chose not to tell me yet blame me for it. it is what it is...so much you know and didn't say. So much you assume, but are far from the truth...but since it was not discussed. Hey, let's just make it up and say what you think right. You think I'm releasing you because of Lenard?!?. Wow! Lady, so far fetch. My decision was made before Lenard came down. It was the lack of caring weeks before Lenard came. The Sunday before the school thing I knew. I wanted to give you a few more chances. I didn't and each time you didn't come thru - should we keep at the same-old, same-old game?! Please. Put yourself in my shoes. But hey, it doesn't matter you were leaving. So I made a call first. The conversation about Lenard is one thing...don't think I'm disconnecting w/ you because of your marriage. That's just one more - "ok, Sierra doesn't listen to my leadership" (honestly the friendship as not as important to me as the other). I messed up bad this time. I really did. At this rate....it's too late. I was wrong. I want to make it right...don't want to look back. So regardless of what's said or discussed about me... I just learn from this and grow in Christ.

Now this I must defend...I didn't give up on you Sierra. I told you in advance what I do and don't want in my life "if" I mentored you. My life is hard enough Sierra. I have many trials, sins, weakness of my own - you don't know all that I deal with. You don't and never will. You think because you live here or hang out w/ me you know. You don't know that 1/2 because I'd never confide in you like that. Never! You so the one thing I disagree with, is that I gave up on you. no. no. no!! You, choose to not allow me to lead you. You want your way all the time it was never that we should be friends...we were connected for ministry. So where do I go from there as a mentor. There's nowhere to go... I'm not throwing you or what G-d showed me ago. I'm releasing it and you to G-d! From the bottom of my heart thanks for finally sharing. And I am sorry, truly sorry. Have a good life. Please call Chad or myself about your rent and lease. Thanks Live life *LOUD* and create a **FANTASTIC DAY!!!**
Rollanda Robertson-Anchorage

March 30, 2009
Dear Diary,

Hmmmm, she could have kept that entire email to herself. I don't want to hear it. You can't apologize for anything you REFUSE to acknowledge. I'm too upset to write right now. I just want her to go away. Disappear. Nothing you say to me matters! You've done enough! LEAVE ME ALONE!!!! If you want to apologize for something, try…Sierra, I'm sorry for using what I knew about you for my own pleasure. I'm sorry for allowing myself to be used to bring the spirit of homosexuality back into your life. SAY WHAT IT IS! Don't apologize to me for no petty stupid stuff until you deal with the root of this whole thing! Ugh! I can't stand you!!!!!

April 5, 2009
Dear Diary,

I cannot believe that Rollanda just told Mariell…wait. Let me start over. Since I sat Mariell down and explained to her every single detail of this horrendous ordeal, she has been seeking counsel on how to handle the situation on her end because she said she can't be under corrupt leadership. Totally understandable. I'm so proud of her. She has confronted Rollanda with it in a respectful and professional manner several times. Ok, but when she spoke to Rollanda the other day, Rollanda called her, actually. But during the phone conversation, Rollanda said to Mariell, "Mariell, its over. It's really not a big deal anyway." ARE YOU KIDDING ME?!?!? She seriously doesn't think, see, or believe this is serious in any way? I'm beginning to believe that she is convinced that it was just sex, or "experimenting" in her words, and nothing more! Nothing that would affect our spiritual walk. Nothing that would potentially cause harm to her ministry or MY life. Really? Really?!?!?

This is extremely disturbing because she's currently mentoring other ladies in other states…and they have no idea who is leading them and where she's leading them to!
Oh my Goooooooooooooooooooood! I just want to scream!!!!! What is wrong with her?!?!?!?!
April 7, 2009
Dear Diary,

It's a shame I had to email Pastor Mela this morning and ask her to please help me because since the meeting, Rollanda has been harassing me. She keeps texting me and emailing me. I really wish she would stop!

From: Sierra
To: Rollanda
Sent: Wed, 8 Apr 2009 3:19 pm
Subject: In response: Regarding balance due for rent

I hope that you are having a marvelous day. This email is in response to your many voice mail messages and the note you left on my car last night regarding my balance due for the rent. I am fully aware of the balance that I owe for the rent and have every intent to pay what I owe. Considering the current circumstances, I am not prepared to pay the balance in full by Friday. I will pay you what I owe as soon as I am able and as the Lord allows. I thank you and Mr. Chad once again for allowing me to stay in your home as long as you did. I do not take it for granted. Again, I never stated that I did not plan to pay the balance. I will pay what I owe, even if I have to pay month to month until it is paid off completely. I will mail any and all payments to your P.O. Box address.

Have a wonderful day

From: Rollanda Robertson-Anchorage
To: Mariell, Myesha, Sierra , Belinda, Chad Anchorage
Cc: Rollanda Robertson-Anchorage
Sent: April 8, 2009
Subject: From Rollanda

Ladies, its Rollanda. I hope you don't mind me addressing you all since you all know about my sin issue, and the accusations made against me.
  Mariell, I sincerely apologize. Please forgive me for letting you down as a leader and a friend. I really, really, really do love you There's so much more to what you have heard. I didn't want or ever meant to hurt you ever!! Mariell, thank you for sincerely reaching out to me with the right motives. You did good. Would

you forgive me?

Myesha, I apologize. Would you please forgive me? I hope I didn't bring shame to your name as advisor of Off Platforms. Thanks for trying to reach me indirectly. Know that next time you can be straight and ask me. I appreciate you coming to me first before repeating it.

Belinda, I only knew you were involved because I was told by two other people. However, I knew Sierra spoke with you last week. So there's been a lot of talking but no one was talking to me and they didn't have to. Just so we are on the same page Belinda...I will not be calling or e-mailing you at any point about this matter, mainly because you spoke w/ Sierra *last week* and as you said she requested a meeting w/ both of us. Rather than come to me (to help me) as a minister; it is my understanding that you heard her side, listen to accusations, didn't confirm that it was truth, didn't check motives, repeated what you heard...THEN contacted me 4 days later about a meeting. By then I had received 4 others calls about this and your needing to talk with me. You'll never know if what you listened to was truth. No matter where I am in my life, I find that hard to come to you after that. There is another minister involved (in fact there are a lot of people involved at this point) so I spoke w/ her because she called me 5 minutes after Sierra spoke to her.

Sierra, once again I sincerely apologize for letting you down as a leader...for causing you to think I don't care about you or that I was only using you. Nothing is farther from the truth. So please forgive me. I'm sorry. It seems from the deliverance meeting last night that you're moving on. I feel better now. Sierras, now that you've shared it with so many people...and many have slandered my name w/o knowing my side or knowing the truth... I hope you feel better about it and are able to move on successfully from here. I wish you the best as you move on from Tampa this weekend.

From: Pastor Mela
To: Rollanda

Bcc: Sierra
Sent: April 9, 2009
Subject: Following Up

Rollanda,

I want to make sure that I follow up on our last conversation. I suggested that you and Trish no longer live together. This is very critical! Also, the fact that you need to be held accountable for Chad's good and for your own good - therefore, I recommend that you sit under a Pastor that can reach out to you and that this would be a more Pastor - sheep relationship (not ministry purposes). Someplace where it's more intimate with your Pastors. What I mean is for the spiritual accountability. Even if they don't know you, remember God does know and He knows why and how and who.

This is also very critical. I will continue to follow up with you. I know that you will comply because otherwise you would open up doors to rebellion and God will then have to hold you accountable for that as well. I don't think that is who you are and I know you want help. This is my job right now. I will be tough, because I care and love you dearly. I need you to give me a Pastor's name and church address by the end of April. No time to waste. As far as Monday nights, I would prefer that Mariell and Samantha would stay in charge and you can be the overseer for now. We don't have to say why, just letting them and the class know that you have other commitments. Thanks for understanding! I know this is only a season & that depends on you on how quickly it goes by. Again love ya, Mela

From: Rollanda Robertson-Anchorage
To: Sierra Brown
Cc: Chad Anchorage, Rollanda Robertson-Anchorage
Sent: April 10, 2009 1:28 am
Subject: URGENT To Sierra: Letter regarding balance owed on lease...

Sierra, maybe you did or maybe you didn't get my many messages. I left a note on your car on Tuesday and had someone to witness it for me and recorded it on video. I left 4 phone messages for you. All of these messages were in regards to the $1,800.00 plus balance you owed on your lease. Last week you called me wanting to know what you owed and you said that you'll get the money to me...that was more than 7 days ago. I have yet to receive the money.

Just, in case you forgot my addresses...it's 1053 Sandmill Ct, Lutz, FL 33333, or P.O.Box 22000, Tampa, FL 33333. Would
you please be so kind and send the money to us asap!!! Thank you in advance.

Sierra, Chad and I have been more than gracious to you...more than patient with you...and I hope that you appreciate that because at this point you don't seems to care. That's ok with us. We still care that you pay us... as long as you pay us, we are good.

Rollanda Robertson-Anchorage

April 10, 2009
Dear Diary,

I really wish this woman would stop calling me. She's called me, everyday for the last 4 days. I have nothing to say to her. Everything I had to say I said in the meeting. I'm soooooo angry right now! All kinds of things are running through my head. Thoughts of how to get revenge, how to make her feel pain the same way I'm hurting now and other stuff. But none of that is in my character. I don't want to expose her like that. I told who I felt needed to know. She has no pastor so I told someone else. I had to get counseling before I could move forward. I remember the day Rollanda decided to kick me out the house... Man, she didn't even have the decency to call ME directly and tell me, but instead she called my friend Mariell and told her that she was kicking me out and that I might come over and stay with her. Mariell had no clue as to what was going on. After Mariell got that phone call, Rollanda sends me a series of texts saying that since our relationship has come down to nothing more than text messages, she'll just text me. She said for me not to worry about telling her that I'm staying out anymore because she's putting me out of the house. I read everything else, but deleted them as they came, well, I deleted them after I sent them to my fiancé and showed them to Mariell. I couldn't believe she had the audacity to TEXT me that she was kickin me out? And WHY?

141

So, that night, while I was staying over Mariell's, I sat her down and said I have something to tell you and I need your attention cause this is a looooong story. I went on to tell her everything that happened between Rollanda and I went from start to present day. I didn't think she was listening because I noticed she was falling asleep. But she heard every word I said. The next day was a horrible day for me. Mariell said that what happened between Rollanda and I was greatly disturbing and she has to figure out what she needs to do because she can't be under leadership that is corrupt. She even said she knew something was wrong with me (over the years) because I was quiet too much and I was sad waaay too much but I never told her why. She felt something was odd about it all anyway because of the hundreds of text messages Rollanda would send me at 2 and 3 in the morning.

So, on Monday, I called Rollanda and asked her when does this go into effect? She said "Oh, it was effective last night." I didn't say anything to that. My next question was, why? You said I was causing strife in your house, so what's the strife? Her response was simply this "The strife was you not talking to me." I wish I could have recorded that conversation. Are you serious? As many times as you and your undercover girlfriend stopped talking to each other while living in the same house together, slamming doors, rolling eyes and all, for weeks at a time until your HUSBAND demanded that you two resolve it, you gon put me out for that? For choosing to stay away from you and her? For not giving you hugs anymore? For not kissing your behind? So, I said ok. After our conversation, I went to class. Now, this is the day I found out that I didn't get the refund from my grant because of the class I had to drop (I couldn't afford to buy the supplies). So now, on the day of my test which would determine rather I pass or fail this class, I can't even get a book to study with. Since I didn't have a job, I couldn't buy any books for class. I sat in the study hall trying to remember what I was supposed to study on because I couldn't find my notes from the last class. Shaking and trying not to cry, I went on to class, not knowing what I was going to do. As I approached the building where my class was, I just broke down in tears. I went on to my car, got in and slammed the door and screamed to the top of my lungs. I knew I was going to fail the class. I was falling apart and didn't know what to do. I called my fiancé and told him what happened at school then called

Mariell and told her what happened and now I need to talk to someone, a minster, quick. She recommended I speak to her dance team counselor on campus who is a deliverance minister. I said cool. I was sooooo glad she said she would go with me.

When we got there, I couldn't even get it out good before crying. My eyes were already red and puffy from crying at school. So I got out what I could and Mariell told her the rest. The minister's response is what shocked me. She said this wasn't the first time she's heard complaints about Rollanda. Never anything like this, but other things from various people. She prayed for me and Mariell as well. Mariell asked for advice as to how she should handle it because she's leaving the company for sure. I was very happy to hear that. I felt horrible though. I kept apologizing to Mariell for keeping this from her because I helped cover it by not speaking out about it. Even though I was a part of it. I could have hindered her walk.

Anyway, after I left there, I went and rented storage space a few miles from Rollanda and Chad's home. I waited til about a little after 5 o'clock so I knew they would be gone to class, and then made my way over to her home to get my stuff. When I pulled up, I saw Mr. Chad. He said "Hey Sierra. How are you? I'm just headed out to (so and so) and I'll be back a little later. The girls went to class already." I said "Ok. Thanks Mr. Chad." And with that, he left. I grabbed my keys to the house and started loading my car as fast as I could. I had no boxes, only the box of garbage bags I bought from the store before I got there. I only managed to get 2 car loads into the storage before it got too dark for me to continue. After I got the second load in the car, I just went back to Mariell's home because my back was throbbing from the injury. I wasn't completely healed yet!

Around 9 pm or so, Rollanda calls me. Of course I didn't answer, so she left a voice message. She said, "Hey Sierra, I see you've already started moving your things! Good girl. Chad said he saw you earlier. That's good. I'm glad you started. However, do me a favor; don't come back over here unless you make an appointment with Chad, myself or Trish because you don't live here anymore. Alright? Thanks."
I looked at the phone and just slowly put it down. I was like, ok Lord. Alright. I'll do that. So the next day, I texted Mr. Chad to

see when he would be home so I could come get the rest of my stuff. He texted his agenda back for the day. The last text said, "Before you come back over for your things, give us the rest of the money you owe. Talk to Rollanda. She knows more about it than I do." At that point, I was fuming. I called my fiancé, my moma and the minster and told them what he said then I told them what I was about to do, which was call the police. They all said that was a great idea. So I did, I called them immediately. The police asked me if I was served any papers regarding eviction or given a court date. I said no, they didn't. Then they gave me wonderful news, the dispatcher said they have no right to withhold any of your belongings. I'm sending an officer to escort you over there, right now. I was toooo excited. I met the officer at the gas station on the corner near their home. I explained the situation then he followed me over there. When we pulled up, the officer told me to wait in my car until he signals for me to come. He also instructed me that I only had 10 minutes to get all of my things and that I was not to say anything to them and he would tell them the same thing, not to talk to me. I was ready to comply.

The officer asked for the homeowner's names before going over to their door. Within moments, I heard Rollanda yelling at the officer and trying to calm her down. All I heard was "Ma'am, please calm down. I'm not yelling at you, so don't yell at me." And I heard her say, "I'm not yelling!!! But you came to MY DOOR..." that's all I could make out. Rollanda was t'd off! After about 2 minutes, the officer signaled for me to come. I got out the car, gave him their house key and gate key held together by a rubber band, then preceded upstairs to my old room. I heard Trish & Rollanda rambling about something. Rollanda was stomping around the house saying "I'ma call Chad. Oh he won't believe this! That's what I get for trying to be nice to somebody! Oh you gon send the police to my house?!?!?" Then Trish yelled out to Rollanda, "Does she still have keys?" The officer replied for me, "I have them." I ran through the room grabbing everything and threw it in the trash bags as fast as I could. I think I made at least 4 trips up and down the stairs. Man, why did Rollanda come in the room with 1 piece of mail, "This came in the mail for you." She stood on the other side of the bed holding this piece of mail out to me for me to grab it. I didn't even look at her, I grabbed the mail and tossed it in the bag with the rest of my stuff.

On my second trip, Trish came to the room and asked me if I needed help. I said no. But I thought to myself, now, why in the WORLD would you ask me NOW if I need help doing ANYTHING when over the last 3 weeks you weren't even talking to me because of some petty mess?!?!? Now all of the sudden you wanna be a friend and help me?! Girl bye! Then she asked me if I wanted her to come over (to Mariell's). I got tongue tied cause that was a dumb question for her to ask. I don't like you right now! Why would I want you to come over? Seriously? So I said, I don't care, that's on you." Fifteen minutes passed before I was done. I needed the extra time.

When I was finished, I told the officer, who stood at the front door the whole time, holding it open for me, then I walked out and he walked out too, closing the door behind him. Omg I was in sooooooo much pain and I'm still a lil upset cause I had to leave my queen size mahogany brown sleigh bed, no, the whole set. The mirror, dresser, side chest, lamp and mattresses. It's cool tho. I don't want to take that with me nowhere. They can BURN it for all I care. We had sex on that bed. I can't even sleep in it. I wouldn't dare have anyone else I know sleep in it. Besides, my life is more valuable than all my possessions I left behind.

From: Ms. Sierra
To: Rollanda Robertson-Anchorage
Sent: April 11, 2009
Subject: Fwd: In response: Regarding balance due for rent

Good afternoon Mrs. Rollanda,

I hope that you are having a marvelous day. This email is in response to your many voice mail messages and the note you left on my car last night regarding my balance due for the rent. I am fully aware of the balance that I owe for the rent and have every intent to pay what I owe. Considering the current circumstances, I am not prepared to pay the balance in full by Friday. I will pay you what I owe as soon as I am able and as the Lord allows. I thank you and Mr. Chad once again for allowing me to stay in your home as long as you did. I do not take it for granted. Again, I never stated that I did not plan to pay the balance. I will pay what

I owe, even if I have to pay month to month until it is paid off completely. I will mail any and all payments to your P.O. Box address. **I would appreciate it if you would please stop calling me now. Thank you.** Sierra

From: Rollanda Robertson-Anchorage
To: Sierra
Cc: Chad
Sent: April 12, 2009
Subject: Re: Fwd: In response: Regarding balance due for rent
cc: Chad, Mr. Gurysone

Sierra, I received your e-mail. Thanks for responding to my many phone calls. This is the 1st e-mail I've received. Sierra, do I detect an attitude in this e-mail? A cockiness??? Listen to me clearly when I tell you this Sierra Brown...I DON'T wish to call you. Not now! Not ever again!!!! Honestly I'd rather have nothing to do with you right now. But, as you know I'm not calling you for pleasantry or personally interest lady. You are no longer a part of my life. I'm calling you regarding a business matter, and business matter ONLY!!! So take care of your business Sierra and I'll stop calling you. It's that simple. You understand that right? So until you pay us in full, the calls will continue...unless you rather resolve this another way. You are too cocky for me woman. I hope it gets you where you are going. How could you "tell" me or Chad to *stop calling* you when you owe me money? You must be crazy. Or you must have misunderstood something about the agreement we made when you asked me to come live here. Your bill is in collections. That's how I see it. I'm not your buddy! I'm not your mama. I'm not your friend. Neither am I trying to be. You are incredible. let me tell you something; when you brought the cops to our home telling them Chad husband suggested or said we won't let you get you stuff -- that was it for us. It was over the top... it was low and dirty. That ended all personal relationship with both Chad and I. so to be polite to you, pay us the $1,845.00 or $1835.00 (whatever the amount) you owe us like you promised you would and we need not bother each other. It's that simple. Be a woman of your word and pay.

146

YOU called me last week asking for the balance saying you would pay it. that's been over a week and nothing...not even $50.00 much less the $1,800 plus ... I've learning that you are not a woman of your word and that you do what suits "you" best without regard for others -- so I guess this doesn't surprise me. That's fine for your life as long as you pay us what you owe us for the time you lived in our home. And since you begged me to live here, you should be begging me how quickly you can pay me. Chad and I have shown you nothing but kindness and love. Never, never pressured you in any way for not paying on time...never threw you out when you didn't pay (we'll never do that anyways) month after month after month when you had excuses and promised you would pay. Let's see how much you are a woman of your word now. Please be FULLY AWARE OF THIS Sierra Brown; until we see a check or money order in the mail box I will continue to call you and continue to believe that you are taking us...and have taken our kindness for granted.

Rollanda Robertson-Anchorage

April 20, 2009
Dear Diary,

I just want to disappear. I feel so numb. To everything. It still hasn't hit me yet, the seriousness and depth of what I just escaped from. I came to Tulsa to get away from Florida to save my life. I would have thought Rollanda would have been happy about that. All of this is crazy. I mean, she still texts me every day, harassing me. This is so unnecessary! I feel like I'm about to crack at any moment. I'm really just trying to lay low for a while. Reclaim my relationship with Christ, get some peace of mind...and...be free. But, Rollanda won't leave me alone! I don't want to express to everyone why I'm always crying or why I don't really want to go visit anyone while I'm here. They won't understand because I'm not going to sit everyone down and tell them what I just went through while they were all under the impression that I was having the time of my life, dancing with an internationally known dancer and working for her as well. Sure I was traveling quite a bit, had a lot of opportunities to perform in different places, marched with one of the biggest (if not the biggest) dance theater in Florida, bla bla bla. It's the behind the scenes stuff that nobody knows about that killed me.

Yesterday, my friend came to get me and took me out to lunch. I tried so hard to keep my composure, but I ended up breaking down in the restaurant and cried so hard I got light headed. This ain't cool at all! I just want to hide away until it's time for me to move back to Michigan.

Chapter 6
How Did I Get Here?

April 23, 2009
Dear Diary,

I really don't feel like dealing with this anymore. But since Rollanda is still constantly contacting me via text message and email, it's best that I get a lawyer. I don't think I can get a restraining order considering the fact that we aren't in the same state. Plus she isn't threatening to cause me any physical harm. Ugh! I don't know what I should do. I'm just going to inquire about what I can do from a legal standpoint to protect myself. I'm guessing I should get a lawyer from Florida that would know about the laws down there. I'll be so glad when this is over.

I'm so glad I kept every single rent receipt from my short stay at that lady's house. I can't believe the amounts she claims that I owe her! That is totally incorrect! I'm so ready to defend myself on this one. Once I find my lease and gather up all my receipts, I'll be ready. It's still insane though. She straight flipped it from being a heart/spiritual issue, to me owing her money. Oh-my-wow.

April 28, 2009 12:28am
Dear Diary,

I'm currently living in Tulsa with my mom. Let's just call this an extended visit. I won't be here too much longer. I've been here since Easter Sunday. I had no choice but to RUN and move abruptly back here from Tampa.

Right after the showcase 2 weeks ago, I arranged for Mariell's friend, Renee', to take me to the airport in my car. I asked if she could just keep my car at her apartment til I figured something out. All that was straight. I stuffed my suitcase with all the clothes, shoes and personal hygiene products I had and went to bed. I had to be at the airport by 5am, which meant I had to leave Mariell's by 4am in order to pick up her friend on time. Somehow I overslept and missed my flight! I had no money to change flights, the airline wouldn't refund my ticket – so I prayed. I called Renee', explained the situation and told her I was on my way.

Once we got to the airport, she asked if I wanted her to wait for me to make sure I could get on a flight. These were my exact words, "No. You just go. Don't worry about me. I'm leaving this state today no matter what it takes. Thank you so much for bringing me here! I appreciate you so much! Bye!" When I got to the counter, all I knew was that I was getting on a plane. God worked it out in an instant! My luggage was overweight – they waived the fee and checked it. The charge for getting on the next flight was $100, regardless to why I missed it. Guess what? That fee was waived too! All I could do was THANK GOD! He saved me once again!

To think, I went through all of this because of something I thought with everything in me that was from God. Well, wait. Since this is my journal and these are my feelings, I can be honest. SO, here it goes. Jesus help me. Um, I did fast about moving to Tampa before I went and I was sure I was doing the right thing. The fact that Pastor Odetta was so dead set against it I guess didn't make a difference to me. But it did stay with me the entire time I was gone. I did have a dream on my WAY to Florida about what my next step was. *I was on the beach (in the dream) and I said "God, I'm here in Florida. So now what?" All I heard was "Go home."* I didn't heed the dream. I didn't heed what I heard. And I told myself I'd never tell anyone about this dream. The question is, do I regret it? I regret not running the day after Rollanda came on to me. Dang man. I can't believe how things turned out. I really can't. I had noooo freakin' clue that she was bisexual. Had I known, there's no way on God's green earth that I would have moved my life down to Tampa to help a corrupt leader and ruin my testimony that I fought to keep? Heck naw! I thank God for His grace. Continuous grace and mercy. For real. It was only that that kept me the while I was away. Out of His will.

He saved my life, again. There were times I kinda wished I would just die. Not that I wanna commit suicide or anything. Well wait, that doesn't sound right. Sooo…. Let me rephrase that. There were times when I would ask God if I could literally just start over. I mean, all the way over. Erase my former life and let me be a new person all together. Or let my past be erased from everyone's mind, even my own, and let me just move forward from that point. I know repentance & forgiveness does that, yea. But that's not what I meant. I meant like, if I could be born again, in my moma's womb and come out grown and not perfect, but just extremely good and SAVED, that woulda been great. Because I feel like I have royally screwed up my life thus far with the decisions I have made. I cried for so many nights because I knew the life I was living was wrong I just prayed I wouldn't die like that but that God would rescue me once again & give me the strength to get out because I couldn't do it on my own strength. I just couldn't. Oooooooooomg.

My feelings for the moment are: I love Jesus. I really do. He's always there. I'm listening to "In Your Grace" by 1NC (and texting Mashon.That's my dawg ya'll!). I love this song. (Lyrics) "For a sinner like me, He gave up His life. It's time to let Him know (once again). Lord, I surrender. I give you all I am. It's not much, but I hear you calling. Oh Lord."

I'm excited about dancing for my little sister's open house. I pray to God that He gives me something powerful to do for her. Something that will bless her life. Something that will stick with her for the rest of her life. Not a performance. Something that will not just pertain to her, but bless every person present. But I want it to be something that ministers to me first. I really gotta pray. First of all, because I'm nervous and although I'm excited, because of all this drama I'm dealing with, I can easily see me trying to get out of doing it. Second, because I know my sister and I know the trials she experienced in dealing with school. Having to switch schools because her parent's relationship was unstable. She had to adjust to being in different places, making new friends, and dealing with stress at home. Getting up eeeextra early every single morning and being really tired. Sometimes too tired to study for classes. But throughout everything, she held on to her faith. There was some temptation, but through JESUS, prayer, and a great support system, she made it. That girl is determined. I just wish I

151

could have been a better example for her. Humm…I try not to beat up on myself too much. I'm full of mistakes. I pray that she doesn't follow my example in them. She will choose to follow God(I'ma have to just pray about this. Not really thinking about this too much at tha moment).

Speaking of following people. I have to go ahead and speak on this leadership thing. I have to seek counseling, on a serious note. Because mentally, I don't want to be messed up for the rest of my life. My spiritual growth stunted due to a mentor, a dance director, a woman of God, someone that I trusted…and one of the shortest friendships I've probably ever had in my life. I guess I am good at suppressing stuff. When I'm ready to put something behind me, it's gone. I would PREFER to suppress this. Forget I ever met a woman named Rollanda Robertson-Anchorage . Just forget about it all together. I wish I could. The good memories, the bad ones, and everything else in between. All because I wanted to dance. Omg. I wonder if I'll ever be able to look at another leader the same? Will my next pastor or dare I say, mentor, be a true man or woman of God? Are they living the lifestyle they preach about? Or are they living a double life like Rollanda was? I used to think, while sleeping in my bedroom (while living in Rollanda's house), while she slept in the bedroom with her best friend, leaving her husband in the room by himself, …how can she sleep at night? Does she honestly believe this is right? Is she for real? Like, wow. I don't know if I was condemning her in my mind? Or what the deal was but I know every time I thought about the life she was living, I thought about my own and asked myself like every week, WHY ARE YOU STILL HERE!!! Sierra, what are you doing?!??!?!?!

And to think, how I was hurting that wonderful man Lenard. He's such a good man. Good is not the best word to describe him, but that's just for the lack of better words (and being somewhat sleepy). I would pray to God that I wouldn't lose him. I feel like I don't deserve him. Is it sad that I still feel this way? I feel fortunate to have a man like this that TRULY loves me for who I am. He told me he fell in love with my spirit first. I don't feel he was lying at all. I don't believe he would lie to me. I am so in love with this man, it's not even funny. I cry for him like I used to cry for my daddy! That was amazing to me.

But I've never been in love before. I know this isn't lust. I know it isn't. I'm in love with his soul. I love him entirely. Everything about him...goodness. I'm the luckiest woman in the world...or one of the luckiest women in the world to have a man, a REAL man, a man of God, that loves me, that is responsible, that is trustworthy, that loves God, that loves his family, that loves & takes care of his son, that loves to be the provider, and loves to love me and make me happy? What? I could cry right now.

I love, I love, I love, looooooooooooooooooooooooooooooove this man. With my whole heart. The day that he told me he was "thinking" about putting this engagement on hold because of the news I dropped on him (another screw up by none other than "me"), I thought I was gonna choke on my own spit while sitting in my car, balling my eyes out...with snot rolling down my face and everything. When I got done crying, my whole face was swollen and my eyes were throbbing. I was crying like I got one of those old school beatings. I don't know if I'll ever be able to laugh at that because my heart was hurting so bad that I once again hurt this man. His heart is just as fragile as mine and he doesn't deserve to be hurt. Not by me. Not by anyone. If I could, I would kiss his heart. With all sincerity, I love him and my intention is not to hurt him. But when sin took a hold of me, I became a prisoner to it. I had no control over my flesh. I would cut somebody if they tried to touch me today (not literally). I have to run for my life, once again. Once again...once again.

I must run. Run with all my might away from people that are living the homosexual lifestyle. I can't even be around my cousin too long because she's a lesbian. Not saying that I'ma wanna sleep with her. No! God forbid! But the spirit. I don't want it on me, near me, nothing. That familiar spirit has got to get away. I love her, but she needs deliverance just as bad as I do. Once again, I want to help her get out of this. But for right now, I need not to be affiliated with it again. Until God says it's time for me to go back and minister to people that are living that way.

My song is still, "I'm Still Here" by Dorinda Clark Cole. I love that song. I will probably dance to that song forever. I'm still here. After being doing things to cause my own hurt, crushed by various people who were close to me, friends literally turned their backs on me, even after an anxiety attack and so much more, I'm still here, and it's by the grace of God.

Let's see... what else has been on my mind... Oh! I'm in the middle of a legal dilemma. I have to decide whether I wanna sue Rollanda & Mr. Chad or not. Which, basically, yeah, I do wanna sue em. Because they were wrong in the way they evicted me which even til this day, I have a legal right to be at their home because they didn't evict me the legal way, which was get the courts involved. Gosh, and now she calls me all the freakin time, harassing me, telling me to be a woman of my word?!?!? Pay the money I owe? Wow. Well my lawyer (Ha! I have a lawyer now!!!) told me from that day forward (when she and I had our phone consultation), not to even think about owing them anything. How she broke it down to me was that they owe me money! Naaa mean?!?!!?! LOL! Heck yeah! About $6000. That's 6 months of rent which is $3000, then the value of my bedroom set and mattresses. That's about another $3000.

I thank GOOOOOOODDDDD I'm out of that! I thank God for giving me the strength to come forward with it. Yeah, I could have easily left and just been evicted and never told another soul about what happened between her and I (and Trish), but Lenard, my love, had a valid point. The blood of the other people would have been on my hands because I left them under corrupt leadership. I knew she was living a double life, but I failed to warn the others about the danger their souls were in. I only pray that God will reveal it the way He wants it done to all the others because yes, ministry is going on. Just like I said before. It's like; she's not even dealing with this stuff for real. Yeah she said "sorry", but I don't believe it was sincere. I believe it was to save face. Like, she did it just to cover herself. I don't believe it was heartfelt.

If she realized the damage that she did to me, not just because we had sex and that alone is a mess. But my soul!!! My soul is in jeopardy and my mental stability, my spiritual walk with Christ has been greatly affected, my testimony has been ruined, and more! I pray that I will be able to study, pray, and laugh my way out of being stressed because it has affected my health for the last month. From the day I strained my back til TODAY, I have been sick. From the back strain, to an annoying sneeze and runny nose, urinary tract infection WHILE on my period & cramping, 4 or 5 sleepless nights in a row, anxiety attack, and now a 2 week cold.

All of this has got to stop! I want my life BACK!

Ok, I'm going to sleep now. I gotta get up in 3 hours to take my daddy to the train station so he can go back to Detroit. Chow for now (as my mother would always say).

LOOKING BACK

"My spiritual growth stunted due to a mentor, a dance director, a woman of God, someone that I trusted...and one of the shortest friendships I've probably ever had in my life."

Self-pity, denial of my own faults, pride and rejection. Again, Rollanda did not force me to stay under her leadership. Even though she was very demanding, I still had to choose. I can't blame her. My spiritual growth was stunted the day I decided to disobey God. It happened when I stopped desiring truth; when I decided not to deal with the root of rejection. I began to have "itching ears". If it wasn't in favor of my plans, then I dismissed it. Rollanda did not stunt my growth, but rather added to the mess that was already there. But she was not the cause of it. This is another instance where I have to take responsibility of my own faults.

"But I've never been in love before. I know this isn't lust. I know it isn't."

Rather I wanted to admit it or not, this was also lust. Lenard and I were involved in fornication with each other prior to marriage. Because lust is Satan's counterfeit of God's love, there was no way we could love each other with the love of Christ. We were in sin, lusting after one another. God's love is patient. Lust is not. God's love is not self-seeking. Lust IS! If we really loved each other with the love of Christ prior to marriage, we would have been able to demonstrate that by not lusting after each other, waiting until we got married to have intercourse with each other, we would have respected God all the way around (and so much more)!

When I wrote this entry, we weren't living in the same state, however, a few months later, we did end up living together. That

155

was wrong. Regardless to our excuses to why we felt the need to live together, if we honored God, He would have made a way for us. Lenard should have had his own home to live in and I should have moved in with my parents. But instead, we decided to live in sin and try to keep it a secret. We can hide nothing from God.

I'd like to share a quote from Bible.com on lust and fornication. "Christians who are living in this situation are out of the will of God and need to repent and seek God as to whether this person is the right one for them. If it is God's will for them to be together they should marry. Otherwise, they need to change their living arrangements..... Living together is shameful and selfish as the parties do not care what others think or how they might affect their families and others. They are living to please their own lust and selfish desires. This type of life style is destructive and especially so for children whose parents are living a bad example before them. No wonder our children are confused about right and wrong when parents degrade the sanctity of marriage by living together out of wedlock. How can living together cause children to love and honor God when their parents break the laws of God before them because they are lustful?"

The word speaks to sexual immorality, specifically. <u>1 Thessalonians 4:3-5</u> ESV *For this is the will of God, your sanctification: that you abstain from sexual immorality; that each one of you know how to control his own body in holiness and honor, not in the passion of lust like the Gentiles who do not know God;*
God is very clear on how He feels about sexual immorality, fornication and lust. There are tons of scriptures throughout the Word of God that speaks to these very issues that we as Christians make allowances for. It is my prayer that every person reading this book, if you found yourself in here, please, begin to go after the heart of God on the matter, repent, and do whatever it takes to get out of sin. If our desire is to please the Father, the One who gives us life every single day, then we need to do whatever it takes to obey His Word. Please don't make excuses to hold on to the

enemy's goods one more day. He means you harm and evil all the days of your life. But God is for your good.

From: Mela Ruiz
To: Rollanda Robertson-Anchorage
Cc: Trish
Bcc: Sierra
Sent: April 28, 2009
Subject: Final email...

Rollanda:

I am writing this letter with pain and regret. *Please hear my heart*. First, know that I love you dearly – both you and Chad. I have not judged you for your sins, however, I am disappointed at your behavior – not about the actual sins you've committed, because we all fall short & God's Grace is sufficient for us, However, the decision you have made – not to heed to the warnings and instructions given to you at our meeting with Sierra and Pastor Regenald Ruiz – this is a form of rebellion and Pride. Those 2 monsters will overtake you if you keep feeding them. You keep saying that "Grace" is the church you visit, but yet that is not the church you are comfortable with, since that is what you said at the meeting. You are not ready to be held accountable by that Pastor. You have mentioned that you have chosen other deliverance ministers, which you have not even been able to give me their names or better yet, refuse and say that you are not obligated to tell us. You are right, you are not obligated to us, however, I have not come to you as a deliverance Minister, but as a long time friend and sister. This is all about God's Kingdom Business anyway and God will hold me accountable for what I know and do (James 4:17 – If you know the right thing to do, yet don't do it – it's sin & you are guilty – TEV).

Perhaps taking sometime to go away by yourself for a retreat so you can really begin to see clearly where you are...just like when God asked Adam, "where are you?" Where is the condition of your soul? Where?

Rollanda, realize that you are not hurting just you by this behavior, but others around you – even if it's indirectly. I have asked you and gave you a certain time frame to ask Trish to move out or even help her find a place to live (isn't this what you did with Sierra?). Yet, you down right told me that you respected my heart on the matter but that Trish was <u>not</u> moving out. This is for not just your own good, but for Chad and Trish's own good. It doesn't matter if you have not sinned anymore – it's the principal.

Sierra, called me yesterday and told me that you keep texting and calling her after we said you needed to let her heal and move on with her life. Surely money can't be more important than that girl's soul? She is requesting my help for advice and inner healing – at least she is seeking help.

I thought that you respected us more than that, after all, we have been friends for 11 years now, my daughter has slept over your house plenty of times, since the age of 5 until now (17), etc. You know I am a woman of God and will not compromise.
<u>See, it's not the sin, but the behavior and stands you have taken after the advice given various times.</u> That is rebellion and pride.

You are still trying to justify and brush us off as if it was us who have chosen ourselves to be who we are in God's Kingdom. It is our responsibility before The Lord, to do what is right.

Rollanda, I don't feel you can mentor anyone at this time, especially since you are not following protocol. The mentoring school is a great idea, however, let others mentor for you <u>for right now</u>. I know you are a great leader and you do love God, but yet there is still lots of SELF in your heart. Also, you owe Samantha some answers as she keeps questioning what happened with play and dance, with Rollanda and Trish??? The group has also asked about you - I released them yesterday completely from under your company and gave them over to Mariell (not sure about Samantha at this point - though I like her and would like her to stay). I will have a new location by May 18th. Please do not text any of them regarding practices.

Well, if you care to discuss this further, I will do this with my husband present in a meeting setting with Chad (your husband) as well, so that it will not just be Rollanda trying to justify or protect herself. Therefore, please do not reply to this email *unless* you are willing to discuss this in person. If Chad, doesn't want to, then

I can understand that and I am willing to bring you into the office with my husband and one witness. This reminds me of the scripture that says...You correct the person in private, but if they don't heed, then you correct them among leaders, then if they don't heed, you correct them before the church - Rollanda, whenever you are ready to heed, just call me – if you truly need me, just call me – I am there for you when you are ready.

You need to be held accountable. If you won't heed, then I will release you into the hands of God...Remember I do LOVE you and that is why I haven't given up, however, this is my final email. You can brush me off and say what you have to, but remember

God does see and He does know and eventually it is He you have to confront, one way or another. ~ P. Mel

From: Sierra
To: Pastor Mela
Sent: April 29, 2009
Subject: Email

Hello Pastor Mela,

I received and read your email to Rollanda and Trish yesterday. This is vvvvvvveeeeerrrrrryyyyyyy disturbing to me. Very. It's just confirming something that keeps coming to me more and more as the days go by and as this sinks in more and more. It's as if Rollanda and Trish are using this "best friend" relationship as a cover up and they are the ones that are "lovers". That comes from a slew of things they have said and done (in my presence) since I moved there. I just didn't pay attention to it. I have so much to say on this matter but I don't know how to go about expressing it to you. The reason why I say this is because I don't want it to seem like I'm trying to get back at either one of them, it's just that things are starting to "click" in my brain. Now that I'm no longer in it & blinded by the sin, I can see. I used to say to myself that they have the most unnatural best-friendship I have ever seen in my life. And if it weren't for the fact that they both proclaim to be women of God, I would have to say they are together.
The email you sent Rollanda hurt me as well. From what you said in response to her, I take it as though she is not sincere in taking

159

steps toward deliverance but instead will do anything to keep Trish near her and not change anything. I honestly, with my whole heart, believe that Mr. Chad does NOT know everything as Rollanda says he does. Why in the world would he allow Trish to stay in the house if he did? The thing that disturbs me the most is that I see things haven't changed with her. I don't believe she's remorseful for any of the things that just happened. She's not sorry for her actions, she's not sorry for all of the people she is affecting, she's not sorry for how she put me out the house, how this has affected my health severely over the last month, the great need for deliverance (for all of us), how we were all sexually involved....all of this and ministry is still going on! That's not how I was taught. If there is sin in the camp, you must get rid of it. Or somebody has to be sat down until it's dealt with. There are consequences to sin and I don't see that she's dealing with any of it. Yet, she's still sending emails about the Southern Baked Camp, preparing conferences and other events for the summer, touring in other countries, etc. I know about the emails because I'm still receiving them (which is nerve wrecking). I asked Rollanda twice to please remove me from every text and email distribution list she has. I no longer want to receive anything regarding DC.

Ok, I'm going to end this email. I could go on and on. As the days go by, and as I get deeper and deeper back into my Word, it sinks in more and more just how serious this thing really is. I have no regrets as far as exposing all of this. I only wish that Trish would have confessed herself instead of it having to come from me. I do not miss them in any way, good times nor sexually. Not dancing with them either. I have come across many pictures of me & the company. I deleted quite a few but just left it alone for now because I don't even want to give the enemy a chance to play with my mind while I'm looking or deleting those pictures.

Thank you soooo much for listening to me. Thank you for sacrificing your time for me as well. I appreciate you more than words can express. I thank you for caring for my soul. Not in word only but in deed.

I thank you soooo much Pastor Mela. Have a wonderful day!

Sierra

April 30, 2009
8:33 am
Dream

This dream took place at Rollanda's house in Florida.

The house wasn't designed like the house she lives in now, but it was hers. I was still there. I suppose I was still living there but I was preparing to leave. I was in the kitchen sweeping up a pile of something that was on the floor. Large articles of stuff. As I proceeded to pick it up, Mr. Chad came and said "Sierra you don't have to worry about that. I know what's in it. I put it there so that he (the service guy) could get it." I said okay, but subtly continued to sort through the items to make sure there was nothing in there that belonged to anybody (like, something we still used). I started to pull out a tank top and something else from that pile when I heard Rollanda and Trish come through the door. They were both laughing and giggling and talking amongst themselves. Mr. Chad was still in the kitchen, at the table I believe. Then I heard them two get kinda quiet for a second (it was at this point I knew they were all over each other). I never saw Trish's face. Just heard her voice when they came in. Rollanda came into the dining area and sat at the open breakfast bar that looks into the kitchen. She looked at me with a devious smile on her face and said "I gotta blllooooooggggg! And you didn't dooooo iiiiiit." I just looked at her.

I had this small rectangle piece of scrap metal in my hand & I just threw it at her. I threw it in a vertical angle so that it would cut the air and hit her. It hit her in her forehead, but it didn't faze her at all. Then I put the pile of things back on the floor and went around the corner (passing Rollanda) and sat at the dining room table where their laptop was. Jas was a part of this dream. She was there, in the house, at the computer before I was. Her things (open book bag, some other papers and things she was working on) were lying on the floor next to where she sat. I glanced down at them then sat down to get on the laptop. Totally ignoring Rollanda's presence. I got on the computer to take my things off, email them to myself then delete them. A few moments later after I sat down to work, Rollanda walked over to me and stood beside

161

me and rested her hand on my shoulder. I didn't acknowledge her, I just kept working. She then put her left hand into the back of my shirt and started rubbing my back. I began to squirm around as if to motion to her "get your hands off of me". Then she began to aggressively rub my back. She stopped, then took her hand out. Next, she reached over with her right hand to touch my left hand (which was on the computer). Once she got close to my hand to touch it, I popped her hand and said with an irritated voice "Don't...touch....me."

She said to me "You know, if you want to use the computer, you should go to Publix. They have a fine computer that you can do so and so on." I looked at her and said "You want to hurt me, huh?" She nodded her head like "as a matter-of-fact, yes". Still looking at her, I said "Why are you so freaking evil? !?!?!" Her whole demeanor changed before my eyes as she responded, "Do you think I care? You thought you were nervous about being with that guy you're with now? Wait until you see what I'm gonna do next!!!!" And began laughing fiendishly.

May 6, 2009
A dream

I just had another disturbing dream. This one involves violence. Here's the dream from start to finish.

Rollanda called me on the phone to let me know I could come back to the company and to the house. I still had some things there. I had been suspended from the company because of the short shorts I had been wearing. They weren't booty shorts, just shorter than normal for me. But instead of talking to me about it, she just kicked me off. So I went back to the house. It was mid evening. I went downstairs and to the backyard to take out a bag of trash. I had on my loose gray shorts and a long t-shirt. Rollanda walked past me and said "Sierra, I said you could come back but if you mess up again, that's it. I mean it!" (her demeanor was so dark, she wasn't herself). I looked at my shorts to see if they were too short. They weren't but I pulled em down anyway to make them longer. When I came back in the house, I took my shoes off. Mr. Chad was doing some remodeling or something so he asked me to put my shoes in a specific area, then he pointed to the spot. I said ok, then neatly placed my shoes there. Next, I

162

*proceeded to walk towards the stairs to go to my room when
Rollanda and Trish came storming downstairs. Rollanda was
furious. Trish was mad too, but she just backed Rollanda. So
Rollanda said "You mean to tell me you told so and so???? when
I told you we don't accept cash for the ????? fund?!?" Trish
jumped in and said something too but they were talking at the
same time so I don't know what she said.*

*They were both yelling at me, charging towards me with accusing
fingers. Rollanda said "then you did it anyway?!?!?!" Trish said
"Yep she sure did!" I couldn't really get a word in. Rollanda
shoved her fingers in my chest. Then that's when I said, "When
you asked me to leave the first time, all I had was cash! I didn't
have time to go get a money order! You just asked me to come
back here...for money??!?!?" I smacked her hand out of my face
and away from my chest. She forcefully bumped me with her body
(as if to punk me). I pushed her back. Trish didn't touch me. She
stood back. {One important detail: When I came around the
corner to go upstairs and Rollanda and Trish were storming
downstairs, in my spirit, I knew Rollanda had just received
something regarding the whole ordeal. Like an email or perhaps a
letter. From who? I don't know. I felt like it was from me to
someone else, but that doesn't make sense how she would have
received it. She was mad because it was revealed to someone
else.}*

*So she bumps me. Then I pushed her and started swinging on her.
She screamed really loud then wrestled me to the ground.
Somehow, the front door opened or was opened. We fought on the
floor and I must have slid her closer to the door or maybe we
were already close to the door. She fought to stay inside. I was on
top of her, shoving her face on the ground, across the metal floor
board of the front door.
I said to her, "Let's take this outside so the world can see who
you really are!" That's when she fought me more to stay inside
the house. Next thing I know, we did end up outside. But we
weren't fighting. Rollanda was yelling obscene things to me.
Basically telling me off. Trish stood slightly behind her with her
arms folded. Next, we were somewhere in the house. Not sure
what room. Rollanda hit me and I fell to the ground. She paced
around me (like predators do when their victims are down and
taunt them). She taunted me as she walked slowly around me. She*

163

was talking, talking, talking. Then she said "And oh! Guess who I ran into today? Or ran over? Your kitty (cat)!" I just laid there on the ground, crouched over. Trish still stood silently behind Rollanda, slightly to her left. I could hear Trish's spirit say "That was so low. You didn't even have to do that."

A moment later, I got up slowly and grabbed a long, rectangular box (with its contents) that was near me and started beating Rollanda with it. I talked to her as I hit her (like one of those old school whooping's where your parents talk to you with each hit). I beat her with that box until its contents fell out. Then I picked that up and beat her with that until the florescent light inside came out. As I hit her, I said "Why would you do this to me? After all I have done for you? I served you! I moved my LIFE down here to help...this...corrupt...ministry!!! I moved my life! I forfeited my career!" At that point I was crying (when I said about my career), I heard myself scream "career". Then I just threw the object to the side and walked out. Trish stood there the whole time, silently watching. She never did help Rollanda. She didn't help me, either. I felt her spirit - she felt that my rage was justified by all of the things Rollanda took me through and the things I dealt with regarding her. She understood why I was so angry, but would not help me because she was Rollanda's friend.

After I walked out, I went to a lower part of the house and called Lenard on my cell phone. I briefly told him what happened. He then asked me what I planned to do. I said "I don't know but I can't stay in this house tonight. I'ma call Rhea and ask if I can stay with her for now" He said "you sure?" I said yes. I can't sleep here tonight. He said ok. Go ahead and call her and let me know. I said ok. After we said our goodbyes, I hung up from him then proceeded to call Rhea.

Just as I was calling her on my phone, I heard somebody calling my name repeatedly. Not in the dream, but in real life. I said huh? Huh? Yes? I woke up hearing myself say "huh?" I thought I would wake to see my moma standing nearby (calling my name), but she wasn't. Then I looked at the time. It was about 3:43am. She was still sleep! So I began to text Lenard the dream.

From: Sierra
To: Mela Ruiz

Subject: Me
Date: May 6, 2009

Good morning Pastor Mela....

I hope you had a safe trip back to Florida. I just wanted to tell you
a few things briefly...before I try to go back to sleep.
For the last 3 nights in a row I have had dreams concerning
Rollanda. I had another one last week before I went to Arkansas
over this past weekend. Jewel was in that dream. You may
recognize her name from MNP. She's one of my good friends. I
only typed out 2 of the 4 dreams because one involved her trying
to kill me, another involved her putting me out the house and she
put her hands on me...and oh! There's another one involving
Ah'shely. Rollanda made sure I was forbidden to come back to
the community where she stays. She called the regional manager
and had her tell me I had to leave the community and never
return. Ah'shely saw it all. She didnt say a word, but her spirit
was deeply grieved. I could see it on her face. So, that's 5 dreams
within the last week. That's too much.

Also, I spoke to my lawyer again yesterday. I want to update you
on that as well. I haven't received any more emails or phone calls
from Rollanda since last Monday when she called me from Mr.
Chad's phone. She did leave a message and I did record it on my
phone.
I'm not worried about the situation...I just feel stressed out. Now
that I'm here, my family and close friends are asking questions
like, what happened in FL? Are you still dancing with that
ministry? How are things with you dancing there? What made you
move here now?

They don't know anything about what went on with me down
there. I don't explain anything. But the questions, the constant
questions, even if it's one person a day asking me something,
that's still too much. Lately, more and more of my friends are
calling me or texting me things like "I don't know what's going on
with you, but you've been on my heart really heavy for the last (x-
amount of time) and I have been interceding for you & crying out
for you". I express my gratitude to them for praying for me and
being sensitive to the Spirit, but I don't go into details. This is all
for now. I'm going to go some reading before I do anything else.

165

Have a wonderful day!
Sierra

From: Pastor Mela
To: Sierra
Sent: May 7, 2009
Subject: Dreams

Sierra, this was my hubby's response to your last email about the dreams. I too agree that you may have ungodly soul-ties (demonic) that need to sever from you. **Please read below this email for my husband's email to me.** Also, read the chapter again on sexual immorality regarding soul-ties and don't forget unforgiveness. The sooner you release Rollanda, the sooner you are free. You definitely need a Pastor to hold you acct. Are you in a home church, yet? Those people who ask you may not have yours nor Rollanda's best interest. Don't slander Rollanda, because that too is sin and then God can't vindicate on your behalf. Remember, God says vengeance is mine - but if you take matters into your hands, then God can't work. Keep me posted. PMR - **See Sierra's email after my husband's response.**

---------- Forwarded Message ----------

From: Regenald Ruiz
To: Mela Ruiz
Subject: Re: give me input on this...
Date: May 6, 2009

She needs to move on. Prayer is the key. However, she just needs to let those who ask, that her season has changed and she is in transition. She needs to be held accountable for her sins as well. She needs to get plugged into a local church and she needs a female to hold her accountable where she is. You could continue to counsel but she needs to find someone local. The more she gets into the word; God will deliver her from the dreams that keep coming. There are still soul ties in BOTH parties! *Rev. Ruiz*

From: Sierra
To: Mela Ruiz
Subject: From Sierra re: Rollanda's emails. .... Fwd: To all

staff/volunteers/ chapperone of SouthernBaked 2K9 Summer Camp. Please read and reply...
Date: May 13, 2009

Good evening Pastor Mela,

Would you please, is it possible, that you could please ask Rollanda once again to take me off of every distribution list she has? I asked her 3 different times to take me off of every one. Not only am I on the distribution list (like this forwarded email about the camp - below), but also Info@DanceChallenger.org and her personal email address, not the old one but her new one. I started to email her myself but figured that wouldn't do any good and I still want to stick with no communication with her. But every time I receive an email from her (sometimes 3-5 in a day) is a constant reminder of the things I don't want to think about. I blocked 2 addresses but this one and another one seems to get thru somehow. I'm getting annoyed all over again.

I have finished the chapter on unforgiveness. I didn't want to rush through it. I'm going to read it again. Everyday I'm speaking to myself "I choose to forgive". I don't want to be one of those people that say, I will forgive her but I'll never forget it. I need this to be over. She also left me a message last week on my voicemail saying she doesn't care who I report to, basically they want their money. I saved the message. But I know she was referring to you. I don't appreciate that. I really need her to go away. This isn't happening fast enough for me....

Have a wonderful day! Sierra Brown

From: Pastor Mela
To: Rollanda
Cc: Pastor Regenald
Bcc: Sierra
Sent: May 14, 2009
Subject: Please hear me

Regenald, please pray about this.
Rollanda, you are still not in compliance with what has been said to you since our first meeting and emails thereafter. I really think you are operating in the flesh - this is not God. I love you

167

regardless of what you are doing or the way you behave, however, you are WRONG, in the ways you are going about your business. I have been ministering to Sierra, because she truly needs to break ungodly soul-ties and forgive you. However, you are not making matters easy. After you and P. Louie and myself have discussed the fact that you needed to step down from some of your venues (perhaps all of them until you finalize the help you are suppose to be getting), yet you will be at Daffy's conference and still doing summer camp and such...You are dishonoring and not heeding to warnings or protocols in God's Kingdom. I am dealing with the inner healing of others that have been wounded by you. I am not saying it's all your fault, but you need to STOP harassing this child in particular. For God's sake and your own. Even if she owes you money - you know very well that she needs to heal. I have read all your emails to her and this one is light - not to mention the ones that have been very direct and with angry tones towards her. I really need you to see clearly.   PM

The following are text messages forwarded to me personally from Rollanda. This is a partial conversation between Rollanda and Pastor Mela.
May 15, 2009

Rollanda: Sure you love me Mela. But you walk by me and not speak... I really believe you.

Rollanda: I am tired of the lies from her. Please don't contact me on her behalf again unless it's for payment. That would close this chapter for both of us.

Rollanda: We'll just take it up in court. Her and you.

June 8, 2009
Dear Diary,

My thoughts - I am so unhappy with the person I have become. I feel fat and useless. I keep having these thoughts that say give up dance. But I love dancing! Plus its great exercise. I'm sad now about Paula's wedding because she asked me to dance. That's fine. The problem is the wedding is only 5 days away and I still don't have the song as of today. That's discouraging. And I feel

168

fat. Me and Lenard's engagement party is in 6 days. I'm supposed to be flying to Tulsa on Monday- 7 days. I love being with Lenard, but I am SO not a home body. I can't just sit up in the house all the time. Just can't do it. Ugh! Today I really feel like I've let so much go. My weight. My attire. My appearance. Sometimes, my joy. My walk with Christ. My standards. I do feel bad – but I can't wallow in it. Life is bigger than my little problems and I can't wallow in self-pity. I have to get up.

I think I've been without a steady job for 2 years now. Since I left the last company I was with. Yep. I need one of those right about now. I need to get back in school. Take some fashion courses, sex therapy/ counseling courses, and some writing courses too because I want to keep working on my book which will consist of a plethora of journal entries, thoughts, actual events, the story of Jonah and more. I have learned that patience really is necessary! There's no need to rush or run into anything. God is still on the throne. Why...who is rushing me- but me? I know the Bible admonishes us to be patient and wait on Him. Be still and know that He is God. But in order for me to be still, that means, I can't be so super busy? Quiet the noise and voices in my ears. NO hasty decisions. That's so hard for me. When my life depends on it, what choice will I make? One that will bring me instant gratification or one that will bring Him glory?

July 16, 2009
Dear Diary,

I'm so upset! I can't stand my cell phone provider right now. If I could get the text message history from my phone, I would have allllllllllllllllllllll the proof I need to show that I didn't make any of this up. I'm NOT lying like she keeps saying I am. Lord knows I'm not lying! Why would I waste my life, my breath trying to conjure up lies on this woman, further ruining my own life, for what? What would this benefit me? Nothing! I would take a lie detector test ANY DAY OF THE WEEK to prove all that I'm saying is true. I'm sick of this! She keeps emailing me, keeps saying I'm lying. And I just heard that Trish is telling people that I fell in love with Rollanda, moved down to Florida and I'm claiming stuff happened. I don't know what else she said, but all that's a lie. I have never fallen "in love" with any woman first of all. Secondly, I had no idea this was going to happen. Whatever.

If I could get those text messages!!! OOoooh!! It would show, from late November 2007 all the way to late January 2009 text messages fromRollanda AND Trish at all hours of the night – conversations we had expressing lustful thoughts. It was more so Rollanda. All Trish text said was "Please don't look at me different, but I always wondered what it would be like to kiss you." Rollanda's would show her saying things such as, "I want to go all the way with you..." "Your touch makes me weak..." "I want you to come over so you can hold me. Chad & Trish r slp..." "I miss u. Wana hold u. Kiss u.Tell u how much I luv u..." etc. etc. Promise to God all of this is true, true, true. And it hurts to know that she's not telling people the truth about it, but rather blaming Trish for her "condition". This is all a huge mess I wish I never would have gotten into! I have to find a way to get my text records. Aaahhhhhh!!!! This sucks!!!!

August 14, 2009
Dear Diary,

Now this I wasn't expecting. Clearly, Rollanda missed the part of my email a few months back requesting to be removed from any and all emailing contact lists she may have. That included MNP. So, now I see that she hasn't removed me. When I checked my email earlier today, I instantly got upset when I saw this email from Rollanda to the MNP Mentees.:

"I love you and I'm praying for you. I know you love God deep in your heart and He knows as well. In due time He will make all things new...please keep in touch.

Loving you, Rollanda"

Lord, please make this stop!!!
October 21, 2009
Dear Diary,

I really don't have much to say. I've spent the last 2 months in seclusion from the world. I feel like my joy is gone. My life is in disarray. My walk with Christ is on life support...and my ministry – well, as far as dance goes, I think I'll just hang that up on the shelf and leave it there. Maybe forever. That's how I'm feeling.

170

The following are text messages sent from Rollanda (out the clear) to my cell phone on 10/24/09. I responded this time because I was highly upset!

Rollanda - 4:20pm Those fighting with me said "I WON!" If UR idea of winning constitutes disunity, revenge, scandal, un4giveness, pain& causing failure, hope you feel good. I'm not fighting.

Sierra - 4:44pm DO NOT TEXT ME. EEEEEEEVER!!!!!!!!!

Rollanda- 6:19pm Sure. Love you lady.

Sierra - 6:25pm Y r u saying this???!?!?

Rollanda - 6:36pm Bc I do and am not fighting w you or hating you or talking about you or trying to destroy you. Never did. Never will. Bye.

Sierra - 6:39pm Good. Great. Grand. Wonderful. GOODBYE!

December 22, 2009
Dear Diary,

Just wanted to include the letter I wrote to my lawyer yesterday. Had to save a copy for myself :0).

December 21, 2009

Dear Attorney R. Watkins,

I received your letter on December 15th stating that my case was closed in your office. I understand that as we discussed that it would be closed/resolved (?) after the letter to cease and desist was sent and received by Ms. Rollanda Robertson-Anchorage .

Enclosed, I have an email that was sent to me from Rollanda's personal email account on December 17, 2009 which shows 2 group pictures of herself, Trish, and new dancers, and statements about a competition they won. I have tried very hard to stay calm and not respond to her many attempts to get a reaction out of me. This is absolutely ridiculous. Not on your part, I'm just saying…for her to repeatedly make attempts to contact or communicate with me. I feel this was sent to me for no other

171

reason than to piss me off. If that was her point, she wasn't very successful.

However, I do consider this harassment. Due to the fact that I have repeatedly, since April 2009, asked and directly told her to take me off of every email and text message distribution list she has. Rollanda called me one time a few months ago and suggested that I tell her which email addresses I'm receiving emails from. I did just that. I emailed her a list of about 4 email addresses, including her personal account, and told her to TAKE ME OFF OF THESE LISTS! Til this day, she has not. It's easy to change my phone number, change my email address or just delete her emails when they come in. But why should I have to do all of that for one person? I'm wondering what should I do at this point? What's the wisest thing for me to do? I honestly don't want to go hard at this until after my wedding is over. This has turned into a huge on-going mess.

It's as if she's sending be things just to show me she's not afraid of the law? Not afraid of a threatening letter. This must come to an end. I have decided not to respond to her in any shape, form or fashion. This is why I'm coming back to you :0(I don't want to take matters into my own hands. That would not be wise. Please help. I'm not sure how to classify my case anymore because initially it was about the rent and everything, but now it's taking a turn towards harassment or something. But why? I don't understand the purpose in this. I considered just building a case against her. Let the text messages and emails build up, then bring it back to you (in the event that this persists). It does not matter to me if the emails are nothing more than general greetings. ANYTHING from her is a huge annoyance. I also considered or wondered if I needed a restraining order? Is it really that serious anyway??? Please help.
Thank you in advance, Sierra

December 28, 2009
Dear Diary,

I just got a letter from my lawyer in response to the letter I sent her on December 21st. I'm entirely fed up! My lawyer said, in a nutshell, I can file a lawsuit against her, but since she's not threatening to sue me anymore, I may consider leaving it alone. Even though her behavior is very annoying, it may not rise to the level of sexual harassment nor do I have grounds for a restraining order. She did advise me to change all of my contact information. So basically, whatever I decided to from this point is in my hands. I will just leave it be and pray she goes away. I don't want to spend any more money on a lawyer for no reason. I pray that I don't have a reason to continue to use a lawyer. Shoot. This stuff is expensive! I am glad I did things the legal way and hired her to defend my case though. I'm still annoyed because Rollanda continues to email me advertisements and ministry stuff and I don't feel like I should have to change my email address or phone number. She should just stop contacting me. Period!

Ok… I'm done. I can't write about this anymore for today.

December 30, 2009
Dear Diary,

Sadly…although I am now in the process of turning this part of my life/diary into a published book, I must continue writing in it because the saga continues. What a shame! Not shame on me…shame on HER! I can't believe how petty she's become. Never saw this coming. After months of dealing with my lawyer, getting a Cease and Desist letter against her to force her to stop all communications with me via snail mail, email, phone call, text message, MySpace or Facebook, she CONTINUES TIL THIS DAY to contact me. But why? I really wonder sometimes- why in the world is this lady being such a pain? Or is it that she is trying to be a pain? Her attempts to contact me don't bother me nearly as bad as they used to because I'm moving on with my life. Learning new things from the Word of God, this situation, and life in general, every day. I want my healing. I so badly desire to just rest in the arms of God and be at peace while I'm yet living. I don't need the drama. From her or anybody.
Back to her contacting me. Since receiving the notice not to contact me anymore, she has sent me 4 text messages (within the same week she received the Cease and Desist letter) and has emailed me approximately 2 times. Why? Does she want me to see that she's thinking of me? Is she trying to get under my skin? It's not working. It's funny that the same person that told me to do her a favor; become like a ghost and disappear; continues to contact me and even requested me as a friend on Facebook.

A few people that I discussed her recent contact attempts with just asked me why don't I block her emails? Hummm, I've been doing that for about 7 months now. I've been back out of Florida for 9 months. I have her emails notified as spam and directed to another folder so I'll never see them unless I open the folder. My spam

173

box doesn't get deleted automatically. Even if I decided to delete every email she sent, they are all missing the point. This is harassment! I shouldn't have to change my phone number, email address or anything because someone chooses to be a pain in my rear end. No. I'm not the problem. They are. I thought about deleting every folder created over the past 2 ½ years with emails regarding OPDATC, MNP, DC and more, but as soon as I thought about it, another thought interrupted my thoughts and said "Don't delete them. Just move them to another folder. You will need them later." I was like cool. Ok. And did just that. Now, all of the emails are documented proof of everything I've stated thus far. Now every email she sends me will be another page added to my best-selling book!

What bothers me more than anything about her and her faithful undercover girlfriend is that she's still doing "ministry" Which to me isn't ministry at all. She's doing "Me, you see?" Like it's not God you see, its ME (her) You See. It's her name in lights. It's her name in bold print. It's her name stamped all over everything. It's her face plastered all over the things she does. As if she wants the world to know her good works. What good does it profit it a man to gain the whole world and lose his own soul?

Truly humble people don't parade the streets trumpeting the great works they've done. Are you doing this for God to see and be pleased or for people to see and applaud you? My goodness. And yet, til this day, hummm I wonder if she's submitted to any leadership yet? As she hasn't been for the last year and a half. I'm still a little heated as this should be a dead subject for me but is very much alive.

I'm tired of receiving phone calls from people in Florida and other states that are truly bothered by her current abnormal behavior. Some people can't even stomach her now. She's beyond rude, nasty, and very controlling. People call me asking me if they are taking things the wrong way or something because they've never known her to be this way and since I used to personally assist her and live with her, maybe I could help clarify some things. Well, I've got news for you. Seems to me she's always been this way. But just like she says, there are two sides to her. If you listen closely, you'll hear her say it.

Many people only know the ministry side of her. But it's what's going on behind closed doors and the issues of her heart that are leaking out. What happens in the dark always comes to the light.

Chapter 7
Turning Point

January 6, 2010
Dear Diary,

I just left drama dance rehearsal at church. Omg. Today was
sooooooooo hard for me. During our warm up, while on the floor,
I started really focusing on my breathing for a second so I could
feel the stretch as I pulled my knee to my chest. As I did that, I
also took notice to the words of the worship music that was
playing. Marvin Sapp. I'm pretty sure it was that Heart of a
Worshipper cd. Awww man, a flood of....SOMETHING just took
over me at that moment and tears began to fall from my face! I
tried to hide it because I didn't want to cause a scene. Then we
had to get up to prepare for across the floor exercises. I don't
know what happened, but it seemed like the dancers took an
unannounced hug break. Mrs. Kim hugged me and kissed me on
the cheek first. I hugged her back. In an instant, a feeling rose up
inside of me that wanted to cringe and push her away. But I
didn't. I struggled to break those feelings of distrust. IT HURT!
At the same time, I had to stop myself from crying again. We
released each other from our hug and I proceeded to turn away
and fan my eyes. Mrs. Kim then hugged me...AGAIN and started
praying. I was screaming inside because of the battle within me.
After that hug, another dancer hugged me, and then another, then
a group hug! I was like is this the hug moment? I noticed
everybody around me was hugging somebody.

We finally got back to dancing. By that time I was all messed up.
I just wanted to ball up in a corner and cry. I was only able to hold
back my tears and barely focus through about 3 across the floor
exercises before I had to excuse myself from class. I went to the
bathroom, sat on the toilet (with my feet up and holding my

knees) and cried. Prayed- cried. And cried some more. I was in there for about 10 minutes. Class was over by the time I came back. My eyes were red. Couldn't hide that one. Dangit. Before class started, I told Mrs. Kela I needed to talk to her after class. so when I went back in, pretty much everyone was gone except Mrs. Kela, Mrs. Kim, the other lady (the hilarious one) and a teen girl that was showing them a dance. Ms. Kela and I went into another room to talk. I was so nervous about talking to her, I totally forgot what I needed or wanted to say. She sat in a chair; I sat on the floor and just blurted out some stuff and tried not to cry. I told her "It's hard for me, not physically, but emotionally and mentally hard for me to be on the dance ministry. I moved to Florida a few years ago to help this lady with her dance ministry. I had no family there. I knew no one. My only intent was to help her. She took advantage of me sexually and it really messed me up. The whole experience was traumatizing and now it's hard for me to trust dance leaders or...just...I don't know what I'm trying to say. I'm not saying I don't trust you, but it's...just hard."

I told myself I would never dance again after that whole ordeal because I had come to a point where ministry was no longer the reason why I was dancing and I had no real desire to try anymore. But because of the call on my life and because dance is my way to worship God, I can't stop dancing. So here I am, trying again. But it hurts! I guess just moving through the pain is what hurts." Ms. Kela said she was sorry for what happened to me and although she can't relate, she does understand moving thru pain. She won't put any undue pressure on me and I need not feel pressured to minister with them or anything. Just take my time. Keep coming. But just let God heal me. If I come and just wanna sit and observe, I can do that. If I need to cry, they will cry with me. If I need to pray, they will pray with me. We talked for a few minutes more then went back into the room where we rehearsing and they all gave me hugs and I went home.

January 18, 2010
Dear Diary,

I googled my name when I got to work today...FINALLY!!! I noticed that my picture was taken off of the DC website. I know she told me it would take a little while, but I don't think it should have taken 10 months to get that done. I saw that not only my picture was gone, but Mariell's and Trish's too. I want no connection to her whatsoever. It still angers me to this day to know that her "ministry" is still going on. I'm not too worried though. Giants do die. The bigger they are, the harder they fall. If she doesn't yield to God, repent, and LET GOD HEAL HER, stop being so deceiving, etc, etc, her self-built empire will come crashing down.

I'm not speaking death to her or anything. In fact, I'm just now getting to a place where I can even ask God, sincerely ask Him to heal her too. Show her who she really is right now. Help her to understand what integrity is, what pride and vain glory is, what it means to really serve Him and His people FOR Him and not for publicity. What it means to really, truly love other people, besides those in your so-called circle.

On another note, I'm so glad I made it to service yesterday. The word was on point, as usual. My pastor preached on walls coming down. Walls that we've built up that hinder us from moving forward. They must come down. Let there be no excuse. Bring them down. So I prayed that God would help me to tear down the walls of rejection, bitterness and/or hatred, distrust and anything else that has come about as a result of that experience. I don't want to carry that forever. I do not want to hate her. I will never promote her ever again in life. But I still don't want to hate her. If I have hate in my heart, it's just like murder. Plus if I hate her, of course that means I haven't forgiven her. And if I don't forgive, God won't forgive me. Yeah, I can say I forgive anyone with my mouth but God knows my heart. And if I'm honest with myself, then I too will know that I haven't truly forgiven. I pray daily that I will die to myself and yield my life to Christ once again. Completely. I need my healing!

Oh, sadly, now I can't help but to watch people in ministry-closely. I hate that feeling. It's like I can't just have that child-like faith that people of God won't hurt me and that they really have my best interest at heart. That isn't so. That's the sad part. Lord, please open my eyes and spiritual ears so that I can be where You would have me to be, connect to only those you want me connected to and discern what to do and how to handle every situation I come across in life. I don't want to become bitter. Bitter people hurt people. Hurting people hurt people. I don't

179

want to be like that.

I often, have to encourage myself to continue on with this book. Telling myself it is worth it and it's not a waste of time. I have to remind myself that the purpose of this book has nothing to do with that woman, but rather the fact that it was a result of me wanting to help in something I thought was God influenced, but was rather self-promoting and the person I thought the world of almost made my world crumble in a matter of months. There was so much involved, I just want to help somebody else so hopefully...my story will prevent someone from making the same mistakes I did. Or even, if they are currently in it, as long as they are still breathing, IT'S NOT TOO LATE TO GET OUT! RUN FOR YOUR LIFE!

I am convinced that this book will help millions of people around the world to come out of hiding. Stop hiding behind their masks. Allow God to heal their hurting, wounded, beaten, broken, torn, mutilated, bleeding hearts. We can't hide behind people, facades, masks, titles, status or anything else. Like it or not...believe it or not...God still sees us! This book will help millions to understand that HOLINESS IS STILL RIGHT! HOMOSEXUALITY REALLY IS AN ABOMINATION TO GOD AND IS NOT ACCEPTABLE. Same sex marriage isn't even honored because it's an abomination. From the beginning of creation, it was never meant to be. Those that just need to be loved or need acceptance will find it in Christ Jesus. He taught me what LOVE really is through His word and the way that He loves me daily. Plus, my wonderful fiancé demonstrated the love of God to me as he loved me thru all this mess. Love isn't impure. It DOES NOT involve sex. It isn't unnatural affection. It isn't perverse. It isn't controlling, manipulative, confusing, domineering, tormenting, or harsh. Love doesn't crush your dreams, but rather cheers you on and supports you. Love loves you just because you are you. Not because you've done anything. We have done NOTHING to deserve God's love. He just, does. That's so awesome. Through God's Word and His agape love for me, I have learned to love myself.

I'm so grateful....for His ever present, pure, true, abundance of love.

January 18, 2010
Dear Diary,

Ok, I'm back. It's 3:12pm and I'm still at work. Working, but thinking. When I first had the thought to write this book, I was like…uh, no! I could say it was something the Lord dropped in my spirit to do, but I wanna be careful about what I pin on God. I will give Him glory for everything I do anyhow… but eh, anyway… I said no because I realized that the world would see just how vulnerable I was. How stupid I was. How I didn't listen and ignored the signs. How I was tormented in this. How I gave up. All my good points and bad ones, strengths and weaknesses. I would be exposing myself totally. Why? Why would I invite the world into my private thoughts? Would it be worth it in the end?

Well, after I thought about it all that day, I decided, yes. It would be worth it. If my story could save even 1 person from spending eternity in hell, from losing their minds while working in ministry, being bound by their so-call God-fearing leader or even if they are just in a homosexual lifestyle they don't know how to get out of…then it's all worth it. No one has to know who I am. It doesn't matter. I just want people to understand the deceitfulness of rejection, lust, homosexuality, perversion. Wait, I don't want to get that twisted. While I DON'T know all there is to know about these things, I am willing to share what I have learned from my own failures and triumphs, studies and many conferences. If this is my only reason for living, I want to make sure I carry out my mission completely and please my God. The process has been very painful thus far. I'm not sure what's ahead, but I can't stop now. Somebody needs to hear my story. And I have to finish so that they can.

January 19, 2010
Dear Diary,

Ok, it's a shame I gotta come right back and say this… but I'm semi-ruffled all over again. I wish I weren't tho. Let me back up. This morning I had a dream that Rollanda called me on my cell phone one day and she was sooooooooooooo mad. *Like I could see smoke coming from my phone she was so mad. (But why would I care about that?) She told me her cousin called her from Atlanta and told her to turn on the news. Rollanda's picture was all over the news and they reported she was being accused of having sex with her ministry staff members. They didn't name the persons*

181

whom they were speaking of. After she told me that, she said now Chad is really mad. I just held the phone in silence for a minute, then said "Wow." I didn't know that." I ended up hanging up on her. Reason being was because although I was shocked, I knew it was only a matter of time before this happened. –The end

Before I got dressed for work, I googled her name, homosexuality and something else. Nothing came up but some sites that I could purchase her book from. Then when I got to work, I told Mariell about my dream. She said she wants our descriptions off of the DC website and asked me to check to see if her picture was still on there. So I went to the website...and lo and behold. Gosh darnit. My freaking picture is STILL THERE! On the darn faculty page for the London instructors. I didn't even teach a class. But anyway...I was on there for a few minutes more. I saw that she's charging folks $1000 to be mentored by her for a year. Who can afford that? And why in God's name is she charging folks that much money? Wow.

On a lighter note, I just received some WONDERFULLY AMAZINGLY SUPER AWESOME news that I've been waiting for! I'll think on this instead...because it's a good report and it's lovely. :0)

January 26, 2010
Dear Diary,

I'm sitting in my Physiology class - lecture E. My instructor is brilliant. I can tell she is veeeeeeeeeeeeeeeeeeeeeeeeeeeery passionate about her work. She loooooooooooves to ramble on about the Nervous System, being left brained vs. right brained, and about the Oculomotor, Cranial Nerves...bla bla bla. Although I need to be here in class and get my $10,000+ worth of education at this school, I wish I were elsewhere. I miss my baby love. My sweet fiancé. Gosh, I love that man so much. I never loved another person like I love him. Perhaps after the wedding is over, I can really focus on my studies :0)

I had a lovely day at work. God is so excellent and awesome to me. He keeps on blessing me. Just a continuation from Saturday when we went to Lenard's co-workers house. Omgosh their home is so beautiful. Long story short, they were a tremendous blessing to us. Lenard's co-workers wife, Trina, really blessed me. She started speaking in my life and I cut that short by asking if she was a prophet. I shouldn't have cut that short, but I've been trying to get away from prophets, mainly because I don't want to hear "Its time, Sierra, walk in your calling". That's a big calling!! I have nothing against them, it's just that God has strategically surrounded me with them everywhere that I go. Anyways, they have very expensive furniture they want to get rid of so they can refurnish their home. So we will have a black leather sectional this week!!! From them!!! There was so much more to that visit. We both left their house overwhelmed by God's love for us. It was one of those moments where you just had to be there. Sunday, while visiting my family, my ma surprised us (me, Lenard, my brother & his fiancée) with tickets to attend a Money Makeover Seminar this Friday! That was our engagement gift. God told her to sow into our lives. WOW! What a way to go into marriage! Preparing for wealth! Then today, I emailed my ma at work and told her I seriously want her to help me find a hairstyle for my wedding. I was thinking, zillions, small zillions. Styled, elegantly. She emails me right back and said as one of my wedding gifts, she will pay for my zillions to get done by the same lady that did her braids. I was like OMG! Another blessing! I receive it as another demonstration of God's love for me because I surely did nothing to deserve this. Oh please! Well, that's all. Just wanted to record what God is doing in my life. He's sooooooo goooooooooood! Not because of what He givesme, but because WHO He is to me!

January 27, 2010
Dear Diary,

I don't ever want to see Wonder Weave again. I have never been so discouraged, so emotionally and mentally torn, so mistreated in all my life. But in MINISTRY of all things! So-called ministry, I am constantly hurt and abused. Before, when I was just coming into the knowledge of Christ, yes, I was susceptible to fall for almost anything because I wasn't mature in Christ and I was just learning the Word. I didn't understand that I was prideful and selfish and I didn't know what real love was. I put my feelings into everything. I put my heart into everything I did. Especially ministry related things. Which is probably why people in church were able to use me, mistreat and manipulate me until my heart was beaten so badly it was unrecognizable? The crap in Florida had me so jacked until not only was my heart almost non-existent, but I barely recognized myself. Now, I KNOW GOD is the ONLY ONE that can keep my heart beating. He is the only One that can make me whole again. I am so sure that if hate was not such a strong word close to murder, I would say I hate her. But since I can't, I'll just say I seriously dislike that conniving, deceitful, manipulative, glory stealing, bisexual minister of hypocrisy!

January 29, 2010
Dear Diary,

Ok...why are all these crazy things coming to my thoughts now??? This morning when I was on my way out the door headed for work, a thought occurred..or rather, something came back to my remembrance. Rollanda once told me of a time that she told Ah'shely that if she doesn't stop talking to so-and-so (one of Ah'shely's friends), then they couldn't be friends anymore. Her reason for saying this is because apparently Ah'shely's friend was talking bad about Rollanda. So she gave Ah'shely an ultimatum. Rollanda ended up cutting her off for 3 months (or something). I don't recall exactly, but it seems like she said Ah'shely begged her to talk to her (Ah'shely begged Rollanda to talk to her) and she dumped her other friend. When she told me that, I was like WOW, that would never be me. But then, this morning, that thought came in the form of it happening again. Rollanda telling Ah'shely not to come to my wedding and/or not to speak to me.

Hummm....I hope this is not going on. I don't talk to Ah'shely often enough to ask. To my knowledge, she still doesn't even know the reason why I left the house, nor why I left the state so fast. However, she will find out in time. Doesn't matter if I want her to or not. She will. Everyone will. Quite frankly,

I don't care. People need to know. Exposure is good medicine for some people. Thinking back though, seeing how Rollanda was is extremely disturbing to me. I see how she told Mariell that her boyfriend of x-amount of years wasn't her husband and that they shouldn't be together. She told me that I shouldn't be with Lenard. She made Ah'shely dump a close friend. She prevents Trollface from having a life because she keeps her attached- like Trollface has an addiction and it's Rollanda. Plus, she's an enabler. Instead of helping Trollface be healed and set free from her issues, she feeds it. What kind of friend is that? I'ma have to continue this later. My view of things from the FLIP SIDE. Now that I'm out, I can see again. Omg, I was so so so so so so very stupid. Straight stupid.

February 7, 2010
Dear Diary,

It's about 2:45 pm on a Sunday afternoon. I should be at school but I couldn't pull myself together enough to sit in class without crying. It stated last night at Lenard's cousin's surprise birthday dinner…which turned into a surprise engagement to his girlfriend of x-amount of years. It was beautiful! As soon as I got out of school, yesterday, Lenard picked me up and took me home to change for the dinner. When we got there, I greeted all familiar faces, waved at a few unfamiliar ones then I sat down in my seat between Lenard and the birthday man and his girlfriend. I sat there quietly observing my surroundings feeling uneasy and out of place, but not sure why. I guess Lenard saw it and he asked how I was feeling. I said somewhat uncomfortable. But I wasn't really feeling uncomfortable; I just didn't know how to describe the way I was feeling. He told me to talk to people. I felt like I just couldn't.

 But anyway, once everyone was done with their dinner and was getting ready to leave, Byron got up and thanked everyone for coming and supporting him on his birthday, but he really wanted to celebrate his girlfriend today… then he went on to drop down to 1 knee and proposed to her while both his family and her's took pictures and screamed. He put a ROCK on her finger. I mean, it was gorgeous!!! Beautiful! There's no denying that one. Lenard asked me if I saw her ring. I said yes, I did see it. But I'll comment on that later. The expression on his face denoted that he instantly became frustrated with me. That wasn't necessary. All I was going to say was that although I love her ring and it suits her and her personality, I'm not flashy so I'm happy with my ring. I wanted to reassure him that I was happy with mine because of the joking comment he made to me about it earlier before I ever saw it. I'm happy for his cousin and his new lovely fiancée. Really, I am. I just wanted to explain that to him in private. Not in front of his cousins.

The timing wasn't right. He and I did have a brief lil conversation about me being so withdrawn and he pointed out all the people that tried to converse with me. When we got back to the apartment, I broke down. I cried for about 3 hours straight. I ended up on the bathroom floor crying my heart out because I sat and analyzed everything. My behavior, the whole night, the conversation Lenard and I had when we got back to the apartment, all up til now. I traced it back to 2007, before I moved to Florida. My behavior then was bubbly, happy, still somewhat loud, laughing always, smiling, welcoming strangers and very sociable. But since leaving there, I have become leery of everyone. It's hard for me to trust even some people that I already knew. I really can't trust new people. I don't wanna be touched. I don't want people kissing on me. The whole 9. Well, anything for that matter. In some way or another, I feel like people have a motive or are out to cause me harm in some way.

After slamming the toilet a few times and kicking the cabinet doors, Lenard eventually came into the bathroom to see what was wrong with me. I told him I analyzed everything and I keep feeling like the problem is everyone else when maybe the problem is really just me. He stated that in his opinion, it all stems back to Florida because of the rejection I encountered there and the trust that I put in those people was betrayed. It made me almost incapable of allowing people to be close to me. It's not people that I've already had a relationship with, but its more so new people. Because I'm too precautious that they will hurt me the way I was hurt in Florida.
Needless to say, I cried some more. I just don't know how to remedy this problem. I don't like the way I feel and I don't want anyone to think that I'm just being stand-offish for no reason. No, there's a reason. Something happened to me!

I cried so much I had a headache. So I fell asleep massaging my own head. I woke up at 6:37 a.m. to hearing my cats banging on the door because they needed water. After getting them water, I went to the restroom, looked in the mirror and saw a horrific sight staring back at me in the mirror. My eyes were sunk in and surrounded with swollen eye tissues??? Idk. But they resemble mini cream puffs. It was awful. I went back to sleep for 2 hrs, woke up from a scary dream and cried some more. I got ready for school and was crying as I got dressed. I was a complete mess. There was no way I could sit thru 8hrs of hot rocks lecture and massaging without crying. So I ran up to the school before class started and got my things I left there from yesterday.

On my way out the door, I ran into someone I knew.

The expression on her face when she saw me was like "Dang! What's wrong with you???" So I just said part of the reason why I was sad, but not why I was crying, which was I'm mourning. Which was true. Anyway, when I got home, I put all my stuff on the couch, threw my keys down, put my pj's back on and got in the bed and balled my eyes out some more while Lenard held me. I asked him if he could pretend like he was a psychologist and ask me questions about how I felt and stuff. He did an amazing job. He asked me questions like; how did I feel once I realized the friendship I sought after with Rollanda wasn't what I expected? How did I feel after the first time she came on to me? He analyzed everything I said and concluded with one statement I made. He said, "It sounds as though, because I'm such a compassionate person, I was more concerned about her spiritual walk than my own and that I can't be so concerned about writing this book for other people so they can learn from it but I have to make sure that I get my deliverance first! Don't want to give people fantasy. Give them what's real. You want to give the whole process. Deliverance. But you can't write about that til you've been through it yourself. You have to <u>live</u> deliverance."

Man....that was some good stuff! That man is so awesome to me.
Afterwards, he kissed me on the forehead and said, "Now will that be cash or credit?"

February 8, 2010
Dear Diary,

Unfortunately, as I sit here in Starbucks thinking back over the last 3 ½ years of my life,....well 3 years, I've changed so much. In some ways I've gotten stronger. But right now, I can only see more areas of weakness. Good thing is I still see the reason why I will forever need Jesus. His saving grace and mercy. I can't function without Him.

I remember when I finally decided that I wanted to leave this double lifestyle I was living, I began to have slight night sweats. Coupled with sleepless nights. Night, after night, after night of restlessness. There were nights I would sit up and cry through the night because I couldn't sleep and I wanted to sleep so bad but for some reason I just couldn't fall asleep. I remember texting my friends on the phone late at night trying to find out what they were doing. Sometimes I was successful in reaching them. Only a few were up. Ultimately, I would try to avoid texting Rollanda, whom I knew was in the bed with Trish, but after so long I would give in. "What cha doin?" I would text her. "Chillaxin with my best friend. U?" "Me?" I would respond . "I can't sleep. Can u come keep me company til I fall asleep?" "Lol. Girl you better pray :0) I'm already comfy in bed. Sorry." The same thing would go down whenever I had a bad dream. "Hey…I jus had a bad dream. Can u come in here with me til I fall aslp?" I would ask. IF I got a response, it was usually "No. Pray and go to bed, lady. See you in the morning"

I felt like I was being toyed with. Whenever she would want my affection and attention, she knew she could get it. But it was just enough to make me want her more. It was like I'm attached to the biggest gallon of dulce de leche ice cream but I'm screaming NOOO inside because I know it will make me fat if I eat it. On the outside, I'm smiling as if everything is A-ok. Constantly lying to myself just made matters worse.

I thank GOD He brought me out of that mess!!! This past weekend has caused me to do a lot of self-examining. Since returning from FL, I have almost completely shut down from the outside world. Excluding the people I already had a relationship with prior to me moving to FL. But now I feel like everyone has a motive. Everybody is out to hurt me in some way. I don't welcome strangers in my life. I look at most pretty females that want to be my friend as gay. That's sad, but true. So since I view people this way, I put a protective barrier up so I won't get hurt. Being sexually violated does more to a person mentally than they even realize. I had no idea that what happened there in Florida would have such an impact on me. I thought it was just in the dance ministry or church. No wait, first I thought it was only dance ministry people I'd have difficulty letting in. Then it expanded to leaders in church. Then church in general. Now its everyone! Strangers, new co-workers, classmates, anyone I didn't already know. Their hugs make me cringe inside. Kisses make me want to cry or just run away. I hate the way I feel right now! I hate distancing myself from people because I'm afraid they will try to hurt me when all they want to do is be a part of my life. Bottom line is, I have come too far to stop now. I'm not going back, I'm moving forward. Running for my deliverance. Running…running…running.. Jesus I'm running..like I should have done a long time ago.

February 23, 2010
Dear Diary,

Just when I was certain this was gonna come to a quiet end, the hefa sends me another email. THIS TIME I failed. I responded. I sent an email in big, bold, all cap letters "STOP SENDING ME YOUR GARBAGE!!! TAKE ME OFF YOUR MAILING LIST!" I failed because I shouldn't have responded at all. This is insane tho. Is she starving for attention or something? I'm not too happy right now because I don't know who to talk to. I could talk to Mariell but she'd be another friend to vent to. I appreciate it and all but I need solutions only God can give me.

During the 8am meeting at work, an idea came to me to send a letter to her former pastors and emails to all of her SO-CALLED Board of Directors. She needs to be held accountable for her actions. I really wish Jesus was in the flesh sometimes so I could literally run in His arms and be safe from harm and have peace of mind and spirit.

I told Lenard if this persists, I'ma need him to intervene. I am trying SO HARD not to blow up on this lady. I'm afraid of what I might do. I really just want her to go away. Out of my life.
For-e-ver!

From: Sierra
To: Pastor Odetta
Sent: February 25, 2010
Subject: Update

Pastor Odetta,

After we spoke the other day, I thought about the entire conversation we had and told Lenard what we discussed as well. He listened to me ramble on about everything then he just kept silent for a while. He finally asked me if I ever felt like I'm always in need of security or help. I answered honestly and said yes. I don't admit that. Long story short... I've been walking around for quite some time (before FL) as if I were a victim of something. One way or another someone was always trying to hurt me for no reason. That's also fear. Which is bondage. I'm glad that was identified. I never looked at it like that. After I got done crying. I thought about all that he had said to me, including telling me to think about my reason for not wanting to go back to WGT. He's helping me get thru this...
You suggested that I block Rollanda on my FB account. I couldn't do that from my phone, but I found out how to permanently block her emails from coming to me. Not just spam (sending to a folder). Thanks for the suggestion. (I wish I would have known this a year ago.)

From: Pastor Odetta
To: Sierra
Sent: February 25, 2010
Subject: Re: Update

Sierra,
I am super glad that you blocked Rollanda. Thank you, Jesus. You can also change your phone number. I think that would be a healthy next step. She needs to not be able to contact you. If you can block or change your email, do so. Break these strings of witchcraft.

Also I would like to ask your forgiveness for any hurt that I caused you, Sierra. It was never my aim. I always want to do what is right and sometimes that can cut in the process. So please forgive me Sierra. My humanness gets in the way sometimes. You and Lenard are important to me. I have always only wanted God's best for you both. And I think that when I drew my line in the sand regarding God's will, I may have hurt your feelings. So forgive me. I could've been a tad more sensitive. Especially at a time when you had just come out of hell. Jesus. I had no clue. I am so sorry.

I am glad that Lenard is helping you process your thoughts and feelings. Take one day at a time. Spend time in God's Word and His presence. Let the Lord refresh you. You will get through this. ~ p.o.

From: Pastor Odetta
To: Sierra
Sent: February 26, 2010
Subject: Re: Update

(Email response from Pastor Odetta in bold)

Pastor Odetta...Pastor Odetta...Pastor Odetta...
My whole reason for not wanting to change my email was because I figured I'd be running. But now that I'm thinking about it, that's stupid. By not doing what I can to prevent her from contacting me is foolish on my part. If I have time, I'm going to create another email address today then over time, I'll just fwd my old emails that I need over to my new one. I planned to change my number after the wedding was over. Right now, I think it would be too much of a hassle because all of the vendors for the wedding, entire wedding party, all of my family and friends coming from out of town...all have this number. So I will most definitely change it. **Good girl. That makes sense to change**

it after the wedding. It will also make your husband to be feel more comfortable.

There's sooooooooooooooooooooooo much more to the story than what I told you the other day. **I know that there is much more. I could sense it. Plus I knew you were giving me the short version because it will take lots of time to catch up to where we are today.** I forgot to tell you about the major anxiety attack that nearly killed me, Rollanda smacking me **I would've never thought she would've put her hands on you. This is just amazing.** How she insulted my family...and I kept silent the whole time...dying from a bleeding heart. I'm writing a book about it. I should be done this summer. I've taken a break from it for a month or so. I can't write the other book until...well, until I stop running from stuff. Eh, anyway, that's another story.

Thank you for your love. Oddly enough, thru this mess, I did realize what GENUINE love is. God is love and its characteristics are found in the Word. I saw next to NONE of these in Rollanda, but all in you. It hurt once I realized yet again I was running from genuine love (not only you but many others) and into the jaws of deceit and death.
I do know you are human. Never doubted it :0). I used to think you were like super-human or something. Ha ha ha. But of course, I know better. **I can run through a troop and leap over a wall.**

In one of our conversations you said you were surprised that I even wanted to be saved anymore after coming thru that. Well, it was either that or die where I was and go to hell. I knew that I had a destiny to reach and that I'm supposed to be doing things for Christ and helping people (and more)... But I would never see those days if I gave up. So, I had to see myself on the other side of this, healed, whole, and in the will of God. **I know it is only by the grace of God. Because for what you've been through, the enemy intended to totally destroy you. If he had been successful, you would not have any desire for the things of God whatsoever. God rescued you. I am most thankful.**

Gotta run & get back to work.

Love u so much more than my vocabulary allows me to express.
-Sierra

March 6, 2010
Dear Diary,

FORGIVE. FORGIVE. FORGIVE. FORGIVE. FORGIVE HER. FORGIVE
YOURSELF. FORGIVE HER. FORGIVE YOURSELF. YOU CAN DO
THIS! FORGIVE HER! FORGIVE YOURSELF. I don't want to be bitter. I
will not be bitter. I will not hate her! I will love her…in the name of Jesus
Lord help me to love her as you love her. Pure. Agape love. I'm not asking to
be friends ever again in life; I just need to forgive wholeheartedly. Forgive.
Forgive. Forgive!

March 17, 2010
Dear Diary,

Ok, I will admit. I was a little in over my head with this one. I shouldn't have
called Ah'shely and said anything. Lenard told me I moved too fast on this
one. I was upset at first, but after I calmed down and listened to him, I saw
that he was right. The one person I was supposed to call because the Lord
gave me a dream about it, I did call her. Now, I called Ms. Tonya and told
her that Rollanda and I had sex and my reason for telling her was because
I'm concerned about her daughter who is still dancing with Rollanda's
company. I apologized for not telling her before. Her initial response was,
"This is a lot to take in right now. I'm going to pray about it. I'm only
hearing one side to this and…this is a lot…wow. Ok. I'm going to do some
investigating and I'll see…" I said ok. I'm just letting you know so you can
protect your daughter. So then after I got off the phone with her, I called
Ah'shely and asked her if she ever knew why I moved out. I wanted to ask
her if she knew anything at all because, man, I don't see how she could be in
that house with all of us, as close as her and Rollanda was and NOT know
that either her and I were too intimate or at least her and Trish were doing
something. Come on!

Then, when I got back from visiting Detroit in January 09, she had already
moved out. I didn't even know she was moving at all. Anyway, I'm all off
subject. I basically told her we had sex, there was a threesome and so forth.
Also, she needs to seriously pray for her friends' deliverance. Do you know
what this lady said? Her response was "Sierra, ok, I hear you. I'm not saying
whether I know anything or not. I don't want to get in that. And why are you
bringing this up now anyway? You've been gone for a year already. You're
about to be a married woman. You've moved on with your life…" Anything
she said after that was like Charlie Brown…waaa waaa waaa. WHAT! Are
you for real? I couldn't believe she said that. WHY am I bringing this up?

192

There was NO concern for my soul or those involved. There was no unction to pray for any of us. Only defense of her friend. WHY!?!? Why won't you challenge her, woman of God? Or at least tell me if you knew something, which would be pointless to know now. But if you knew something THEN it would have been great to tell me or at least ask or do something. I was so pissed. But that's not the end. I got a voicemail from Ms. Tonya right after that saying that my story doesn't agree with her spirit and something else. I deleted it. Wow. I was so shocked by their responses. Loyal followers of Rollanda, I guess. I wish people wouldn't think that someone with a great name in the community is incapable of sinning or doing something like this. IT'S POSSIBLE! WAKE UP! Ugh! But I was wrong for calling them and now I really wish I never did. It was a waste of breath.

April 26, 2010
Dear Diary,

I hate the fact that I still think about her at all. Not in a perverted way, but just the thought of her makes me gag, or just slightly irritated. Why? Hummmm, well what young girl doesn't want to have fond memories of her dance teacher when she grows up? What young boy /teen doesn't want to think about his karate teacher and how hard he was on him because he saw potential in him even as a youth and accredits his success and discipline in his career to his teacher? Or the gymnast that spent countless hours with their coach training, pressing through the pain, strains, getting up early and staying up late, also to make their coach proud? I'm sure none of these children, teens or young adults imagined being taken advantage of by their leaders, instructors, coaches or teachers in any kind of way to the point that all memories of this person they once trusted are now tainted with vicious acts done to them.

I hate that I'm even writing this. I hate that I can't drink tea and not think about her no matter how hard I try. I used to love the Warm Vanilla Sugar fragrance but now I can't stand it because it reminds me of her. I can't even listen to some Christian songs because it reminds me of her or the company and all the deceit! I don't get upset. Those are actually good memories. But the point is, any memory, good or bad at this point is an annoyance. My first introduction to Island dance and soca music was during a workshop she taught at her conference in Detroit 2006. I really enjoyed that class! It was wonderful and I learned a lot. Now today, I have soca/carnival music on my MP3 player. My mind went back to the 2006 African/Caribbean dance class. Then it flashed back to us dancing to soca music in her living room. All 3 of us would dance around the living room in circles until we fell out into a laughing fit. But that's as far as I would want my memories to go because after that would come the not so fond memories.

I actually had a passing thought to text her and tell her how thinking of her was beginning to piss me off because our relationship couldn't be just business or about mentoring or about dance...WHY did she have to involve sex?!?!? WHY WHY WHY!??! WHY me? And all this time has gone by without a sincere apology from her. It's okay. What I mean is even though I never received a sincere, heartfelt apology, I have to completely let it go. I have gone on with my life but these memories are imprinted on my brain. I wish I could make them all disappear forever.

I kinda wish I could call her just to say "hello" and see how she's doing. How's Sparky and puppy (if he's still alive). I wouldn't ask about the "ministry" because I have lost all faith in it. My desire to see her healed and completely delivered is still alive. Well, my desire for God to do it still stands. I don't have to literally see her. Anyway, that's enough of that.

I'm excited about my desire to dance again. I will be going back to dance at church next Wednesday. It's soothing to my soul. Worship in dance. I probably won't dance with the dance ministry til like, June, but I'm ready to start going again. I thank God there's no pressure on me to do anything. That's the last thing I need.

Gosh...I really feel like, if you don't do the thing you are anointed to do, you are allowing a great part of you to just die. One of the things I'm anointed to do is dance for Jesus. It brings me so much joy. It ministers to me first. Then I just minister it back to the Lord from my heart. Doesn't matter if I have an audience or not, just as long as He's watching.

I would be content with dancing for Jesus and my husband only, but that's not what the Lord wants me to do. He said that I'm a light on a hill not easily hidden. I have to let my light shine so that other people can see it and glorify my God in Heaven. This time around, I'm going to do it right. I'm doing it all for His glory, not my own nor anyone else's. I didn't give myself this gift. I will give the glory to the giver of all. My life sustainer, the air I breathe, my reason for smiling, my heart's desire, my savior, my Lord, my comforter, my redeemer, my righteous judge, my healer, my deliverer, my shield and defense, my strong tower and my best friend. Omnipotent, omnipresent, soon coming King! Alpha-Omega, Lord of everything! He is holy! (Exhales) I'm just thankful He thought enough of me to keep me here. His grace...surely goodness and mercy shall follow me all the days of my life. Amen.

May 3, 2010
Dear Diary,

It's been 1 year since I left Florida. My, I feel great! I owe it all to the Lord. It's all because of Jesus that I'm still alive and in my right mind. It's amazing how faithful God is to me even when I'm not faithful to Him. He never left me…it was me that left Him. Even when I can't see my way, His word gives light to my pathway. When I choose my own path, I'm therefore choosing to walk in total darkness. I love the Lord so much and I intend to spend the rest of my days serving Him and serving others with a heart abounding in love to seal the deal. I choose to flow with the simplicity of the Word of God. Love the Lord thy God with all your heart, soul and strength. And love others as I love myself. I couldn't truly love other people if I didn't love myself. And I couldn't love myself or anyone else truly until I began to understand the love God has for me. There's none like it!

On another note…this isn't May 2010! I wasn't even sure if I'd make it to April 2009! It was so horrific. But it was also my breaking point. It was the month in which I broke free. I decided to run and not look back. Now, April 2010, I have seen miracles in me and my husband's lives. I've seen favor upon favor in our lives. I had the wedding I asked God for and married the man of my dreams. I gained a very intelligent and handsome son, another wonderful mother, 2 bodyguards (my new sisters!) another prince and princess (nephew and niece, and a host of other sisters, brothers, cousins, favorite aunts, uncles and more! I am surrounded by genuine love. I am in love with love. God is love. So…you know the rest. :0))

It simply doesn't make sense to trade real love for "fun", or a fictitious and deceptive image of love. IT'S NOT REAL! How can one who is unable to love themselves possibly know how to genuinely love someone else? Their lack of knowledge of LOVE (God) leaves them incapable of loving you completely and without merit. If you're open, the Lord will show you. If your heart had tasted the goodness of Jesus, as you go through life, you'll be able to see, there is no greater love than His. Homosexuality is a trick, a trap, a lie. It's NOT love. I have been there. So I speak from experience. Its unnatural affection; lust and perversion, not love.

Drugs, porn, abuse (of any kind), addictions, obsessions, none of these can provide love. None can fulfill. Only Jesus can.

Through God's grace, this is one mistake I pray to never make again. To all that are bound by any of these things, to the non-believer and yes, even to the believer, CALL IT OUT! Call on the name of Jesus! The name that is above every name! He is able to rescue you from a life of death and destruction. Do not hide in guilt, pain, hurt, shame, indecisiveness, threats or opinions of others, hopelessness, helplessness…whatever it may be. Just do it! If you want to be free…you will need to put on your running shoes and a pair of boxing gloves because you will have to fight! Oh wait, back up. Duh. This is a spiritual fight. Run in the natural but FIGHT in the spirit. Grab your weapon, the Word of God. Can't win a spiritual battle without it. For many, you'll need to run. Run away from these things that have you bound. If you feel you can't do it alone and need help, confide in someone you trust that will help you get out. No excuses. Get an accountability partner. Crawl if you can't walk…but GET UP! Don't stay down! There were days I had no strength to get up because I was spiritually and emotionally drained. All I could do was lay on the floor and cry. Those were my liquid prayers. I didn't know what to say or pray…so…I cried to Him.

It is possible to break free from rejection, homosexuality, lesbianism and bi-sexuality. It IS worth it. Free is so much better than bound. Break free from the opinions of others. Who cares what the naysayer thinks? Those who don't want to see you succeed aren't worth a moment more of your time. No one on earth has a heaven or hell to put you in.

We all must die one day and will have to answer to one GOD! Doesn't matter who doesn't believe if He exists. He still IS! He is the only One we should seek to please. In serving Him, we will be able to whole heartedly love and even serve our enemies, our neighbors, our community, our families, etc.

I'm so glad… I thank God for everything I went through. Because… I went "through" it. I'm now on the other side. I almost lost my mind in the midst of it all, but God kept me. I can't keep my testimony to myself! If this book only helps 1 person, it would have been worth it. That's 1 soul saved. One soul delivered. One soul snatched out of the enemy's grasp. One soul added to the Kingdom of God. One more soul that's determined to pull others out of the fire. Thank you Jesus!

May 21, 2010
Dear Diary,

Maybe this is my last entry for the book. I'll see what the Lord says :0)
Well, yesterday and today, I've had this feeling …. I just can't seem to shake… an urgency to expose Rollanda to another nationally known dance

leader (that came via dream 2 days ago) and the urgency to get my book done. Everywhere I look there's something about gay this, homosexual that, rainbow or gay pride. Well, let me say this before someone gets upset. I believe those that choose to live the lifestyle of a homosexual (be it male or female) are still people. They will never be anything less than human. However, the spirit that they have allowed themselves to become joined with is heinous. It's out to destroy them and they don't even see it. I love people, but I detest that spirit with a passion. Some may wonder why I can speak about this so boldly. Well, it's because I've been entangled by its lusts, its false sense of love and security for YEARS! It's deception. I've been bound by its chains and so caught up in it that I had no true desire to get out. It was as if I was in the middle of an ocean made of quicksand. I don't want to drown, but…it seems useless to try and get out because I'm so deep in it already. Why try? Plus, no one can see me. No one will hear my cries for help. So why try?

That's a lie. There's always hope and God will make a way of escape. The question is, are you looking? Do you really want it? I think even some Christians have been blinded to the stench of homosexuality because it's globally accepted. It's everywhere. It's in our churches, choirs, dance ministries, it's in our government, all over Hollywood, in the media, in the videos, promoting it in music, soft porn in magazines and advertisements everywhere, it's even in the cartoons now. Is this what we are to tell our children that is acceptable?!?!? That this is morally correct? That it's okay for Sue to kiss Jan or for Tom to kiss Chad? NO! It's not! God doesn't accept it so why should we? It's time to fight. I do not care about what type of backlash comes from this. I will continue to pray for my loved ones until I see a change.

I will take a stand. I will. All those who want to get out, I will be interceding for them. Whatever God wants me to say, I will say. It's a must. Somebody has to speak out about this demon that's taking over our media, our kids, in the school system…everywhere.
Lord, please save us.

May 26, 2010
Dear Diary,

THE DEVIL IS A LIE!!! I know this is the enemy planting seeds in my mind to make me believe I'm crazy and that I'm just making this stuff up. There's no way that's true. I recall very clearly…very vividly, Rollanda and Trish doing explicit things…like there was no tomorrow. I know that's rather graphic but that's just how it was. No exaggeration added to the statement. I remember the nights she snuck into the guest bedroom and laid with me. I remember the night when she was about to go lay with Trish in her bedroom but instead asked me if I still wanted to go all the way with her. I said "yeah", and she replied "ok let's go before I change my mind." And so it was, we had sex for the first time. I never once initiated anything with her. If she started something, I'd finish. I'm not saying this to say it's all her fault and she brought me out. Oh no. I'm just as guilty. But I MUST bring light to this truth. IT HAPPENED! It's not just something I can get over. I can't sweep it under the rug. I can't just go on with life. This must be addressed and dealt with. The spirit must be destroyed in my life.

So as much exposure as I'm bringing to her, I'm also bringing it to myself. And if someone were to ask her if these events really occurred... well, can you get blood from a turnip? No. So it is you can't get the truth from a liar. I'm just sayin! She won't admit nothing like that. Her friends, I'm sure, have never seen this side of her. Master deceivers KNOW how to deceive people. They can do it their whole lives. So you can't say "well I know she wouldn't do that. I've known her for 10 years and she's never done that before." It's a spiritual thing. You must have discernment to see it. And if you see it, CALL IT OUT!!! It's time to unmask before Him (how about that!?!??!). Be real with Him and be transparent before the people.

After all, we are all human and have to answer to the same God once we die. We can judge each other all day and all night but we don't have a heaven or hell to put one another in. It's time to get back to holiness. There's a war going on and we can't walk around like we won't get hit! We must put up our shields of faith, put on the breastplate of righteousness, the helmet of truth, the sword of the spirit and the shoes of peace ;. The WHOLE ARMOR OF GOD. Not just parts of it. We have no time for wardrobe dysfunctions in this day and age. The enemy is busy recruiting anyone who is willing and we must be just as busy doing our Father's business. Leading people to HIM, not to OURSELVES!!! Lord help us!!!

Regardless to the tricks the enemy tries to play with me, he is a liar and the truth is not in him. I will open my mouth and speak out against this spirit as the Lord has told me to. I know it won't be easy, but He told me to go forth. So I must continue forward in Jesus name...giving Him all the glory every step of the way. Amen!

LOOKING BACK

I have to point this out. When I walked down the aisle to marry my husband, the spirit of lust, rejection, fornication and homosexuality went with me. I still wasn't delivered! I know in the natural I wasn't involved in any homosexual acts anymore, BUT all it would have taken was the right moment, the right person, and this could have happened all over again. WHY? Because I wasn't delivered! Those spirits still needed to be addressed.

When this was brought to my attention, it was NOT well received! Not at all! I wanted to be delivered of everything. I did not want to bring homosexuality or lust into my marriage. I didn't realize that both me AND my husband needed deliverance even after we got married. Marriage in itself will not grant me salvation nor will it deliver my soul. I can ONLY gain these through Christ! Once we got married, intercourse was no longer considered fornication, but because we were involved before we got married, the SPIRIT of that thing was still there. That's the dangerous part that a lot of Christians don't understand! Neither did we! If we never got delivered of these things, you could just time it – adultery was coming for our marriage! But I thank GOD that HE loves us enough to show us what's in us so that we can be fully delivered. Psalm 18:19 *He delivered me because he delighted in me.*

On another note, looking back, I found this to be quite disturbing. It <u>seems</u> like in December 2009, I was still wrestling with everything I had just come out of, then in January 2010, I was back on the road to being saved, I was dancing again and everything was ok. NOT SO! I was still messed up! As I stated above, I was not delivered of lust, fornication, homosexuality or rejection. I was still fornicating and still living in sin. The only thing that changed was my surroundings. My mind hadn't been renewed. I still didn't fully give my life back to Christ. I still compromised the Gospel, and more. Once I decided to be honest with myself about where I was I was still in sin, not delivered, I had to be honest about the thoughts I still entertained, get rid of the "old" man, old mindset, old way of doing things, etc., truly repent and turn away from my sin, then deliverance can begin. This was the hardest thing for me to do! Admitting how messed up I was and taking responsibility for my own sins didn't happen over night because I thought I was "good". But the WORD says our righteousness is as FILTHY RAGS!

I wanted to blame everybody else. I wanted to blame Rollanda for coming on to me because if she never would have touched me, then I wouldn't had been caught up in lust and fornication again and I wouldn't had fell with Lenard and...blah blah blah. All of that is wrong. It was my fault because prior to me even meeting Rollanda, when the Lord was using my mentor to help me deal with the root of REJECTION in my life, I refused. I stopped right there. And when I decided I didn't want to deal with the root of rejection in my life, I allowed all of these things (and more) to grow in me from the roots of rejection. In order for these things to die - rejection had to be plucked up from the root! But I decided to let it stay because it was too painful. As a result of my decision, this story was born.

Even after I had given my life back to Christ again, it was still hard for me to go back to the alter for prayer. You know, when a call is made for those who are dealing with certain things, you can go down for prayer? Well, when the alter call was made for those dealing with lust, fornication, homosexuality, etc., I didn't get up immediately. It was a fight for me to get up, once again, and get prayer for the same thing I went to the alter for before. Once I realized sitting in my seat would do me no good, dismissed who might be looking, and went after God - I got up out of my seat and down to the altar. Even if no one prayed for me, I went to God for myself because I want to be free for real.

So, dear reader, I do not want to leave you with the wrong impression. Marriage did not deliver me. I wasn't messed up one day, then everything was great the next. No, no no. This is a process. I must continue to study the Word of God as if my very life depended on it, be obedient to every instruction given to me, guard myself (what I watch, listen to, what I speak, who I allow myself to get close to), and put no confidence in my flesh. Ever! God is delivering me. He is faithful and just to complete the work He has begun in me! Philippians 1:6 *And I am certain that God, who began the good work within you, will continue his work until it is finally finished on the day when Christ Jesus returns.*

August 5, 2010
Dear Diary,

It's 6:00a.m. and I'm awake. Still thinking about prayer yesterday. It's funny because I had to press to go. Part of me wanted to go back to bed; the other part was screaming "PRESS!!!!" After my husband told me ever so politely "Baby, go to prayer", I knew it was a wrap. I thank God I went! All of this is just so....different...in a good way. I mean, I'm at a loss for words. Tuesday, when I woke up at 5am, this feeling came over me like I can't wait to go to church tonight!!! And that thought alone shocked me because just a few months ago, I didn't even want to step foot in this church! But during my prayer time that morning, I asked the Lord to help me and let this feeling stay and increase. There was a time when I was excited about going to church, everyday. Even if I was sick, I would still go because I knew the Lord would heal me. Then something happened....oh yeah, I backslid. Then my mindset was I need to go to church so I can lie under the altar! It was more so out of guilt from sin rather than having Godly sorrow and truly desiring to be delivered or even being excited about being amongst other believers. But here I am again...round 3. It's time to fight! I have lost soooo much ground due to my own disobedience. That poor choice almost cost me my life. If not for the GRACE of God, I would be dead. Since He's kept me, I must give Him, me. All of me. I want His peace, His joy, His righteousness, His truth....all of Him. In Him I must live, move and have my being. I have to obey God. I have to trust God completely. But first and foremost, I must spend time with God; worshipping Him, loving on Him, praying and studying His word. I want my relationship with Him to be fully restored. The joy that I once had is gone. No person on earth can substitute the unspeakable joy that Jesus gives. I'm honestly tired of looking like I'm depressed all the time. My smile is only momentarily. I'm happy for a while but happiness isn't lasting. Joy is. None of this is a reflection on my husband. Bless that wonderful man! This is only about my personal relationship with Christ.

I chose the carnal things of this life (which are fleeting) over an eternity with the lover of my soul. In doing so, I lost the most precious thing in my life- my relationship with Christ. Although I'm alive in the natural, I feel like I died in the spirit. Only God can revive me...and He has! I'm so grateful for Him! Not one more day will I block the Lord out of my heart. I need Him so badly. So deeply. His love to penetrate my being. I can't get enough of it. Every single day of my life, I need Him. I will not sit back and watch my brother, my sister, my cousins, my friends, nor strangers DIE from this disease because I don't want to offend them. The sin is offensive to God! What's more important!?! Hurt feelings or saving a soul from eternal flames? I will open my mouth! I will share my testimony! People must know that HE can and He will deliver! He loves us! He stayed on that cross and paid the price for my sin, for our sins, so that we can be free. He died so that we can have access to the Father. So that we can spend eternity with Him. So that we may know the depth and width of His love and acceptance. So that we can become the children of God. So that we would be adopted into His family. So that we can have joy unspeakable, peace that passes all understanding, the favor of God, and have an everyday love affair with HIM! With all that said...it's time to fight! I'm not saying it's going to be easy, but it must be done. I want it all back! And in Jesus name, I win!

August 26, 2010
Dear Diary,

All I can say at this point is THANK YOU JESUS! The Lord is soooo
amazing! Since I've given my life back to Christ and surrendered my attitude
to Him, I can honestly say His love in my life has been very evident! My
heart is filled with joy again. I forgot to mention that my husband and I
joined our old church again! We were welcomed by everyone with open
arms. I LOVE being back at Worship God Tabernacle. I'm so excited about
our transition! I never thought I'd be in a place where I could say that. But
that's where the Lord has us and we are glad about it. I'm almost speechless!
I've been happily married for 4 ½ months now. I passed my therapeutic exam
today and I have one more day of class left! I thank God for keeping me! I
can say now I'm in a wealthy place! No more idols (G-Yes insider!). No
more murmuring and complaining. NO more compromise! I must have total
obedience and ultimate trust in the Lord. Oh God. I sleep peacefully at night
now. NO more mental torment. And I can forgive all those who hurt me. I
learned that forgiveness is more so for me. If I hold on to unforgiveness, God
won't forgive me. I know holding on to unforgiveness will also affect my
physical and mental health. I've got too much to do in my lifetime to die
early, walk around with a cold, bitter heart, or lose one more night of sleep.
This was a bad situation, but God brought me out!
And He said He will redeem the time that was lost! Hey! I feel a shout
coming on!!!

Back to forgiveness…It's a humbling thing. It's necessary. For me and the
ones who offended me. After all the mess I got myself into, I just gotta come
back and testify of the goodness of God. I have peace of mind! Joy in my
heart! Bless His name! I'm a new business owner. I'm living in the place
where I want to live, got a new car, me and my husband are both published
authors (very soon!), we have a handsome son with standards and realistic
long-term goals at the age of 13, our family adores us (and we love ya'll right
back!), and our church home is moving in a wealthy place! How can I say
thanks for the things He has done for me? Things so undeserved…yet He
came to prove His love for me!

He did it just for me! He brought me out. Cleaned me up and put me back on
the path of righteousness. He can and will do the same for you. He loves you.

September 1, 2010
Dear Diary,

I know I was supposed to be done writing weeks ago, but I had to come back and say...Great is the Lord and He IS greatly to be praised! I love me some Jesus and He loves me. He...loves...me. Wow... He is soooo good! No...wait..he's been so AAAHHHHH to me! Good is an understatement. There is NO OTHER NAME under the sun by which man can be saved. What can wash away my sin? Nothing but the Blood of Jesus! Not a title! Not a job! Not a false promise! No relationship with any man or woman! No friend! No contract! NOTHING but His blood! And in the name of Jesus, I am delivered and totally free from homosexuality and I denounce it's power and grip over my life in the name of Jesus! My mind has to line up with His word! My thoughts will glorify Him! In His name, I am healed! I am whole! I AM forgiven and I can forgive others! I have His joy in my heart! I can trust people! I will obey Him! I have peace of mind! Thank you Jesus!

Not one more day will I cover up this heinous spirit for the sake of not exposing someone. People are out here DYING DAILY while I glory in my deliverance. NOT SO! It's time to be about my Father's business. This time...it's for real. I will speak His truth to the ends of the earth. I WILL NOT KEEP SILENT! I will take a stand against the very thing that was set out to destroy me. And because he brought me out...because He saved my life, I have set my heart to go and pull others out of the fire. I will not be one to sit on His goodness. I will not walk pass people that are dying for hope and I have the hope of Glory inside of me. He did it for me and He can do it for you! I'm not ashamed to say THANK YOU JESUS FOR FREEING ME FROM HOMOSEXUALITY! I am free to love my husband purely...desiring NO OTHER! Now I will crush this spirit every-chance-I-get. In Jesus name! Be free!

Chapter 8
Broken For The Master

February 18, 2011
Dear Diary,

I'm all smiles today. I'm just so full of the joy of the Lord. I can't stop
smiling and laughing! Not that I want to. But when I think on the goodness
of Jesus, and ALL that He's done for me, my soul cries Hallelujah! Thank
God for blessing me! I'm so grateful today. For the last 3 weeks or so, I've
been bursting with joy unspeakable. Like, nothing spectacular happened (in
the natural) that caused me to be so happy. It's just, Jesus! It feels sooooo
good to have peace of mind. It's the best feeling to have His joy in my heart.
He's so grand!

As I sit and reflect on the last 2 years of my life, I can see the hand of God
over me. I can see where the prayers of the righteous helped me to get
through the day. I can see how God's grace and mercy kept me. I can see
how much I've grown in Christ since I gave my life back to Him. I see that
my desires have changed from what I want to what He wants. Honestly, I
just want to be pleasing to Him in every way. I want my life to glorify Him,
my marriage, my business, my home, the words that come out of my mouth,
my thoughts, my dance, everything I do…I want Him to receive the glory.
He's just done so much for me. I know that I am nothing without Him. So I
will offer Him my nothingness.

Just reading over the things I've been through since 2007 is enough for me to
be grateful and thank God for keeping me from year to year. I don't need
another horrific thing to happen to me in my life before I finally surrender to
the Lord. Noooo.. This is it! God is so merciful and kind. I can't stop
thinking about how good He's been to me. He forgave me for turning my
back on Him. For spitting in His face. For making a mockery of Him. For

205

becoming those same people that crucified Jesus long ago. When I chose to return to my sin instead of running to the One I know could save me and keep me from falling, I hurt His heart. I don't ever want that to happen again. He loves me so much!

Speaking of forgiveness; This is so huge for me. I can honestly say that I whole-heartedly forgive myself for the things I've done over the last few years. I had to understand God's love for me and His forgiveness so that I could finally forgive myself. It was certainly a process. I hurt so many people when I made the decision to sin against God and chase after the desires of my own heart. The young people that were looking up to me. My mentees, mainly. I hurt my parents, my pastors, my friends, my little sister...and Lenard. As soon as I returned to Michigan for the last time, I made personal visits to quite a few people to apologize to them for ignoring them over the years, for lying to them, for offending them if I did, and for anything else I may have done to cause pain to them. It was necessary and I'm so glad I did it!

I can honestly say that I forgive Rollanda, Trish and Mr. Chad as well. I cannot blame anyone for my own sin. I have to take responsibility for my own faults. I was drawn away by my own desires. Rollanda was just used by the devil to lure me in and tempt me. At the point when I was tempted, I had a decision to make. I had 6 seconds to say "I'm going to take the bait!" or "The devil is a liar! For God I live, for God I die! I will serve Him and only Him!" I could have spoken the word of God to my situation, listened to what He told me to do (which was GO HOME), and I wouldn't have went through all of that mess. I don't believe it was intended for me to experience that. The devil's plan was to kill me. To take my very life. But thanks be to God, he wasn't successful! So it was my choice to fall into homosexual sin again. No one forced me to do it. I wanted to. I was not an innocent bystander. I was a willing participant.

I chose to be lukewarm. I chose to rebel against my pastors. I chose not to listen to my mom when she pleaded for me daily to come home. I chose to ignore wise counsel. I chose to fear for my life every single day for nearly 2 years straight. It was my decision. When I wanted to get out, of course the devil wasn't going to let me go without a fight. That's why I had to tell somebody in authority to help me, to pray with and for us. My life depended on it. In the multitude of counsel, there truly is safety! And those same people I tried to shut out of my life were praying for me all along. I can't say thank you enough! I don't regret telling and exposing myself or anyone else involved. It was needed. I no longer beat myself up for the mistakes or decisions I've made. Remember, no test, no testimony. When I was tempted, I consider that choice as being a test of my faith and commitment. I failed the test. But GOD is a God of 2nd, 3rd, 4th, 5th, 100 chances! I'm so grateful!

On another note, I must bring this up. There was a point in time where I said that I hated Rollanda. Now, this too is sin. Under no circumstances is it okay to "hate" anyone. The Bible says in 1 John 3:15 *"Whoever hates his brother is a murderer, and you know that no murderer has eternal life abiding in him."* Also in 1 John 4:20 it says, *"If someone says, "I love God," and hates his brother, he is a liar; for he who does not love his brother whom he has seen, how can he love God whom he has not seen?"* So according to the Word of God, I was a liar. And I agree! I knew within myself that if I loved God, I would stop sinning; I would obey His word and follow Him. His word tells us that if we love Him, then we will keep His commandments. I wasn't doing that! Plus I thought evil in my heart towards Rollanda, constantly. I thank God that I am able to pray for her now. I pray for her deliverance in Christ by any means necessary so that her soul may be saved. I pray the same for Trish and Mr. Chad. I rejoice in the day that the scales will fall off their eyes.

I pray that if you are holding hate in your heart, no matter who or what it is regarding, that you allow God to heal your heart. Keep in mind that He sent His ONLY son, Jesus, to die for our sins. We were just as guilty, filthy, horrible, ungodly, sinful and hateful as the people or person you may claim to hate right now. Or maybe even worse. But Jesus died so that we wouldn't have to pay the price for our sin – which is eternal flames. We deserved to be on that cross being beaten for the things we have done to our Creator. But He loved us with an everlasting love that goes far beyond our comprehension. He died for us so that we could have a relationship with the Father. So that, we could have peace of mind. The chastisement of our peace was upon Him. Nothing is worth going to hell for. And in order for us to be forgiven, we must first forgive. Freely we receive forgiveness…then we ought to freely give it.

Through all of this, I was finally able to come to the realization that rejection was the culprit in the majority of my issues. It was my root issue. Rejection can lead to so many different things. It can cause a person to become a drug abuser, an alcoholic, stay in an abusive relationship or become the abuser, rejection can lead to hate, rebellion, all types of sexual perversion, deep rooted fear, or need for approval…and so much more. In my case, it drove me to homosexuality. I was looking for acceptance. I fell into the arms of whoever appeared to care. All the while, missing the One who truly cares for

207

my soul. My rejection stemmed from growing up without my father. I was looking for fulfillment for many years, but was never satisfied until I came to Christ. This last time, rejection played a major role in my life once again. Only this time, I was in the church. What I thought to be rejection from my pastors, was nothing more than correction. I couldn't handle the correction because of the deep rooted rejection that was already in my heart. I wasn't able to receive their love for me. If I wasn't being praised for something, I felt I wasn't liked. I wasn't needed or appreciated. That is rejection and pride. These things drove me away from that church and I pushed my pastors out of my life. Or so, I tried. Lol. I thank God for showing me this. Today, I am pleased to say that I am back at my church, serving under awesome leaders. My church family is my family. I love them all so much. I understand correction is necessary. The Bible says so. I understand that if they correct me, that IS showing they love me. They care for my soul. My pastors truly love God and want nothing less than His will to be done in my life. I know that now. I can see that and I appreciate them so very much for all the time spent ministering to me, praying for me, wisdom poured into me, laboring with me, and just showing me the love of God. I wouldn't trade my spiritual parents for anything in the world. They are invaluable.

I just gotta say that I thank God for His delivering power. Because of His love for me, I know that I am not rejected, but I am accepted by Him. He reminds me of His love for me, daily. I was created in His image and for His glory. Everybody is not against me. No one is out to get me. My husband loves everything about me. This man L-O-V-E-S me, completely! He shows me every single day. He reminds me of who I am in Christ. We pray for each other daily. He appreciates me. He adores me. I am the happily married wife of one man. I am all his, forever. I am deeply loved by all of my family members. My parents adore me. My pastors love me. My awesome friends love me. Even my cats show me love every day. I am surrounded by love. I have the mind of Christ. No longer do I walk around as if I'm defeated. The devil is defeated. As a child of God, I win! The blessing is on me and my family – NOW! I expect the great – NOW! I don't have to agree with the lies the enemy tries to whisper in my ear. He is the father of lies and the truth is not in him. God's Word is true. Everything He said about me is wonderful. He has plans to prosper me and bring me to an expected end. I will dance for His glory! I will be that broken praise dancer for the Lord! I am victorious through Him! Gosh, I could go on and on and on…just like the song says. To sum it up, I'm just plain grateful.

August 2, 2011
Dear Diary,

As I sit here and reflect on today's events, I am amazed by the intensity of God's love for me. Although my day didn't involve much of anything, this day was a defining "moment" in my life. The Lord told me that I need deliverance from not only lust, but homosexuality, fornication and rejection. When He shared this with me, it hit me kind of hard.

Well, I was in the middle of unpacking boxes from our recent move – for 1, and 2, of course, all this time I'm walking around thinking I'm delivered of homosexuality and rejection. Needless to say, I had to have a seat and talk to the Lord about this! Once my prayer time was over, I understood that the Lord was showing me these spirits are laying dormant, they hadn't left.

I was too shocked at that moment to realize that this was **great news** for several reasons! 1- He's calling me to come closer to Him. In order for that to happen, some things (like this) must be released! 2 - He chastens those that He loves. 3 - He (desires for me to be) delivered because He delights in me. 4 - He would not have us ignorant of Satan's devices (residue is a device). 5 - This confirms that He hears my prayers. 6 - I am getting understanding! 7 - He's still speaking to me!

So after all that, I went to Bible study and had a much needed time of refreshing in prayer. Thank you Lord! Well, I am now asking the Lord to direct me in the way He would have me to go in order to walk out my full deliverance. I don't want to play games with this and pretend that I am delivered right now just to save face.

No, I want God to create in me a CLEAN heart and renew a RIGHT spirit within me! These unclean spirits that are lying dormant (inactive) have to GO in the name of Jesus! This house is NOT their home! There's only room for one spirit in this temple – and that's the Holy Spirit. All others must exit, stage left!

Chapter 9
Prayer

It would be a shame to travel all over the world ministering for the Lord and be well-known in the dance community or just in your own community, touching the lives of thousands of people, or even a congregation of 3; go from conference to conference, teaching, learning and ministering, move prophetically, witness God's healing power manifest through your ministry, be used of God to minister a powerful dance of deliverance that brings people to their knees, only for YOU to be lost. We don't want to find ourselves in Matthew 7:21-23 *"Many will say to Me in that day, 'Lord, have we not prophesied in Your name, cast out demons in Your name, and done many wonders in Your name?' And then I will declare to them, 'I never knew you; depart from Me, you who practice lawlessness!"*

If you found yourself anywhere in this book, I pray that you would seek the Lord. It doesn't matter if your struggle isn't homosexuality. If you were/are a fornicator, like I was, please repent and turn. The only thing that stopped me from fornicating was getting married. But that did NOT save me or deliver me from the spirit of fornication, homosexuality, lust or rejection. Those spirits are yet lying dormant. I too am seeking God for my process of deliverance. I must walk this thing out to its entirety.

If your struggle is lust, perverse thoughts, masturbation, pornography, lying, being a false witness of the gospel, operating in a spirit of control and/or manipulation, being a hypocrite, living a double lifestyle, if you're caught up in idolatry (looking to man vs. looking to Christ our Savior) or anything that was not named, please, I beg of you, repent. God has been so gracious, loving and kind to all of us. He sent His Son, Jesus, to die for us. He paid the price for our sin and we now have access to the Father. He's extended to us the gift of forgiveness. Let's accept His gift.

211

If we confess our sins, He is faithful and just to forgive us our sins and to cleanse us from all unrighteousness. 1 John 1:9

Below is a prayer you can pray. There were times when I knew I needed to pray, but I didn't know where to start. You can pray this prayer or take it and make it more personal.

Dear Heavenly Father,

Lord, I come to you as humble as I know how, asking you to please forgive me of my sins. I know that Your word says that if I confess my sins, that You are faithful and just to forgive me and purify me. Lord, I need you to cleanse me right now and help me to walk upright before you. I admit I am guilty of walking in pride, selfishness, wickedness, rebellion and engaging the sin of witchcraft through the spirit of lust. Lord I repent of these things right now in the name of Jesus and I ask that You would wash me with Your blood and make me clean. I want to be free. I desire to do Your will. Please help me to identify every root cause of the sins I have committed against you so that I can be free. I bind the spirit of rejection, deceit, control, depression, suicide, false love, perversion, lust, torment, fear, fornication, rebellion, homosexuality, every mute, deaf and dumb spirit that would cause me to not speak Your word, hear or receive Your truth, and every spirit that would cause me to believe a lie. I ask now God, that You would help me to live a life of purity. I loose holiness, righteousness, and peace in my life right now. I desire to live for You and You alone!

Lord, sanctify this gift that You've given me. I want to minister for Your glory, not my own. I repent for being a glory stealer. I want to find joy and contentment in the what You've given me, if that means never dancing on another platform again. I will dance for an audience of 1 – You.

Father, I ask that You would now create in me a clean heart and renew a right spirit within me. Help me to be more like You. Show me what You want me to do and what You want me to get rid of so that I can break the power of Satan over my life. No longer will guilt and shame rule my life. I thank You that Your word says who the Son sets free, is free indeed! And in the name of Jesus, I receive my freedom! I believe Your word is true! I believe You died on the cross for MY sins! I thank You that Your word says that I shall not die, but live and declare Your works! So even when I feel like it's too much for me to bear, I can turn to You, God, knowing that You will not give me more than I can handle. But I can cast my cares upon You because I know and fully believe that You care for me and You love me. Thank You Lord!

In Jesus mighty name, Amen!

Chapter 10
The Path to Deliverance

Now I rejoice, not that you were made sorry, but that your sorrow led to repentance. For you were made sorry in a godly manner, that you might suffer loss from us in nothing. For godly sorrow produces repentance leading to salvation, not to be regretted; but the sorrow of the world produces death. [11] For observe this very thing, that you sorrowed in a godly manner: What diligence it produced in you, what clearing of yourselves, what indignation, what fear, what vehement desire, what zeal, what vindication! In all things you proved yourselves to be clear in this matter.
2 Corinthians 7:9-10

My process of deliverance started here. I was able to stop lying to myself, acknowledge the fact that I was in sin and stop making excuses for the spirits that were lying dormant- waiting for an opportune time to resurface and destroy me. I was ready to call myself on the carpet, no matter how shameful or painful it would be, and say, Lord, here I am. From my heart, I am sorry! Help me. Cleanse me. Deliver me.

Yes, deliverance is a process. Just like the children of Israel were to be delivered out of the hands of Pharaoh and go into the Promised Land. We too are walking that same journey. The outcome will be up to us. If we decide to murmur, complain, worship idols (including ourselves), become prideful, forget God, operate in the spirit of witchcraft, etc, and then we'll keep going around the same mountain until we get it right. If we don't choose to enter the process, then we'll die there and never get delivered. But the moment we say YES to the will of God, regardless to if we understand His plan or not, that's when we can say we're on the right path -the path to deliverance. During each person's process, God may require something different of them. Follow His plan for your life. He is the Author and the Finisher of your faith.

If you desire to be fully delivered, it is vital that you are able to identify the point of entry of the demonic influence so that you will know what to denounce and pray against. This thing must be plucked up from the root! Although I believe there are many more ways for demons to gain entry into our lives, I'd like to share a few examples of common entry points:

Abortion
Abuse (Mental, Physical, Sexual or Verbal)
Adultery
Child Abuse
False Religion
Fear
Fornication
Idol worship
Incest
Molestation
Music
Occult Practices (Such as sexual sorcery, astrology, horoscope, levitation, incantation, homosexuality, orgies and lesbianism to name a few)
Piercing the flesh (i.e. Body piercings)
Pride
Rape
Rebellion
Rejection
Sin (In general)
Soul Ties
Substance Abuse
Thoughts
Transference
Unforgiveness

Here's what one must do to receive deliverance

*Humble themselves: Acknowledge their need for Christ and His provisions for deliverance. (James 4:6)
* Be completely honest about where they are spiritually and the acts they have committed against God and their own bodies. (Psalm 32:5; 1 Corinthians 6:18)
*Confess their sins. (1 John 1:9)
*Repent (Revelation 3:19)
*Renounce all demonic influences/ strongholds over their life.
*Forgive themselves and any/all offenders
*Call on the Name of the Lord (Acts 2:21)

Your daily decisions determine your outcome.

Here are some practical things you can do daily to maintain your deliverance. Everything that I name, please believe me, I have and do practice myself.

<u>Guard your spirit:</u> What we allow our eyes to see and our ears to hear go into our spirit. Therefore, we should be mindful of our surroundings at all times. Since we are not fighting a physical fight, but a spiritual one (Eph. 6:12), we must guard our spirit by guarding our heart. The word tells us in Proverbs 4:23 to guard our hearts with all diligence. We do this by hiding the Word of God in our hearts, daily casting down evil imaginations (2 Corinth. 10:4-5), letting go of "stinking thinking" (Phil. 4:8), putting on the whole armor of God (Eph. 6:13-18), resisting the devil [and all evil temptations] (James 4:7) and forgiving one another.

<u>Guard your eye gate:</u> Be careful of what you watch. Rid your environment of pornography. Avoid soft porn on television, sexual scenes in movies, in magazines and any other type of advertisement. Avoid looking at people lustfully (desiring them in your mind, body, or spirit).

<u>Guard your ear gate:</u> Be careful of what you listen to, avoid talk radio that promotes sin, certain music, and ungodly conversations.

<u>Guard your body:</u> Make sure you dress modestly. Avoid walking in a sensual or suggestive manner. Completely shun drawing any sexual attention to the body.

Relationships

Til this day, I am very cautious of how I handle relationships. I am becoming more sensitive in discerning the spirit of homosexuality and lust in people, more now than ever before. If I see the spirit plain as day on someone, I am extremely careful of how I conduct myself with that individual. It's not done in a way that they feel uncomfortable or as if I am homophobic, but I must guard my spirit.

I am not quick to befriend someone who is in actively engaging in that lifestyle. I do not want to find myself in a place of compromise. It's not wise. I cannot and will not put any confidence in my flesh.

For we are the circumcision, who worship God in the Spirit, rejoice in Christ Jesus, and have no confidence in the flesh. Philippians 3:3

I recommend asking God to help you establish Godly relationships. Ask the

Lord to sanctify your relationships so that you can be free to have healthy, normal relationships with others. Honor God in all of your relationships. Trust that He is able to lead and guide your relationships in a way that is pleasing to Him. Even if you are in a situation where building a relationship with an individual(s) seems perfect, please do not put confidence in your flesh. Pray and ask God to give you discernment and show you the purpose of that relationship – *if* it's His will for you to establish it.

Trust in the Lord with all your heart, lean not on your own understanding; In all your ways acknowledge Him, and He shall direct your paths. Proverbs 3:5-6

One important relationship to develop while on the path to deliverance is one between yourself and an accountability partner. This person should be a believer in Jesus Christ (not backslidden), full of the Holy Spirit and mature in the things of God. They must be able to give you pray with you, encourage you in the things of God, and give you Godly advice (according to the Word of God) and to help you to walk circumspect. It is important to seek God on who He wants to help you while on this path. In times of weakness or temptation, call them and be honest about how you are feeling. They should encourage you to obey God in all points, making no allowances for sin or compromise, pray/intercede on your behalf and check on you periodically.

Disconnecting

When breaking ungodly soul ties, it is very necessary to take drastic measures when disassociating yourself from the spirit of witchcraft, control, lasciviousness, perversion, lust, fornication, homosexuality and any demonic influence, such as, disconnecting yourself from any person(s) you were involved with sexually (this includes masturbation, phone sex, sexting, cyber sex, and all those who you may have fanaticized about/with), changing email addresses, phone numbers, social networking accounts, untagging pictures, and removing yourself from certain groups.

Gifts also play a symbolic part in a relationship and can hold a soul tie in place. Discard all personal gifts, love letters, love notes, greeting cards (of any kind, including electronic), autographed books, jewelry, clothing (this includes company t-shirts, dance garments, jackets, etc.), shoes, souvenirs, etc., from that person(s). Holding on to such gifts symbolizes that the relationship is still in tact and the soul tie can still be held in place, even after it has been renounced. It's time to get rid of these things.

Verbally renounce all demonic influences over your life. Whether you were oppressed by someone operating in a spirit of control, manipulation, or witchcraft – or if you were the oppressor, you need to verbally renounce all spoken covenants between you and the individual(s). For example, if you made a verbal commitment to love this individual forever and never leave them, you now need to verbally take it back in order to break this soul tie. You can release these verbal covenants by speaking (from your heart) something like this:

"In the name of Jesus, I now renounce and loose myself from any and all ungodly soul ties created between myself and so and so, and I break these ungodly soul ties right now, in Jesus' name. Amen"

Most importantly, you must forgive the person(s) of any wrong doing. Holding on to unforgiveness will only keep the bond knit together longer. We must choose to release the poison of bitterness and unforgiveness, knowing this is required of us in order to receive forgiveness from God. Accept responsibility for your fault in the matter, repent, and then forgive yourself.

Whatever it takes to be free, do it.

Maintaining Your Deliverance

In Ephesians 5:15, the scripture tells us that we ought to walk circumspect. The word *circumspect* means to [be] careful to consider all circumstances and possible consequences (Meriman-Webster Dictionary). I take this to mean that in everything I do, I ought to be wise and carefully think it through. The wisest thing to do, in any situation, is to pray and ask God to direct us.

Study the Word

In order for us to be able to discern all circumstances and all possible consequences; we must know what the Word of God says. Search the scriptures to hear God's heart on the matter. For example, since my sin/struggle was lust, fornication and homosexuality – all rooted in rejection, my assignment was to study the scriptures on those things and see how God feels about them. When I say study, I mean do more than just read the scripture. Search out every key word and its counterparts. Use the dictionary to get a clear understanding of what each word means. Lust is also connected to perversion, lasciviousness, debauchery, etc. Next, I would suggest studying on what it means to be pure and holy. Study the Word on sanctification, temperance, righteousness and humility. Search them all out to get a clear understanding of what God is communicating to us in His word.

217

Fill the House

Once I grasped the understanding of what it was that kept me from pursuing the things of God, I found purpose in keeping myself filled with the Word for the assurance that this sin would not return.

"When an unclean spirit goes out of a man, he goes through dry places, seeking rest, and finds none. Then he says, 'I will return to my house from which I came.' And when he comes, he finds it empty, swept, and put in order. Then he goes and takes with him seven other spirits more wicked than himself, and they enter and dwell there; and the last state of that man is worse than the first. So shall it also be with this wicked generation."
Matthew 12:43-45.

So filling yourself with the Word of God becomes your defense from the enemy who wishes to return and overtake you.

Pray the Word

After studying and filling oneself with the Word, the acknowledgement of what's been learned must be done. The only preventative measure that will keep the sin that once had us bound from returning, is praying the Word of God as a defense mechanism. The Bible tells us that the weapons of our warfare are not carnal, meaning we cannot fight a spiritual battle with natural means nor empty words. The scripture goes on to say that the weapons of our warfare are MIGHTY in GOD for pulling down strongholds! There is POWER in the Word of God! (2 Corinth. 10:4) God gave us His Word to use as a weapon against the enemy!

Obey God in all things

But God be thanked that though you were slaves of sin, yet you obeyed from the heart that form of doctrine to which you were delivered. And having been set free from sin, you became slaves of righteousness. I speak in human terms because of the weakness of your flesh. For just as you presented your members as slaves of uncleanness, and of lawlessness leading to more lawlessness, so now present your members as slaves of righteousness for holiness. Romans 6:17-19

Now that you have studied the Word, filled your temple with His Word, and prayed His Word, now it's time to obey His Word. Any instructions He gives you, rather it be through prayer, your study of the Word, or through your spiritual leaders, obey them to their entirety. The Lord said if we love Him, (we will) keep His commandments. (John 14:15)
Remember, no matter what, God is able to deliver us out of anything.

218

Nothing is impossible for Him. If you are discouraged and not sure how you will make it out of "this one", remember that He is more than able! You can do ALL things through Christ who gives you strength! This includes living holy! Throughout the Bible, we see God as the Divine Deliverer. I would like to share a few scriptures with you. Please read them and be encouraged!

" ...*who delivered us from so great a death, and does deliver us; in whom we trust that He will still deliver us.*" 2 Corinthians 1:10

"*...then the Lord knows how to deliver the godly out of temptations and to reserve the unjust under punishment for the day of judgment, and especially those who walk according to the flesh in the lust of uncleanness and despise authority. They are presumptuous, self-willed. They are not afraid to speak evil of dignitaries.*"
2 Peter 2:9-10

"*And he said: 'The LORD is my rock and my fortress and my deliverer.'*"
2 Samuel 22:2

"*He delivered me from my strong enemy, From those who hated me, For they were too strong for me.*" Psalm 18:17

"I *sought the LORD, and He heard me, And delivered me from all my fears.*" Psalm 34:4

"*For You have delivered my soul from death. Have You not kept my feet from falling, That I may walk before God In the light of the living?*" Psalm 56:13

"*Even to your old age, I am He, And even to gray hairs I will carry you! I have made, and I will bear; Even I will carry, and will deliver you.*" Isaiah 46:4

"Do *not be afraid of their faces, For I am with you to deliver you, says the LORD.*" Jeremiah 1:8

"*He delivers and rescues, And He works signs and wonders in heaven and on earth, Who has delivered Daniel from the power of the lions.*" Daniel 6:27

"*And the Lord will deliver me from every evil work and preserve me for His heavenly kingdom. To Him be glory forever and ever.* " 2 Timothy 4:18

Amen!

Chapter 11
Scriptures

1 John 1:9 NLT
But if we confess our sins to him, he is faithful and just to forgive us our
sins and to cleanse us from all wickedness.

Ephesians 2:8-9 NLT
God saved you by his grace when you believed. And you can't take credit for
this; it is a gift from God. Salvation is not a reward for the good things we
have done, so none of us can boast about it.

Romans 5:8 AMP
But God shows and clearly proves His [own] love for us by the fact that
while we were still sinners, Christ (the Messiah, the Anointed One) died for
us.

Romans 10:9-10 NLT
If you confess with your mouth that Jesus is Lord and believe in your heart
that God raised him from the dead, you will be saved. For it is by believing
in your heart that you are made right with God, and it is by confessing with
your mouth that you are saved.

John 8:36 AMP
So if the Son liberates you [makes you free men], then you are really and
unquestionably free.

1 Corinthians 10:13 NLT
The temptations in your life are no different from what others experience.
And God is faithful. He will not allow the temptation to be more than you
can stand. When you are tempted, he will show you a way out so that you
can endure.

2 Corinthians 5:17 AMP

Therefore if any person is [engrafted] in Christ (the Messiah) he is a new creation (a new creature altogether); the old [previous moral and spiritual condition] has passed away. Behold, the fresh and new has come!

Leviticus 18:22 NLT

"Do not practice homosexuality, having sex with another man as with a woman. It is a detestable sin.

Leviticus 20:13 (Entire Chapter)

"If a man practices homosexuality, having sex with another man as with a woman, both men have committed a detestable act. They must both be put to death, for they are guilty of a capital offense.

Romans 1:18-32 NLT

But God shows his anger from heaven against all sinful, wicked people who suppress the truth by their wickedness. [19] They know the truth about God because he has made it obvious to them. [20] For ever since the world was created, people have seen the earth and sky. Through everything God made, they can clearly see his invisible qualities—his eternal power and divine nature. So they have no excuse for not knowing God.

[21] Yes, they knew God, but they wouldn't worship him as God or even give him thanks. And they began to think up foolish ideas of what God was like. As a result, their minds became dark and confused. [22] Claiming to be wise, they instead became utter fools. [23] And instead of worshiping the glorious, ever-living God, they worshiped idols made to look like mere people and birds and animals and reptiles.

[24] So God abandoned them to do whatever shameful things their hearts desired. As a result, they did vile and degrading things with each other's bodies. [25] They traded the truth about God for a lie. So they worshiped and served the things God created instead of the Creator himself, who is worthy of eternal praise! Amen. [26] That is why God abandoned them to their shameful desires. Even the women turned against the natural way to have sex and instead indulged in sex with each other. [27] And the men, instead of having normal sexual relations with women, burned with lust for each other. Men did shameful things with other men, and as a result of this sin, they suffered within themselves the penalty they deserved.

^{28} Since they thought it foolish to acknowledge God, he abandoned them to their foolish thinking and let them do things that should never be done. ^{29} Their lives became full of every kind of wickedness, sin, greed, hate, envy, murder, quarreling, deception, malicious behavior, and gossip. ^{30} They are backstabbers, haters of God, insolent, proud, and boastful. They invent new ways of sinning, and they disobey their parents. ^{31} They refuse to understand, break their promises, are heartless, and have no mercy. ^{32} They know God's justice requires that those who do these things deserve to die, yet they do them anyway. Worse yet, they encourage others to do them, too.

1 Corinthians 6:9 NLT

Don't you realize that those who do wrong will not inherit the Kingdom of God? Don't fool yourselves. Those who indulge in sexual sin, or who worship idols, or commit adultery, or are male prostitutes, or practice homosexuality, or are thieves, or greedy people, or drunkards, or are abusive, or cheat people—none of these will inherit the Kingdom of God.

1 Timothy 1:10 NLT

The law is for people who are sexually immoral, or who practice homosexuality, or are slave traders, [Or kidnappers.] liars, promise breakers, or who do anything else that contradicts the wholesome teaching.

Ephesians 3:20-21 AMP

Now to Him Who, by (in consequence of) the [action of His] power that is at work within us, is able to [carry out His purpose and] do superabundantly, far over and above all that we [dare] ask or think [infinitely beyond our highest prayers, desires, thoughts, hopes, or dreams]-- ^{21}To Him be glory in the church and in Christ Jesus throughout all generations forever and ever. Amen (so be it).

Chapter 12
Suggested Listening

The Bible on CD
Nothing but the Blood - Hillsong
God Wants To Heal You – Angelo & Veronica
Heart That Forgives – Kevin Le'Var
Chains – Kirk Franklin
Living For – J. Moss
Mighty to Save - Hillsong
I'm Free - by Marvin Winans
I'll Trust You Lord - Pastor Donnie McClurken
Help Me Believe - Kirk Franklin
Moving Forward - Israel & New Breed
If Not For Your Grace - Israel & New Breed
Saved By Grace - Israel & New Breed
It Will Be Alright - Tye Tribbett
I'm Still Here - Dorinda Clark Cole
East to West- Casting Crowns
Strong Enough - Stacie Orrico
Free - 1NC
My Help - Ron & Cece Winans
Still My Child - Mary Mary
Grateful - Hezikiah Walker
Holding On - J. Moss
Encourage Yourself - Donald Lawrence
Great & Mighty Is Our God- Donnie McClurken (psalms & hyms)
The Real Me- Natalie Grant
Count It All Joy - The Winans
Standing In Your Grace - 1NC
Grace, Grace, Grace- Lisa McClendon
I Need You Now – Smokie Norful

Free – Darwin Hobbs
Only Help- Tye Tribbett
When The Rocks Hit The Ground – Tye Tribbett

Chapter 13
Suggested Reading

The Holy Bible

God's Remedy for Rejection –Derek Prince

Naked Surrender – Andrew Comiskey

Root Issues – Mayra Leon

Pigs In The Parlor – Frank and Ida Mae Hammond

Destroying The Spirit of Witchcraft – Starr Lewis

The Kingdom of God & The Homosexual – Andrew Comiskey

Approval Addiction – Joyce Meyer

Total Forgiveness – R.T. Kendall

Tell Them I Love Them – Joyce Meyer

Pursuing Sexual Wholeness: How Jesus Heals
The Homosexual – Andrew Comiskey

For more resources on help for how to leave the homosexual lifestyle, I recommend seeking out Exodus International (exodusinternational.org). Their ministry is specifically geared towards those who desire to be free from homosexuality and approach it with grace and love in Christ Jesus.

Made in the USA
Charleston, SC
18 March 2012